wholefood
from the ground up

TO YOU, DEAR READER – MAY THERE
BE MUCH JOY AND DELICIOUSNESS IN
YOUR LIFE, AND AT YOUR TABLE.

OPPOSITE: HONEY AND BANANA CAKE WITH MOCK BUTTERCREAM, PAGE 234

jude blereau

wholefood
from the ground up

MURDOCH BOOKS
SYDNEY · LONDON

contents

> Long after we've achieved everything on our list, long after we've tried to do it all by skipping meals, grabbing the latest energy bar or eating the fastest 30-minute meal, we will still do best – and indeed thrive – with whole and real food. We will still yearn to slow down and come home to the smell of food cooking, and to sit with the people that matter to talk, share and eat.

nourishing wisdoms

Born in the 1950s to a mother of Italian descent, I was fortunate enough to grow up in a family and society that understood food; how to grow and source it, supply and prepare it so that it nourished both body and soul. We collected our eggs from the backyard, my younger sister Kate and I loved climbing the fig and almond tree to eat our fill when in season, and harvested simple vegetables from the back garden – with a fair amount of wonder at the thrilling mystery of it all.

These foods were supplemented with seasonal fruits, vegetables, dairy, meats and grains that were produced in the hills that surrounded the city, or the farming lands a few hours' drive away, with seafood from the ocean and nearby river. We also foraged for foods – Kate and I knew that there was only a short time of the year we could collect the pine cones that fell to the ground at the local church, which we would take home and crack open to find the oh-so-delicious nuts, and adored going to my aunt's house to play all day in the mulberry tree, eating ourselves silly. Families and friends also shared their crops. From these humble fresh and seasonal foods, Mum cooked simple but delicious food to feed and grow a large family.

Starting in the 1960s and 1970s this way of life began to noticeably change. With industrialisation, the work of growing and sourcing our food and then transforming that food into delicious meals to grow and nourish lost its value. Accompanying that loss was another: the vast body of food knowledge built up over generations. This knowledge – how we think about food and then act upon that knowledge – is what I call food culture. There is a societal food culture, and the personal food culture we hold within the home. With this loss, these nourishing wisdoms have largely disappeared – indeed they are no longer considered central to our nourishment and well-being any longer. That bottle of pasteurised, homogenised low-fat milk might look like milk, have the word milk on the label, suit the bottom line of the company producing it and represent the current politically correct views on health, but no amount of spin can change the way your body is able to relate to and use that product – it simply won't, because it simply cannot.

∞

We call this inability of nature to interact with imitation foods by many names – intolerance, allergy or disease. While I am a huge believer that each of us is a spiritual being having a human experience, here on earth our physical body is formed of and governed by the forces of nature, and this is something that has been well understood by all traditional cultures that enjoyed good health and happiness. Although it would be overly simplistic to dismiss the many benefits that industry, technology and society have delivered, it remains that we are asking the human body, which has changed very little over millennia, to suddenly adapt to very different and novel fuel sources and indeed, we are sicker and unhappier than ever before.

I started my wholefood journey some 23 years ago because I was (and remain) deeply interested in food and living a real and full life. When I first started along this path, I thought it was as simple as eating less or no meat and having wholegrain and wholemeal (whole-wheat) flours. I even went through a stage of considering dairy to be unhealthy. But these were the norms of the day. I now see the principles that make up wholesome and nourishing food quite differently from when I started out. I love being older, having seen a full lay of the land.

What is apparent now is how fortunate I was to have had the benefit of growing up with a strong, intact food culture. How blessed I was to have had such a deep connection with the actual growing of food and the subsequent preparation and transformation into tasty meals that nourished both body and soul. By collecting those eggs and harvesting food from the soil, trees or water I learnt where food came from, and the seasons and cycles of nature. I certainly knew that nothing tasted as good as the fruit straight from the tree, or the fish Kate and I caught with my dad and ate for breakfast. I absolutely understood that our nourishment depended on the sun, rain, wind and soil and, in doing so, was tethered to and a part of the great interconnected web of life. Yet, for many, without the benefit of that connection to the source of our nourishment and without a strong grasp of food culture, it is very easy to become confused about the many conflicting messages about what wholesome and healthy food is.

This book is about restoring some of the forgotten wisdoms in regards to what healthy, wholesome and nourishing food really is. It's about giving you the tools, skills and recipes to translate that knowledge into nourishing and delicious foods as a workable part of your everyday life. My experience with teaching hundreds of people wholefood cooking over the years is that once you acquire this knowledge you will be empowered to make informed choices about why, where and how you source food, and then translate that food into delicious meals to nourish yourself and loved ones. I can't lie to you and say it is a quick journey. It's taken me years to learn what I know about wholefood cooking, but a lifetime to truly understand what I know and place it within a holistic framework – two to five years is a normal time frame, but I can promise you it gets easier as you go. Please don't try to do everything at once – take the time to carefully read through the pages of this book, and then begin with one area in which to act upon, such as where to source good food. My aim isn't for you to become a purist – I cook old-fashioned food with a common sense approach and have what I call 'a funky wholefood thing' going on. I can promise you, however, that the wholefood journey is a deeply rewarding path. Food is the most fundamental way we interact with our environment and it informs all we are and who we can be. I'd love to help you on your way to making nourishing and delicious food a realistic part of your everyday life.

nourishing foundations

As a society, and as individuals, we make many assumptions in regards to what makes food good, what it is that makes eating wholesome, nourishing and healthy, and what makes it an ethical and sustainable choice. For millennia, this information or 'nourishing wisdom' was handed down within the home, in the garden, on the farm or through older members of the community. But with the deterioration of our food culture (and the societal constructs that support them) and the rise of an industrialised food system, this wisdom has been largely forgotten and even lost. Disconnected and without a nourishing context on which to make an informed choice, it can be very easy to become confused by the many dietary and lifestyle paradigms that abound, each telling us that their path is more ethical, sustainable, healthier, or wholesome. Put simply, it's incredibly confusing and there is often conflicting information. Ultimately, I don't think things are that black and white, and I believe there are more important and fundamental issues that truly matter. The simple nourishing foundations that follow reflect the understandings I now have after more than 23 years working in the 'healthy' food industry and over 60 odd years of living.

SOIL MATTERS Your food will only be as good as the soil in which it grows, and it should also be good enough to eat. Synthetic pesticides (herbicides, fungicides) (derivatives of nerve gases left over after the early wars) are designed to interrupt and kill living systems. For these reasons, I am a huge supporter of certified organic and bio-dynamic farming systems. Buying your food direct from the farmer or farmers' market is probably one of the most important things you can do. Talking to and forming a relationship with those who grow your food empowers you to make informed choices about the growing systems you support and the food you eat.

WHOLE, NATURAL AND UNREFINED MATTERS Food should be as close to its natural state as possible, with as little that is edible taken away, and as little that is inedible added to it. I won't be talking about the broad range of additives in this book, as I am interested in the food before these are added and this is what I mean by 'cooking from scratch'. Wholefood as a concept also understands that the whole is always far greater than the sum of the nutrient parts and that our bodies use food to its maximum nutritional potential when it is consumed as a synergistic whole, not processed and broken into parts.

HAVING GOOD GUT ECOLOGY MATTERS Beneficial biota coat our entire digestive system, creating a natural protection for the gut wall while at the same time, nourishing our digestive system, keeping pathogenic bacteria under control, creating B vitamins and forming an important part of our immune system. A healthy gut is absolutely critical for an optimal digestive system, especially gluten and dairy.

EATING FOOD THAT MATCHES YOU MATTERS While I'm not a believer in food paradigms and labelling our food, if I had to choose one that I've actually seen to be working over the years, it would be Ayurveda. Without being fanatical, knowing what suits your body makes a huge difference. Some people may be fine with cold raw food in winter while others will suffer. Some do best with cooked vegetables, some with grain, some with no grain. Know yourself, and what suits your body.

ANIMAL FATS MATTER Fats, such as marrow, offal, eggs and milk fats are rich sources of the fat-soluble vitamins A and D, and omega-3 derivatives. You don't need to eat a lot of them to make a vast or positive difference to all aspects of your health – this has been well understood by all healthy and traditional cultures, as well as the value of bones (used in stocks).

SWEETNESS IS NOT A DIRTY WORD A bit of sweetness in a whole and balanced diet is not going to kill you. Eating a lot of refined white sugar and flour, low-fat, processed vegetable oil, nutrient-deficient, additive-laden food in a stressful life possibly will.

THE CONTEXT OF YOUR LIFE MATTERS: LIFESTYLE AND STRESS The human body can handle hard work (my mum for example walked miles to school and home every day and certainly didn't have a dishwasher or even a washing machine until later years), but it is not built to live a crazy life. Working long hours each week, leaving and coming home in darkness and always doing ten things at the same time are all aspects of a crazy life. Humans, like nature, require quiet, still and calm seasons and to be supported, loved and nourished, both physically and spiritually.

DELICIOUSNESS IS A NUTRIENT IN ITS OWN RIGHT AND IT MATTERS Fractionalising food into its components and eating the 'healthiest' meal on the planet can never satisfy, fulfil and truly nourish if that food (and the context in which it is eaten) is not enjoyed. In ways I cannot understand, deliciousness and joy invite food into the body and enable its nutrients to be fully utilised.

CHOOSING GOOD MEAT (AND ANIMAL PRODUCTS) I had my vegetarian days, which I now see stemmed from my desire to express the view that all was not well with the food industry and the establishment supporting it. But my view has shifted and evolved over time. I still love to eat a wide range of plant-based foods, but I do include and enjoy some meat and animal products. At its heart, I believe that not eating animals or their products because of the ethical or sustainable issues they pose is overly simplistic. As I've grown my vegetables in my small suburban garden, I have become intimately involved with many aspects of nature, including death. Killing bugs, rats, snails, slaters or moths – albeit in an organic

and environmentally conscious way – is simply an essential part of the process. I try to apply ethical, sustainable and environmental issues to sourcing all food, including animals and their products, and strongly believe in the principle of thanksgiving and gratitude. I consider animals raised within an industrialised food production system, with no respect or honour, to be unsustainable, unethical and immoral, and not the mark of a civilised society.

When I source meat and animal products, I look for farming systems in line with my own beliefs above, and where animals are able to express their essential cowness, chickeness or such and are fed the food they are meant to eat. In the case of cows, sheep, and chickens this is pasture not grain, with chickens requiring protein and some grain. Chickens also need to scratch for worms and such, and dust themselves in dirt. In the case of pigs, they need to furrow, roll in mud and have a wide omnivorous diet.

CHOOSING GOOD FISH Fish and seafood are powerful nourishment, but sourcing them can be tricky. Just like fruit and vegetables, all species of fish and seafood are not plentiful or available all the time – these are the basic rules of nature and so we have to adapt to when they are either scarce or not in season. But today, the fishing industry circumvents these natural conditions by farming or importing fish, and these artificial practices spawn a myriad of issues that impact negatively on the environment as well as the quality and integrity of the fish itself. (It should be noted that traditional aquaculture systems such as integrated vegetable and herbivorous fish farming are entirely different things, and have been practised for centuries.)

My views have been formed by extensive research over the years, but corrected and enriched by Dr Jeremy Prince, who has worked in fishing sustainability for over 30 years. He has worked in every capacity, including sitting on and consulting to governmental bodies about fishing sustainability. I encourage you to explore and learn more about the issues, particularly around fish farming. In the meantime, my simple formula is clean, local, sustainable, unfarmed and seasonal. A quick internet search will provide you with a good local guide for sustainable seafood these days and this is a great place to start. But first and foremost, I try to focus on where the fish comes from rather than its variety, preferring local first, my country second and never, ever choosing imported fish or seafood products.

COOKED VERSUS RAW Such is the nature of the 'healthy' food industry that the classification of raw versus cooked food as good versus bad respectively predominates as a perception of healthy, wholesome and nourishing food today. I believe it is an overly simplistic view to say that cooked food (anything over 42°C/108°F) is dead food, with diminished life force and nutrient value, when it has, in the successful evolution and survival of man, been spectacularly successful. While we might share a large amount of DNA with the chimpanzee, evolution has given us a smaller colon to gut ratio, a weaker jaw and smaller teeth – all perfect for cooked foods, which require less energy to digest. So while cooking can lessen an ingredient's nutritional value, these practices still provide incredible nutrient density and energy that is easily accessible, making meat, fibrous greens and complex carbohydrates more easily digestible.

Again, very little in life is black and white, and I believe it is the same with raw and cooked foods. All healthy human groups include raw foods in their diet and understand the value of that life force. When choosing vegetables to eat raw, it pays to bear in mind that nature tends to provide season-appropriate foods – lighter, less carbohydrate dense and higher water content vegetables and fruits in summer and warmer climates (for example, lettuce, cucumber, tomatoes, zucchini/courgettes), strawberries, stone fruits, melons, tropical fruits). These require no cooking and are easy to eat raw. And it gives us almost the opposite in the cooler months and cooler climates – denser carbohydrate root vegetables, with thicker and more cellulose-dense leaves (for example, root vegetables, cabbage, broccoli, kale), which, once cooked to make that goodness accessible, provide us with more fuel to keep us warm.

=======================================

As the nourishing foundations above demonstrate, it's generally not what the food IS that makes it good, wholesome, healthy, ethical or sustainable, but rather how we grow it, process and prepare it. The context in which we source it, eat it and the life we live is equally important. I don't believe it's as simple as not eating meat, or not cooking your food. Neither is it about spending large amounts of money on 'superfoods' – all foods that fulfil these nourishing foundations can be considered super in some way and of value.

=======================================

a word about the recipes

You won't see a lot of fashionable 'superfoods' in this book (really this is often just another word for expensive). The recipes you will find here use simple vegetables, most of which can be easily grown at home, and often in abundance. Whilst I don't have chickens, a cow or a pig I find them awe-inspiring – chickens provide eggs (that most perfect of digestible proteins), roosters make some of the best stock, the cow gives us milk which we concentrate to cream, then butter and ultimately pure butterfat, all their meats are delicious and their bones, organs and fats, and together with seafoods are some of our most nutrient-dense food sources. I don't say this lightly nor do I use these foods lightly, but source them carefully, and use them in smaller amounts, with gratitude, respect and no waste. But then, shouldn't that be how we treat all our foodstuffs – animal and vegetable? While there is no room for preserving the harvest in this book, it remains a core part of who I am.

the mechanics of food

The way in which our bodies turn food into life-giving, life-enriching fuel is both incredibly intricate and delicately balanced. And in this balance, all foods are not equal – they differ in the amount of energy provided, the speed in which that energy is delivered and how long that energy lasts. Given that we talk about 'burning' fuel, it's a good idea to equate how different foods behave to fuel for a fire. Carbohydrate is like the kindling; complex carbohydrates (for example sourdough bread, whole grains, legumes) burn quickly like twigs, while refined carbohydrates (for example, white bread, white sugar, white rice, lollies, fruit juice, soft drinks) burn faster still, like paper. Both give a lot of flame (energetic warmth) but burn out quickly, though the complex carbs give a slightly lower flame for a longer period. But fats, such as butter, avocado and those in nuts are like the big, slow-burning log that gives a steady flame for longer. Not only do fats supply double the energetic value of carbohydrates, they take far longer for the body to convert into usable energy, having the effect of making you feel fuller for longer. Fats also stimulate hormones, telling our brains when we've 'had enough to eat'. Although protein can be converted to energy, it's not the body's preferred fuel. I consider protein, which provides the structure in our bodies, to be exceptionally grounding.

Refined carbohydrates are especially damaging because not only are they nutrient shallow, they also provide the fastest yet most short-lived fuel. This kind of fuel is the worst for our body because sugar is released into the bloodstream quickly, stressing the insulin response resulting in a sugar low. This is exceptionally stressful to the body, but especially to the adrenal glands. We can, however, buffer the effects of carbohydrate by including longer-burning foods such as fats and proteins in the same meal, which not only helps to slow down the release of sugar into the bloodstream but also adds a far greater range of longer lasting nutrients for fuel. This is why a fat such as avocado or butter (or indeed an egg) on wholegrain sourdough bread, or ghee or butter in porridge is such a good idea. Adding a coconut-based vegetable curry to white basmati rice, wholegrain and/or legume is another example. Add some pure protein such as meat, egg or fish to this curry and that fuel density and buffering effect increases yet again. It is more important that we provide our body with the fuel it needs, when it needs it rather than be bound by strict guidelines for breakfast, lunch and dinner. An egg breakfast such as on page 108 is a more nutrient-dense option that will fuel you over a longer period of time than the Oat Kernel and Spelt Berry Porridge on page 124. But equally, it could be some leftover Chicken with Buttermilk Herb Dumplings (page 202). Any recipe in this book can be for anytime, it's the nutrient fuel load and how that fuel load burns that really matters.

how to eat

The food culture handed to me by my mother was all things in balance and moderation. I understand this to mean all real food, in balance and moderation. Eating is about giving your body the fuel it needs, at every level. Traditionally, we used to meet that need with 'square meals', to which we enjoyed sitting down – not only did they provide a steady supply of fuel, a balance of essential nutrients, they were also delicious. We ate these as breakfast, lunch and dinner with nourishing snacks where needed. This is entirely opposite today, where people exist on snacks – of questionable nourishment value – all day long. Eating in balance means balancing our nutrient requirements, our life force requirements (raw and fresh) our non-physical requirements for deliciousness and joy, seasonal requirements (hot or cold) and our own digestive temperament. In terms of moderation, a small amount of refined carbohydrate isn't a disaster as long as the other fundamentals are in place.

What does a nourishing and balanced day look like?

● You should look to your main meals to provide the bulk of your nutrients and fuel for the day – your reliance on snacks will immediately lessen.

● Consider the nutrient and fuel density of your meals, as discussed on page 12. Remember that protein and fat will always be more sustaining than carbohydrate. For some, it will also be more grounding, especially for breakfast.

● Balance nutrient groups and avoid eating from just one all day long.

● Balance cooked and raw.

● Include some of nature's most nutrient-dense foods – butterfat, egg yolk, offal, fish and seafood.

● Include cultured foods to aid digestion (see page 39).

come into the kitchen

===================================

A wholefood kitchen is a living, breathing space where we translate intent and knowledge into food that can heal, nourish and delight. But it is also so much more than this ...

===================================

A kitchen filled with whole and natural foods is a powerful place – it is where our most fundamental needs for nourishment are met – from the food we eat to sitting around a table with our loved ones and laying down our burdens of the day. I believe that we need these comforting places in our ever-increasingly busy lives – I know I most certainly do. The kitchen matters more than we know.

Having some good foundations and some good tools will help you to make good-for-you delicious meals with less stress. And, it all begins with a whole and natural foods pantry.

good-quality fats

Fats are a primary source of many of our most nourishing and essential nutrients. Unfortunately, the molecular structure of fat makes it very vulnerable to light, heat and oxygen and creates perfect conditions for the formation of free radicals. By definition, a free radical is a molecule that has one extra or one missing electron – this is problematic because molecules prefer to have paired electrons, giving them stability, holding them together, so to speak. Oxygen-containing molecules are particularly susceptible to radicalisation. These unbalanced molecules (the free radical) will literally tear through cell walls, damaging cellular structures and DNA, trying to rebalance themselves (free-radical damage is arguably considered to be at the root cause of many degenerative diseases). Nature can protect us against some free-radical damage with antioxidants – in effect, they generously give hydrogen atoms to the free radical, thus stopping its quest to steal them from other atoms (and thus forming more free radicals) – vitamin E for example. Whilst all fats will ultimately become rancid from light, heat and oxygen those with double bonds (mono-unsaturated and polyunsaturated fatty acids) will do so more quickly – the more double bonds (polyunsaturated) the more damage. Saturated fats have no double bond and are amongst the most stable fats.

In the words of nutritionist Marion Nestle, 'The problem with nutrient-by-nutrient nutrition science, is that it takes the nutrient out of the context of food, the food out of the context of diet and the diet out of the context of lifestyle.'

The way an oil has been processed is incredibly important. Petroleum solvent extraction may be cheap, but it results in a highly damaged (rancid) end result, however, you won't smell this because it has been bleached and deodorised, with many of the nutrients destroyed in the process. I choose oils that are extracted by stone pressing (olive oil) or expeller pressed. These oils have a naturally higher flavour and colour and this is as it should be – an oil should always reflect in look and in taste the plant seed from which it comes. Highly unsaturated oils (such as flax, walnut and chia) should always be extracted in the absence of oxygen and light. Good-quality oils are bottled under nitrogen into dark-coloured bottles, with an inert gas added to fill the gap between the oil and the lid (thus leaving no room for oxygen). All this will help protect it from oxidising, but the less saturated it is (the more double bonds it has) and the more it is exposed to heat, light and oxygen (from when it is pressed, and then removing the lid) the faster it will begin to deteriorate.

Below is a list of the fats and oils I prefer to use and these have nourished traditional peoples for hundreds of years. As any chemical or pesticide will store in fat, it is especially important to use organic fats and oils. Xenoestrogens will also store in fat, and for this reason fat is always best stored in glass, rather than plastic.

STABLE FATS AND OILS FOR HEATING
*Store at room temperature except where noted.

Butter is my first choice for baking and eating, and I tend to make cultured butter for its delicious flavour and beneficial bacteria. Because butter is made up of about 20 per cent water and milk solids, it's not the best option for frying as the milk solids burn. Ghee (page 44) is very easy to make and is my personal favourite as it enhances the flavour of all it touches.

Rendered fat or drippings from roasting a bird, frying bacon or chicken skin, have the ability to intensely flavour a dish. Keep these rendered fats separated, sealed in small containers in the fridge. Lard is especially good for frying and baking.

Coconut One of the most highly saturated fats, thus very stable. This delicious fat is also rich in easily digestible short and medium chain fatty acids that are also powerful antivirals, antifungals and antimicrobials.

Full-flavoured coconut oil Comes in two forms – with and without flavour and often labelled 'extra virgin' and 'virgin' respectively. Don't rely on that however, different brands call them different things, so it's worth getting to know your brand. Perfect for frying and deep-frying.

Desiccated or shredded fresh/dried coconut Use on its own, or grind into coconut butter. It contains everything that coconut contains – protein, fibre, vitamins, minerals, including the fat, but it is important to note coconut butter is not pure fat as above. Coconut butter is a wonderful choice when making dairy-free chocolate, nut and seed balls and such, as it holds its shape even when hot – pure coconut oil will melt at body temperature. Coconut milk/cream should be free from additives and full fat. Once opened, store in the fridge.

Extra virgin olive oil I like to taste before I buy, choosing one with a full and fruity flavour. This monounsaturated oil is great for shallow-frying, baking and in dressings.

Unrefined sesame oil While not as stable as olive or macadamia oil, because it has its own heat-activated antioxidant (sesamin), it can withstand gentle heating. I love it for its fragrance and use it in dressings or drizzled over stir-fries or steamed vegetables.

Nut-based oils *Store in a very cold and dark place. Even more stable to heat than olive oil, monounsaturated macadamia oil is a wonderful option for shallow-frying, baking and dressings.

I use the less stable monounsaturated peanut oil for flavour – in dressings and for drizzling over a stir-fry or cooked vegetables.

NEVER HEAT
*Store in a very cold, dark place.

Walnut oil Delicious drizzled over a salad or cooked vegetables.

Flax oil I take this as is, for dressings or smoothie additions.

whole grains, flours, pasta and noodles

Whole is the best possible way to have your grain, but for easier and quicker cooking they can be broken into smaller pieces (in a food processor or blender), flattened by rolling, or ground into a meal or flour. Having a broad range of whole and semi-refined grains, meals and flours in your pantry and fridge will guarantee that you have a nourishing meal at your fingertips.

Whole grains are a rich store of protein, numerous vitamins and minerals, quality fats and complex carbohydrates in many forms, including fibre, and have fabulous nutritional value. When referring to whole grains, I am talking about grains that have only had the inedible hull removed, with as much of its bran intact as possible. In some countries this hull is referred to as the husk. Once the inedible hull is removed, a grain is made up of three parts: germ, endosperm and bran.

● *Germ* rich in B vitamins and fat, it also contains some protein and minerals.
● *Endosperm* at the very core of the kernel lies the starch, with some protein and small amounts of vitamins and minerals.

● *Bran* this is the outer skin of the seed. It protects the valuable fat stored in the germ and endosperm from light and insect damage. It is rich in B vitamins, antioxidants and fibre.

In keeping with my philosophy that we shouldn't be ultra-focused on the nutritional profile of a food, I'm not going to go into their individual nutritional strengths – honestly, they are all fabulous. Without their inedible hull, grains as they are, will be called different things by different grain consortiums. For example, wheat and its ancient relatives are known as berries but oats or buckwheat are known as kernels or groats. When you take that and break it to a smaller size it is commonly called a meal (polenta or grits), if steamed and rolled it will be called rolled or flaked, and when ground to a very small size it becomes flour. Those flours will often have different names and meanings from country to country.

Buying and storing It's worthwhile finding a brand of whole grains and flours that you like. I prefer to buy whole grains from bulk bins, as with the higher turnovers the grains tend to be fresher. I store them in an airtight dark glass jar in a cool dry pantry. If you have hot summers, put them in the fridge. The minute you break that grain into pieces and the germ is exposed (rolled, flaked, cracked grains and flour) it degrades very quickly.

A NOTE ON PUFFED AND CRISPY FLAKED GRAINS Puffed and crispy flaked grains, albeit organic or labelled 'health food', are nowhere near close to their natural state. Often, they will be added to crackers and coated with a high amount of sugar. They are highly processed using extreme pressure and heat, which makes the protein especially vulnerable and, some believe, toxic to the nervous system.

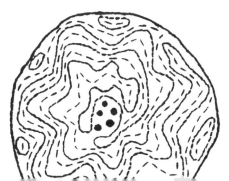

GLUTEN GRAINS

Barley (low gluten) I like to use organic 'pearled' barley, with an obvious presence of the buff-coloured germ intact. Natural, naked or 'hulled' barley is an heirloom variety that grows with very little hull. With an earthy and honest flavour, barley flour is one of my favourites. How it is made varies among producers, but I prefer the flour to have some obvious bran and germ throughout.

How to use Barley is a high-starch, low-gluten grain. It is great added to soups and stews, and makes a welcome alternative to rice on its own or in a pilaf. Barley can also be used in grain salads or in stuffing mixtures.

Oats (low gluten) There's a fair amount of controversy over whether oats contain gluten or not – I lean towards the 'yes they do' side. Oats are sold as kernels (or groats) and if you have a roller mill, you can roll them – making them quicker to cook – when needed. Because the fats in oats are so vulnerable, shop-bought oats are almost always steamed before rolling, and called 'stabilised' rolled oats. In Australia, oatmeal is most widely accepted as stabilised oat kernels that are ground into a rough meal. However, elsewhere oatmeal may simply be the unstabilised oat kernel, or rolled oats, ground into meal. Oat flour is made from sifting oatmeal to get rid of the bran and germ.

How to use Oat kernels do not cook into separate grains – moreover, they burst open, and impart distinct creaminess to any dish they are added to. Add them to soups or stews or use as porridge. With a high fat content, oats (rolled, meal and flour) add sweetness and moisture to most baking, but beware that too much meal or flour can result in a gummy texture.

The wheat and ancient wheat family This is a large and complex family, consisting of newer hybridised wheat grains, and the ancient form from which they are descended. Wheat is most commonly sold in three varieties:

- *Hard (winter)* a high-protein variety, for making bread and pizza
- *Soft (spring)* a low-protein variety, for baking cakes and biscuits
- *Durum* a high-protein, very hard wheat used for pasta.

Before wheat as we know it, there was a huge range of 'original wheats' – einkorn (farro and piccolo), emmer (farro medio), spelt (farro grande) and kamut (khorasan).

Spelt is my favourite grain. While technically it is an ancient 'wheat', I tend to think of it as an entirely independent grain to common wheat. Spelt has a slightly different gluten profile, is highly water soluble and easier to digest.

I store a limited range of pasta and noodles, in particular, spelt lasagne sheets, spaghetti and a couple of pasta shapes. For baking, my go-to flour is both white and wholemeal spelt flour, for its flavour and crumb. In wholemeal spelt flour, the bran should be visible. With white spelt flour, how much bran or germ that is visible can vary enormously between brands. Some are quite 'white' and others are similar to a light wholemeal. It's good to bear in mind that the more 'wholemeal' your white spelt is, the more liquid it will absorb. For example if your recipe calls for white spelt flour but yours looks more like a light wholemeal, I recommend sifting the flour to catch most of the germ and bran, which you can discard. Then measure out the required quantity from the sifted flour. I also keep the nutty and buttery sweet-flavoured kamut flour, which makes a beautiful shortcrust pastry, and a low-protein cake flour from wheat – both white and wholemeal.

Rye (low gluten) While closely related to wheat, rye is lower in gluten and consequently makes heavier and denser bread. Rye is high in phytase, and for this reason is very popular for sourdough starters.

sprouted
whole oats

sifted oatmeal
for oat flour

rolled oats

steelcut oats
(from whole)

whole oat kernels

GLUTEN-FREE GRAINS

Amaranth Incredibly nutrient dense and considered to be a complete protein, this carbohydrate grain smells of grass and earth and is easy to digest. I also keep flakes (steamed and rolled amaranth, and flour).
How to use With a high level of amylopectin starch, amaranth becomes silken in texture when cooked. It is best served in a soup or broth, or mixed with another grain, such as rice and perfect for porridge, too. The flakes can be used in place of rolled oats for texture in baking, but be careful using the flour – its strong beetroot (beet) flavour can easily overwhelm.

Buckwheat Along with rhubarb, buckwheat is a member of the high-oxalate knotweed family. By all means sprout it if you wish, but it is best eaten cooked. It is often sold with its dark brown hull attached but I prefer it hulled, showing its glorious tan/green colour bran, and often called a groat. Once toasted, it's called kasha.
How to use I prefer toasting the buckwheat groats before using. This helps tame buckwheat's desire to explode like cotton wool into a starchy mess once cooked. Whole buckwheat is delicious in salads (particularly with earthy root vegetables), pilaf or pudding. I like buckwheat flour to be ground from the hulled groat and have some bran visible. Be careful as the flour is assertive and perfumed in flavour, and is best used with other flours, especially brown rice flour. Soba noodles are absolutely delicious for Asian-inspired noodle bowls, stir-fries or salads.

Maize (corn) Nothing is more confusing to the consumer than maize. This is partly due to the fact that it is called by both its technical name maize (Zea mays) and corn(e) – the name given to it by the English settlers upon first seeing it. Both terms, maize and corn, are correct, but in this book I will refer to it as the latter. 'Corn' encompasses far more than the vegetable variety (sweet corn). The other varieties, known as field corns, are treated as grains:

- *Flint corn* hard and flinty and remaining so when coarsely or finely ground.
- *Dent corn* softer than flint corn with kernels that have a noticeable 'dent'. This is most commonly used for cornmeal and cornflour (cornstarch).
- *Flour corn* softer starch good for flour. When buying, look for corn products that are milled from the whole corn with its germ intact.

- *Polenta* Most often made from hard flint corn. The hardness is what gives true polenta its creamy and toothsome texture. In many cases the skin and germ are removed to extend shelf life.

- *Pozole (masa, masa harina, maseca)* When dent or flint corn is soaked and cooked in an alkaline solution – or nixtamalised – you get pozole (or hominy). This technique is a wonderful example of traditional wisdoms. Native Americans always soaked their corn in water that had run through the ash from woodfires – making it highly alkaline. This removes the skin and germ, releases the vitamin B3 (nicotinamide) and increases the bio-availability of the protein. These are either dried to use in stews or ground into masa, masa harina or maseca.
How to use Masa is a true wonder, intensely delicious and is used most commonly to make tortillas (page 190) and nacho chips. It is a great tool for binding patties and is an essential in the gluten-free household.

- *Cornmeal or maizemeal* Both are correct and indicate a coarsely ground meal, but they are not quite the same as polenta. Cornmeal is most commonly made from dent or flour corn.

- *Corn (maize) flour* This is often referred to as 'golden cornflour' due to its obvious golden hue. It is a finely ground wholegrain flour that is excellent as a gluten-free coating for fritters and patties.

What we know as cornflour or cornstarch (the white one used to thicken things, see above) is the white starch inside the highly refined grain.

Millet Vastly underrated, millet is a superb, gluten-free grain with a buttery flavour and one of the very few alkaline grains. I prefer the inedible hull removed, called hulled millet.
How to use Millet is very similar to buckwheat – it likes to explode to a rather mushy mess when cooked. For using in salads, it is best given the tea towel treatment (page 67) and then fluffed up with a fork. If millet is left to sit, once cooked, covered, it will stick together making it ideal for using in stuffing or patties. Millet is often considered to be the original polenta and you can use it in this manner (see page 186).

Quinoa Another high-protein (considered complete) and low-carbohydrate grain, quinoa grows with its own bitter insecticide (Saponin). This is usually rinsed off before being sold, but if your quinoa is bitter, it most likely has not been and will need to be very well rinsed before soaking.
How to use Quinoa is an incredibly flexible grain that cooks up to a delicious, intact grain ideal for salads, stuffings or side dishes. The flakes can be used in place of rolled oats for texture in baking, but be careful of the flour – it can be strong in flavour and brands vary enormously.

Rice The rice family is made up of so many varieties, but in essence, we can classify rice as short/medium grain and long grain. No rice is naturally white; it is the bran and germ that determines its colour and this varies between types of rice. White rice is made by removing the bran and germ (refining it). Semi-refined rice, consists of grain with just some of the bran and germ removed, offering the best of both worlds. Short-grain rice is generally sticky and is the best choice for puddings or sushi. Medium-grain rice is not as sticky but lends itself well to salads, and long-grain is great for savoury dishes such as fried rice or pilaf.

● *Fragrant rice* The long and slender basmati rice and jasmine rice are two very well-known members of this family.

● *Brown rice* This is what I most commonly use and buy as the bran and germ have not been removed. Look for brown rice that has obvious green kernels – an indication that the rice has not been gassed for ripening.
● *Sticky or glutinous rice* With a high amylopectin starch level, these rices are very sticky. When cooked, this starch becomes translucent, giving a sheen to dishes cooked with it. Used for traditional puddings, desserts and porridges, but also the essential ingredient for amasake (see page 24) and mochi.
● *Wild rice* Technically, this is not part of the rice family, but an aquatic grass seed. Because this seed is fermented after harvest, it is rich in B vitamins, with an assertive and nutty flavour.

Rice flour This is my first choice for gluten-free baking. If grinding it yourself, use medium and shorter grains as they will give a starchier end result. Rice flour is available in brown or white, and it is worth having both in your pantry.

● *Sweet rice flour* Flour from sweet, sticky or glutinous rice. Starchier than other rice flours, this is a good choice in gluten-free baking.
● *Mochi* This is pounded sweet rice that has been dried, cut and packaged. Baked, grilled or fried, it will puff up to a delicious snack – it's delicious fried in coconut oil, with honey.

Teff Many traditional cultures pride their strength on a grain, and the Ethiopian teff is no exception. With tiny seeds, teff is one of the highest grain sources of calcium and vitamin C. Teff flour is particularly good for gluten-free baking; being subtle in flavour it won't overpower like other gluten-free flours and it gives a uniquely moist and delicate crumb.

Chickpea (besan) flour Because chickpeas contain easy to digest complex carbohydrates, they are often ground into a gluten-free flour, which adds a wonderfully soft and moist texture to baking.

STARCHES AND THICKENERS Cornflour (cornstarch), arrowroot, tapioca flour and kudzu (kuzu) are all starch-based thickening agents that can also be used to help provide structure in baked goods.

Kudzu (kuzu) I cannot imagine my pantry without kudzu. Made from the root of the kudzu plant, this thickener is well known for its medicinal qualities in China and Japan, where it is traditionally used to treat digestive problems, such as an upset stomach or to soothe the nerves. When used to thicken sauces, it imparts a beautiful, clear sheen to the finished sauce. Good kudzu can be a little lumpy and it is best crushed before measuring. Two teaspoons will set one cup of liquid to a sauce consistency and one tablespoon to a pudding consistency.

Arrowroot Similar in appearance to cornflour (cornstarch), true arrowroot comes from the root of a tropical plant and is gluten free. Look for it as an ingredient on packets when buying, as much of the arrowroot sold is actually tapioca flour. True arrowroot is a rich source of trace minerals and calcium, and it is this mineral content which differentiates it from tapioca flour. I prefer to use true arrowroot as it's more nutritious, but it's fine to use the more commonly available form of tapioca flour.

Cornflour (cornstarch) This is the finely ground endosperm of corn (maize) (see also page 20), which has little nutrient value. It is, however, particularly useful to help provide body, for example in dairy-free 'cream' or panna cotta. In small amounts, it is also useful as a flour, to aid binding, especially in gluten-free baking. Check the packet when you buy cornflour as it is often actually made from wheat and therefore not gluten free.

Potato starch Many potato starches are actually 'flours' (made from cooked, dried and ground potatoes). Real potato starch is made from the extracted starch of the potato. Used in gluten-free baking or as a thickening agent.

LEAVENING/RAISING AGENTS These allow us to incorporate air in baked goods, thus making them lighter. Chemical leaveners work by mixing together an acid and alkaline ingredient, which when liquid and heat are added, react, creating carbon dioxide.

- *Baking powder* Many commercial baking powders use bicarbonate of soda (baking soda) for alkaline as opposed to the healthier option of potassium bicarbonate. I am happy with either. Be aware of aluminium-based acids used in many commercial baking powders (sodium aluminium sulphate, phosphate aerator, sodium aluminium phosphate) as they are not only bitter in taste but add aluminium to the body. The healthier blends commonly use calcium phosphate.
- *Alkaline alone:* Bicarbonate of soda (baking soda) – when mixed (activated) with an acid, baking soda is a sturdy lifter.
- *Acid alone: Cream of tartar* is a by-product of the wine industry, made from the sediment found in wine casks. Cultured buttermilk, yoghurt, sour cream, vinegar and citrus are all good choices for the acid.

GELLING AGENTS

Agar (kanten) is a nutrient-rich gelling agent made from seaweed. I prefer the powdered form as this provides the most reliable results. Agar will set at room temperature and can be boiled and reheated without losing its gelling ability. It dissolves best in high-pectin fruit juices, however it will not set in vinegars or high-oxalic acid foods, such as chocolate, rhubarb or spinach. To achieve a good, but not too firm, jelly, the basic equation is 3 teaspoons of agar flakes or ½ teaspoon of agar powder per 250 ml (9 fl oz/1 cup) of liquid.

Gelatine aids digestion, especially in cooked and high-protein foods, and one of the reasons why bone broths are so nourishing. I use a powdered one I trust, made from the healthiest, grass-pastured cows. There are ethical brands available and you will find them online at websites such as gpawholefoods.com.au or radiantlifecatalog.com.

chocolate and cocoa (cacao)

Chocolate, as we know it, is the result of a long process. Seeds from the cacao tree are fermented and then spread out to dry. At this stage, the beans are raw. The seeds are then roasted and shelled, resulting in cocoa 'nibs'. Cocoa is high in phytates and oxalates and this traditional manner of preparation has its wisdom. Fermentation and heat delivers many benefits to the seed, helping to reduce its anti-nutrients, including phytic acid (see also page 58). Other than cacao butter, none of the chocolate or cocoa products I keep are raw. I love cocoa nibs for their subtle chocolate flavour and nutty crunch, and keep both natural (undutched) and dutched cocoa powders. They are very different in terms of colour and flavour. Natural cocoa powders are slightly more tart and acidic but give good results for chocolate work. 'Dutched' cocoa powder has been alkalised, which neutralises acidity and softens the cocoa flavour producing a deep chocolatey reddish tone. I like using dutched cocoa for baking and undutched for chocolate work.

Chocolate bars are made of a mixture of cocoa liquor (ground nibs), sweeteners, flavouring, possibly milk powder and emulsifier. The proportions determine the mouthfeel, flavour and use. When buying chocolate, check the percentage on the packet. This determines the percentage of cocoa liquor, and the higher it is the more bitter the chocolate will be. Brands vary, and it is worthwhile to check the sugar used. Most organic brands use raw sugar, but my favourite, the German Rapunzel brand, uses rapadura sugar, and it makes for a beautifully sweetened chocolate. I prefer the dark and bittersweet chocolates and keep both 70 and 56 per cent dark chocolates, along with white chocolate.

extracts and colouring

Although my preference is to use the real ingredient for flavour or colour, I do keep a few high-quality options: rose and orange water, Boyajian citrus oils, rose and almond essence (my favourites are Nielsen-Massey). As for colouring agents, the brands I trust include Dancing Deer Earth-Grown Food Colors, Hullabaloo and India Tree.

sweeteners

I like to have a variety of sweeteners in my pantry, not only to bake with, but to use in savoury dishes to balance the flavours. The following are sweeteners that I consider to be wholesome and that are essentials in my pantry.

Rapadura sugar Rapadura (also known as panela, gur, palm sugar/jaggery, chancaca and papelon) is made from sugarcane and is the most unrefined cane sugar available. Juice is pressed from the sugarcane without heat, and simmered over gentle heat evaporating the water content. The resulting dark granules retain the minerals that are essential for the digestion of sucrose. This vitamin- and mineral-rich rapadura is considered a nourishing food in its traditional home of Latin America. These nutrients, along with polyphenols help to slow down the absorption of sucrose, giving it a naturally low glycaemic index. Rapadura contains about 73–83 per cent sucrose, compared with 99 per cent sucrose in a white sugar.

The production of what we commonly know as sugar, be it white or brown, is very different from that of the rapadura process. Sugarcane juice is boiled under vacuum (to achieve high temperatures without caramelising the sugar) to evaporate the water, forming sugar crystals (hence, we refer to it as a crystallised sugar). All traces of vitamins, minerals, polyphenols and such found in the whole juice are separated off (often sold as golden syrup, treacle and molasses, molasses being the most mineral rich) and the sugar is then, often, bleached. Most often, common brown sugars are simply a white sugar with controlled amounts of molasses, syrup and polyphenols added back. Although rapadura has many wonderful properties, the strong flavour and colour may not always be what you are after.

Slightly more refined cane sugars Often labelled as 'unrefined cane sugar' or 'golden' these are nonetheless slightly more refined than rapadura, being crystallised cane sugars. They have much more of their molasses still intact after the processing path, and are markedly less sweet and more flavourful than their generic counterparts. These vary in crystal size, and I like to have a store of icing (confectioners'), caster (superfine), muscovado and the robust demerara sugar to hand. Although they are never the same as the more body-compatible product that is rapadura, if used in moderation, they are an excellent compromise from time to time. I am particularly fond of golden icing and caster sugars for when I want more sweetness, and less colour and flavour than rapadura.

Maple syrup I love maple syrup. It's such a beautifully flavoured sweetener to use, and it's rich in trace minerals, including calcium. I prefer organic as non-organic can contain formaldehyde traces (used to extend sap flow in the trees and not permitted by the Canadian government).

Palm sugar and coconut palm sugar (jaggery) Palm sugar is made from the sap of the sugar palm, whereas coconut palm sugar is made from the nectar from the blossom of the coconut palm. They are delicious, darkly fragrant and mineral-rich sweeteners. Compared to rapadura sugar, both are less sweet. Palm sugar is sold in logs, which are easily shaved with a sharp knife. Granulated coconut sugars are popular and very widely available.

Maltose-based sweeteners These are some of the most whole sweeteners, made by steeping grains with enzymes that break down the starches into simpler sugars. These complex sugars take much longer to digest than other sweeteners. Brown rice syrup is delicious but can be tricky to use in baking so I tend to stick to using it only in biscuits or creams. Brown rice syrup works well with maple syrup, thinning it out and making it a touch sweeter. Amasake is enzyme rich and made from fermented rice. As a tool in the dairy-free arsenal, amasake is highly underrated. The original rice milk was watered-down amasake, and this method remains superior to many of those commercially available today.

Other useful natural sweeteners
• *Raw, unprocessed honey* with all its enzymes intact.
• *Apple and pear juice concentrates* for adding in small amounts as flavour accents.
• *Dried fruit* – drying fruits is one of the oldest forms of preserving and I love to use them in the cooler months. They are always organic, sulphur-free and never coated in oil. This means they are expensive. I store them in the fridge as it's the only way I can keep them free from parasites.
• *Vincotto* has a delicious, earthy sweetness. It is made from overripe grape juice, evaporated to a thick consistency over a gentle heat (see page 28 for more). It is then left to sit in oak casks where the flavour continues to develop.

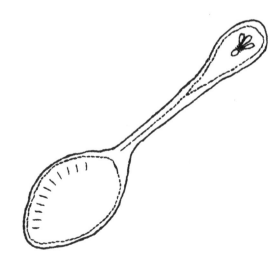

legumes

Beans, lentils and peas (including split) are all legumes and provide a rich source of protein and complex carbohydrate. Unlike meat, poultry, fish and eggs they are not a complete protein, bar one exception being the soya bean. Legumes can also be a rich source of B complex vitamins and a host of minerals including iron. It's important to note, however, that the iron in legumes is of the non-heme variety meaning it is not absorbed readily by the body. When eating them, you can aid the absorption process by incorporating foods that are rich in vitamin C such as leafy green vegetables, berries, tomatoes and capsicums (peppers).

I keep jars and jars of legumes above my stove and on the shelves in my pantry and love that they are so economical while providing a nutrient-dense and delicious meal.

Within this large family (*Leguminosae* or *Fabaceae*) there are many sub-families, and some of these, such as the beans we find from the *Phaseolus vulgaris* (meaning common) sub-family are harder to digest. To put it simply, they can be split into two groups: beans that require long soaking and cooking times and lentils and split peas, which have shorter soaking times and are easier to digest.

BEANS Beans differ from lentils and the pea family as they contain long chain sugars called oligosaccharides, which require an enzyme the human stomach does not make to break them down. Those long chain sugars essentially reach the large intestine intact where they are metabolised by bacteria, producing methane and carbon dioxide gas, one of the contributing factors to the flatulence problem associated with beans. Not all beans have such long chain sugars, namely adzuki and mung beans, and chickpeas.

The life of a bean goes through a few stages. When very young, we can eat the pod and the very immature seed within – that pod will still be moist and delicious, but as the seed matures the pod loses that moisture and eventually becomes a fibrous, inedible shell. The moist fresh seed is the most delicious way to eat a bean, requiring no soaking. Those oligosaccharides develop as the bean dries (its sugars transform into starch) and this older bean must be properly prepared and well cooked (see page 59). Many organic dried beans that are available are old and do not cook well. I tend to buy and use what is more local (to my country) or what I can grow. My favourites include adzuki, black (turtle), borlotti (cranberry) and pinto, Christmas lima and cannellini beans, and chickpeas (garbanzo beans).

Tempeh

To make tempeh, soya beans are soaked, dehulled, cooked and sometimes split. Any other legume or grain can be used to make tempeh – it is not always strictly a soya product – and I am lucky to have access to chickpea tempeh. Once cooked, the beans are inoculated with the *Rhizopus oligosporus* bacteria and left to ferment for the spores to spread, forming a thin fuzz (mycelium) over the beans, transforming them into a firm cake. Along with miso, tempeh is my preferred soya medium and is probably one of the most 'body compatible' of the soya products. Fermentation delivers many benefits to the soya bean: it greatly reduces oligosaccharides – those nasty complex sugars in beans that can cause flatulence, it makes the protein easy to digest and most importantly, deactivates the phytates and enzyme inhibitors present. Tempeh must be cooked. I love the nutty flavour of tempeh. I buy uncooked tempeh, often sold frozen.

I think we also often forget that beans contain some very complex carbohydrates and require a robust and healthy digestive system – children with immature digestive systems or those with compromised digestive systems (such as the sick, elderly, allergic and intolerant) are not always able to digest them well.

LENTILS AND PEAS Lentils or peas that have been husked and split are also known as dal, and there are many varieties. My favourites include mung dal, French green lentils, black beluga lentils, whole and split red lentils, yellow and green split peas, and black-eyed peas.

While lentils and peas don't have the issue of oligosaccharides, they are seeds so are best soaked to reduce the anti-nutrients (see page 59). These legumes are the handiest things to have in your pantry – quick to cook and even without soaking they are much easier to digest than beans. If you run out of time to soak them, the world won't end, but just like an unsoaked grain, if you have some bone stock or butterfat on hand, it will act as a buffer to some of the effects of the anti-nutrients.

nuts and seeds

I don't keep a large range of nuts and seeds as I prefer to use them in balance and moderation – not as a primary fuel or primary nourishment source. I believe we eat far too many today, mostly because we're hungry. I love using them to provide texture and flavour in a dish – especially baking and to help build a protein profile in a vegetarian or vegan dish. For paleo, vegan, gluten-free and dairy-free diets that heavily rely on nuts and seeds, it is essential that these are activated with a good fermentation time (see pages 58–59).

With large amounts of polyunsaturated fatty acids, nature goes to a lot of trouble to protect nuts and seeds from light, heat and oxygen. Take for example, the thick and dark colour of the shell, the hull and bran of the seed. When these are removed, they will immediately begin to deteriorate and the more unsaturated that fat, the quicker they will become rancid. When that nut or seed is ground, rancidity will occur more quickly. The nuts I use most often are almonds, macadamias, hazelnuts, pecans and walnuts, all of which I store in the fridge or freezer. When buying almond meal (also known as almond flour), I choose meal made from blanched almonds, as this is free from tannins and phytic acid. I keep sunflower, sesame and pumpkin seeds (pepitas).

sea vegetables

You will always find a broad range of sea vegetables in my pantry, waiting to add their nutritional bounty to many dishes. They are rich sources of protein, vitamins A (in the form of beta carotenes), B, C, E and K, trace elements, carbohydrates and unsaturated fats and some of the richest and most concentrated sources of minerals, including calcium, zinc, iron and iodine. *These foods are traditionally used in small amounts within the context of a broader diet.*

When buying, choose sea vegetables that are sourced from clean waters – these will invariably be more expensive, and knowing your brand is absolutely essential. Trustworthy brands include Maine Coast Sea Vegetables, Spiral, Eden, Pacific Harvest, Santos Organics, Kai Ho/Ocean's Treasure, Mitoku and Muso (available from good health food, organic or wholefood shops). But there are many more, so I encourage you to look around and talk to people at your local health food store. Sea vegetables are easily stored in an airtight container and will keep indefinitely in a cool, dark and dry place.

How to use Most dried sea vegetables need to be rehydrated before use and will be easier to digest this way. Simply cover well with water and soak for 15–30 minutes. Strain and squeeze out the excess liquid and rinse before using. Agar, kombu or wakame can be added to stock, legumes or grains, infusing all the goodness into the pot.

As they are all rich sources of iodine (some more so than others), you may need to reduce the salt used in the dish, adding further tamari, miso or salt towards the end of cooking, to taste. When soaked, sea vegetables are especially tasty in salads and stir-fries. In their dried form, many can be toasted and sprinkled over grains for extra texture and flavour.

- *Arame* is strong-tasting and noted for its high levels of iron. It comes pre-cooked, in noodle-like pieces, and needs to be rehydrated before use.
- *Dulse* is a beautiful purple almost cerise colour, noted for its high protein and iron levels, it is ready to eat from the packet and has a soft, chewy consistency.
- *Kombu,* known for its high iodine content and amino acid glutamine is a natural flavour enhancer, the flavour being umami. It is my essential ingredient when making vegetarian or vegan stocks, and because it contains the enzyme alpha-galactosidase required to break down the oligosaccharides in beans, it is my first choice when soaking and cooking those. We should not be overzealous about eating every scrap of kombu that we cook, with the issues of kombu and iodine. Soak and cook with it, yes, include some in what you make, yes, but don't go crazy eating lots of it.
- *Wakame* – when rehydrated, this subtle-flavoured green leaf is especially wonderful in salads and I've roasted it for the Wakame Gomasio (page 80). It can be used to enhance flavour and make beans more digestible, though not to the same extent as kombu.
- *Nori* – in its original state, the deep purple–red leaves are beautiful when soaked and used in salads. Commonly sold as nori sheets, these are made by drying the leaves and pressing them between bamboo sheets. Only when this sheet is toasted will it be green. The toasted nori sheets are great crumbled into miso soup or over a bowl of steamed vegetables and brown rice.

vinegars

Unpasteurised and unfiltered vinegars are rich in amino acids, trace elements and minerals. Vinegar should always be bought and stored in glass, never plastic. Try your best to choose high-quality and artisanal vinegars.

My favourites are the slightly sweet and fruity apple cider vinegar, which is my all-purpose vinegar, brown rice vinegar for Asian influences, balsamic for stronger, fruitier and sharper Mediterranean background notes and a well-aged Pedro Ximénez sherry vinegar. Raspberry vinegar is especially delicious with beetroot and strawberries, but of all the vinegars, vincotto vinegar remains the most special. Vincotto is a dark sweet reduction, made from slow-cooked overripe grapes. The syrup is left to mature for three years in oak barrels, and at this time vinegar made from the same grapes as the vincotto is added to the barrel and left to ferment over many months until the flavour is mellow. Pure vincotto vinegars should not be heated or cooked but rather drizzled over foods, imparting its acidic yet mellow flavour.

herbs and spices

Herbs and spices help add dimensions of flavour to your cooking. Herbs can be used both fresh and dried – in general, fresh herbs will have a more fragrant, lighter and brighter flavour than their dried counterparts. I grow a simple range of herbs that I like such as basil, coriander, fennel, oregano, rosemary, lemon thyme and thyme. I use them both fresh and hang them to dry.

Because the multi-dimensional flavours of spices are carried on volatile oils that once exposed to oxygen can diminish quite rapidly, I prefer to buy spices as the whole seed, rather than ground. I then toast (where applicable) and grind small amounts as needed, or enough for a short period of time stored in a small glass jar, in a cool, dark place.

SPICES I KEEP Allspice, cinnamon, nutmeg, cloves, cardamom, cumin, coriander, yellow and brown mustard seeds, fennel seeds, ginger, juniper berries, black, white and red peppercorns, turmeric, mustard powder, mace, smoked paprika (brands vary widely in bitterness and smokiness), chipotle chillies (whole and ground), and New Mexico red chilli powder.

VANILLA Vanilla is one of my favourite flavours. I keep vanilla pods (which should be plump and soft), extract and paste. Although there are rules that govern what an extract or essence should be, I've found these vary from country to country. I refer to it in my recipes as natural vanilla extract and recommend you look for one that only has vanilla and alcohol and no sweeteners or additives.

salty things

Everything we use in a dish contributes to how delicious the end result is, however, there are some key ingredients that work wonders to lift or balance the flavour of a dish.

Salt plays a vital role in cooking – just as light allows objects to be seen, salt allows flavours to be tasted. This does not mean that adding a whole heap of salt will make a dish delicious – it means that the flavour must already be present, and a judicious use of salt will allow that flavour to be more 'visible'. These are my favourite ways of adding salt to a dish:

SEA SALT Good-quality salt is an important part of a wholesome diet. Not only is it essential for the gut, it is also a rich source of minerals, including iodine. There is a huge difference between a mineral-rich, unrefined sea salt and a refined, bleached and concentrated sodium chloride that is sold as 'salt'. I prefer unrefined sea salt, which contains over 80 trace minerals that match the mineral profile of our blood. Land salts will have this mineral profile subtly altered, as they take on minerals from the soil or rocks

– for example iron – and this will often colour them. I also like to have a couple of salts that have been infused with herbs or sea vegetable; these allow me to add a unique dimension of flavour to any given dish.

ANCHOVIES AND FISH SAUCE Anchovies alone, or left to ferment over time with salt to make fish sauce, have been used for thousands of years to add a umami kick and saltiness. Look for fish sauces that are labelled First Press, have the highest level of fish (shown on the label as degrees) and no sugar, and anchovies packed in olive oil.

CAPERS IN SALT The unopened flower bud of the *Capparis spinosa* plant, capers are a delicious and unique savoury taste – a little like green olives, yet more lemony. I absolutely prefer capers preserved in salt as opposed to cured in vinegar, and even when the salt is rinsed off (before using) they can still add quite a salty hit to a dish.

OLIVES In their raw state, olives are inedible with high levels of bitter phenolic compounds so they require curing or soaking in salt brine (and fermentation) to make them edible. Unfortunately, not everyone does a good job of this and many still have a noticeable bitterness. I am a big fan of tasting olives before I buy.

SHOYU, TAMARI AND MISO These are all salty, soya-based sauces or pastes, fermented over varying lengths of time with koji. Fermentation delivers many benefits to the soya bean, making it far more digestible – for example, breaking down phytic acid, enzyme inhibitors and transforming complex carbohydrates into simpler ones. It pays to be brand savvy when buying soya products such as shoyu, tamari and miso (see opposite) and where possible, choose organic (although expensive they are worth it). Cheaper brands use genetically modified soya beans, but quicker industrial processes reduce what was originally a deeply nutrient-dense food to its simplest and nutrient-shallow version. Some brands will use free amino acids to speed up the brewing process, which can have similar effects to MSG (monosodium glutamate).

Shoyu and tamari These sauces are beautiful ways to salt your dish, adding complex flavour and grounding it at the same time. Aged over years, shoyu has a deeply delicious and complex flavour rich in B vitamins, protein and enzymes to aid digestion, but wheat is involved in its production. Made over a shorter period of time, I find tamari lighter in flavour and choose a wheat-free option. When the weather is hot, I keep these in the fridge.

Miso Whilst traditionally made with cooked soya beans, and sometimes a grain, it can equally be made with legumes – chickpeas for example, with no soya or grain at all. For the most potent effect, miso should be unpasteurised – in this way it is a rich source of beneficial bacteria and enzymes. There are many varieties of miso, with length of fermentation and/or other grains used, all affecting the end taste. Miso has a long shelf life – once opened, store in an airtight container in the fridge for up to 12 months.

Some of my favourites are:
- *Unpasteurised brown rice genmai miso* Mellow and mild, genmai miso is delicious on bread or crackers (page 113), or added to dressings or sauces. Pasteurised miso is much cheaper and I use it in stews or soups as a salty, savoury and earthy stock base.
- *Shiro (white) miso* Also known as sweet or mellow miso, white rice and soya beans are fermented with less salt, over a short period of time. I use this a lot to replace dairy – for example in dairy-free dips or dressings. With its noticeably sweet taste, a small amount helps to replicate the full, velvety flavours of dairy in the mouth.
- *Chickpea miso* Similar to shiro miso, this has a sweet and mellow taste but with more depth of flavour.

UMEBOSHI PLUMS Fermented in a salty brine, with the herb shiso (perilla), umeboshi plums are one of the most alkaline foodstuffs around. Umeboshi plums are traditionally used to balance expanded states (jet lag, tiredness, nausea, hangovers, too much sugar). Available as whole plums or paste, I use these as my 'salt' when I also desire a fruity addition to the dish. They will keep in an airtight container in the fridge indefinitely. To use simply cut as much plum as you require into small pieces and add to the dish, tasting as you go.

MUSTARD Good mustard is one of the most common foods that represents the flavour of pungency. Other foods that represent this flavour are chilli, garlic, some herbs and spices. Pungency stimulates digestion and it is classically used Ayurvedically for this. Mustard is also an emulsifier, and is used in this manner, for example, in a dressing. I keep both wholegrain and a Dijon mustard.

MIRIN Made from sweet brown rice, rice koji and water, this is a glorious fermented product, with an alcohol content around 10 per cent (this is higher in organic brands). Traditionally called 'the mother of taste', it smoothes out what is discordant and harsh. It is a classic and wonderful match to the astringent lentil, gives the sticky gloss to many a savoury and sweet glaze, but even simply paired with shoyu or tamari as a marinade or dipping sauce it is superb. Be wary of imitation mirin – it is mostly sugar, corn syrup, ethyl alcohol and fermenting agents – cheap, but nasty.

WORCESTERSHIRE SAUCE Worcestershire sauce belongs to a large group of fermented sauces that all include fish, with the end result being a high glutamate/umami sauce that delivers flavour to everything it touches. Soy, fish, tamarind, vinegar and molasses are the traditional ingredients.

DRIED SHIITAKE MUSHROOMS are my number one go-to dried mushrooms, when an earthy, grounding and meaty flavour is called for. Donko is a highly prized shiitake mushroom and refers to its traditional outdoors growing method on wood, rather than inside on an artificial substrate. This is the one I buy. The shiitake is considered to be a premium immune-boosting food, rich in protein and B vitamins, and one of the few vegetarian sources of vitamin D (in the form of ergosterol), but this will require conversion and I would not base my requirements for this critical fat-soluble vitamin on shiitake, but rather the animal sources.

CURRY PASTES Incredibly handy in an emergency, I keep massaman and laksa curry pastes in glass jars in a cool, dark place, or in the fridge.

PESTO I cannot imagine my kitchen without pesto, which I consider to be a paste of seasonal herbs, with added extras – commonly nuts and cheese or miso. In a sense, it is the Mediterranean equivalent of the Asian curry pastes. If I have a jar of pesto in the fridge over summer, or freezer and pantry over winter, I can deliver deliciousness in a minute.

bottled and tinned basics

I love preserving the bounty of the season and use jams, marmalades, fruit butters, chutneys and relish to achieve the end result I am after. A touch of quince butter might be the earthy sweetness that a lentil braise requires, a spoonful of lime marmalade will make that fish curry sing or a touch of chutney will bring a dal together.

I also keep high-quality options of bottled or tinned basics on hand. Where possible, I will buy preserved fruit or vegetables in glass jars rather than tinned as so many tins are plastic lined. Although if buying tinned tomatoes, for example, I look for brands that are BPA-free (such as Honest to Goodness) and don't use plastic. It is also handy to have a select few tins of beans, I like black or pinto beans. They can be a lifesaver when making a quick minestrone or Mexican chilli beans. Also, tinned chickpeas for a last-minute soup or dip.

eggs

There are many unethical practices involved in egg production – confining hens in cages, stocking densities, not providing nests or perches or enough space to flap their wings, no access to outdoor ranges and de-beaking. At the very worst end will be caged eggs, with barn-laid, free-range and animal-welfare approved eggs varying in degrees. While free-range and animal-welfare approved are the best of this bunch, de-beaking may or may not be allowed depending on the certifying body. Certified organic or biodynamic eggs will guarantee that none of those practices take place, including eating GM-free feed, but they won't guarantee that male chicks are not killed at birth, or hens are sent to slaughter after egg production slows down (usually around 18 months old). This practice is common to all commercial egg productions and a huge inducement to having chickens at home where possible (roosters can be used as stock or for eating). As the best eggs come from chickens that range widely on grass grown on good soil, eat certified organic or preferably bio-dynamic grain and peck for insects as they roam, I look for eggs that are labelled certified bio-dynamic and grass pastured. I also get to know who the farmer is, and choose eggs that fit the above description in the area I live, but also from a farm where chickens live out their natural life also. These eggs will not be cheap, but will have a far richer omega-3 and fat-soluble vitamin profile, and given how critical both these things are, I consider their cost to be a great investment. Eggs are best kept on the kitchen counter, unless the weather is warm in which case it's a good idea to store them in the fridge as they can deteriorate rapidly in warmer temperatures.

A LITTLE PREP FOR AN EASIER, MORE DELICIOUS LIFE

FOUNDATION
recipes

build good foundations

Having stocked the pantry, and sourced beautiful fresh foods, it will make a huge difference to your week if you can stock your fridge and freezer with basic ingredients to have on hand. Many of the recipes in this section are your primary nutrient-dense foods that will enable you to quickly put together a nourishing and nutrient-packed, delicious meal. These are recipes best made in advance, which will be ready to use at a moment's notice.

Along with vegetables from the market (and fruits where required) you will find full-cream non-homogenised organic or bio-dynamic milks (both pasteurised and unpasteurised), cream, yoghurt and butter, cheeses, miso, opened condiments such as pastes, chutneys and jams, leftovers and any summer visitors such as tamari or shoyu, grains, seeds and nuts in my fridge. In the freezer will be chicken stock and vegetarian stock, and sometimes a fish or duck stock. Pastry, bones, meats and bread also live here along with prepared meals for an emergency. But further to this, my fridge is where I can store my foundations to make my week easier.

stock: the basics

Stocks are so easy to make, simply requiring a lovely big saucepan and a degree of time. They all freeze exceptionally well. Finally, as if this isn't enough encouragement, they cost virtually nothing – they are the original frugal, thrifty food. I find commercial stocks overbearing in flavour, and those made from bones (such as fish, chicken and beef) carry none of the rich, nutrient-dense bounty of gelatine contained in your own homemade stocks.

BONE STOCKS Bone stocks have been used by just about all traditional cultures for nourishment and healing. The original nature doctor, Dr Vogel, describes its use in Europe for healing; in New York chicken soup is known as Jewish penicillin; and throughout Asia, fish stock is the restorer of chi – life force. With its rich store of calcium and other bio-available minerals,

Stock cubes and powders

Originally, many stock cubes, such as Bovril bouillon cubes, were essentially reduced beef stock. Today, however, stock cubes, powders or concentrates often have a large percentage of additives and while some may sound natural (lactose-, glucose- or salt-free), they will almost always be refined. Of most concern is MSG or its many mimics such as hydrolysed vegetable protein. This is a protein obtained from foods (most commonly soya, corn or wheat), which is then broken down into amino acids by a chemical process called acid hydrolysis. When meat is browned, the protein (amino acids) reacts with the sugar – this is known as the Maillard reaction. In the 1950s it was discovered how to induce a Maillard reaction and thus create meat-like flavours in the laboratory. Any protein can be hydrolysed in this way, making free glutamic acid or MSG.

it is invaluable when used to cook grains as it helps to buffer the effects of phytic acid and aids digestion.

Bone stocks are a rich source of minerals and trace elements, which are pulled from the vegetables, bone, marrow, cartilage and tendons as they cook, in the form of electrolytes, a most highly bio-available format. A rich store of calcium and other bio-available minerals means it is invaluable for cooking grains helping to buffer the effects of phytic acid in the grain, and when used to cook beans, the gelatine makes them much easier to digest. Also, bone stock provides valuable calcium in a dairy-free diet, and is a great sources of glucosamine and chondroitin, which are crucial for healthy joints.

Here are just some of the key benefits of using bone stock:
- It is a good source of amino acids – arginine, glycine and especially proline (gelatine).
- Gelatine is an especially valuable tool. It allows the body to use more of the complete protein it eats – this is called 'sparing protein'. This is why you don't need a lot of expensive meat to gain the protein benefits, for example, in an Irish stew (lamb neck) or osso buco (shank). Using meat on the bone is a great way to add extra nourishment to a meal when you don't have bone stock on hand.
- The gelatine in bone stock is exceptionally healing to the gut – soothing and lining the mucous membrane and aiding digestion.
- It helps to protect against and lessen infectious disease. The fat in chicken stock contains palmitoleic acid, which is a microbial monounsaturated fat that is also a powerful immune booster.

Note: You will achieve better results with the recipes in this book with a well-flavoured, well-gelled homemade chicken, duck, beef or fish stock. Alternatively, reduce your stock to intensify its flavour.

VEGETARIAN AND VEGAN STOCKS I like to keep it simple when making a vegetarian stock and prefer earthy vegetables that don't overpower. Dried shiitake mushrooms (see page 32) add both nutrients and a welcome depth of flavour in the cooler weather, while kombu sea vegetable (and to a lesser extent wakame) (see page 26) will add a umami flavour and valuable nutrients, especially minerals. Agar sea vegetable will add mineral and nutrient density, and also gel your stock if needed.

STORAGE This depends on how much space you have. If short on space, once made, stock can be reduced after straining, over medium heat until the desired amount is reached. This can be poured into a dish, covered and kept in the fridge for a considerable length of time, taking out what you need from time to time. It rarely goes mouldy, and if it does, simply remove that bit and reboil the rest. Stock can be poured into ice-cube trays and frozen to make stock ice cubes. Or store in containers for up to three months. I like to freeze the stock in small 250 ml (9 fl oz/1 cup) and 500 ml (17 fl oz/2 cup) containers, giving me the option to use a little or a lot.

dairy: the basics

I love dairy, and enjoy using milk, cream and butter as they come, but I also know that with a little extra work I can make them more digestible with the addional bonus of good bacteria to aid my gut health. On pages 44–54 you'll find easy recipes to transform your regular dairy products into beautiful, and useful, products like ghee, yoghurt and labne.

LACTO-FERMENTED AND CULTURED GOODNESS

Essentially, any foods can be fermented and when we eat them, we ingest the good bacteria that are so important for our gut health. But for myself, I only prepare a limited amount at home, because I just can't do it all. I choose to focus on what I consider to be the most important and easy for me – dairy milk. From this I can make yoghurt or use dairy kefir 'grains' to culture milk to use as desired, or cream, giving me cultured (sour) cream. I can use this delicious, good bacteria-rich cream as it is, or whip it to make cultured butter and cultured buttermilk. In all of these products except for yoghurt I prefer to use raw milk, but I cannot advocate to you that you use this as it is illegal in Australia.

KEFIR 'grains' look like little cauliflowers, but are indeed a symbiotic community of bacteria and yeasts (SCOBY). Rather than just one or two strains of beneficial bacteria, such as you might find in yoghurt, kefir is a deeply complex, multi-strained community and is far more powerful. But, better still, it is incredibly easy to use. You can buy them on the internet or get them from someone who has some extras to spare. Kefir powder is available, but honestly I wouldn't bother as it doesn't usually work.

I love kefir as it's easy to prepare at home. When the grains are added to milk, they find a welcome food source: lactose. As this is consumed, the bacteria and yeasts grow, reproduce and the by-products are lactic acid (which makes it sour), carbon dioxide (which can make it a little bit fizzy) and enzymes. During this process, the milk protein (casein) can also be consumed making the end result an easily digestible product with the added bonus of good bacteria and yeasts.

MY FAVOURITE WAYS TO USE CULTURED DAIRY PRODUCTS
Rich in lactic acid, I use all of these cultured dairy products — kefir milk, yoghurt, sour cream, buttermilk and their whey (dripped from making labne), when soaking my legumes (page 59) and grains (page 63).

If you are dairy free, you can use the lactic acid produced when using other scobies, such as kombucha, water kefir, or when culturing vegetables instead.

40

fish stock

DIETARY INFO GLUTEN FREE | EGG FREE
MAKES ABOUT 3 LITRES (105 FL OZ/12 CUPS)

Fish makes a surprisingly tasty and sweet stock. It's particularly rich in minerals – especially iodine – and other thyroid-strengthening substances. My preference is to avoid using oily fish as this tends to produce an overpowering stock. Most often, I buy the bones and head of the most beautiful fish, such as red mullet, red emperor, pink snapper and so on, for very, very little money from the fishmonger. I often get the wings (which are really quite meaty) thrown in and if the fish is large, they are more than happy to cut the head in half, and the bones into pieces for me. It is always a good idea when buying a whole fish, and having it filleted, to ask for the bones and head to turn into stock.

1 tablespoon butter or ghee
1 large brown onion, coarsely chopped
2 carrots, coarsely chopped
2 celery stalks, coarsely chopped
60 ml (2 fl oz/¼ cup) white wine, or
  2 teaspoons apple cider vinegar
4 thyme sprigs

4 parsley sprigs
1 bay leaf
1–2 fish carcasses (about 600–700 g/
  1 lb 5 oz–1 lb 9 oz)
1–2 fish heads (at least 1 kg/2 lb 4 oz),
  cut in half

Melt the butter in a stockpot or very large heavy-based saucepan over medium heat. Add the onion, carrot and celery, and cook, stirring occasionally for 15 minutes, or until lightly coloured. Pour in the wine and allow it to sizzle and boil, then add the remaining ingredients along with 5–6 litres (175–210 fl oz/20–24 cups) water or enough to cover and bring to a gentle boil. As soon as the stock comes to the boil, reduce the heat to low and simmer gently for 1 hour, skimming any scum from the surface regularly during cooking.

Strain the stock through a colander placed over a bowl, then discard the solids. Allow to cool, then place the stock in airtight containers (see Storage, page 38) and refrigerate for up to 1 week or freeze for up to 3 months.

vegetable stock

DIETARY INFO GLUTEN FREE | DAIRY-FREE OPTION | EGG FREE
MAKES ABOUT 1.5 LITRES (53 FL OZ/6 CUPS)

This is the basic vegetarian stock I invariably make. I like to brown the vegetables in ghee as the fat enables more access to the minerals released from the vegetables. Caramelising the vegetables also deepens the flavour of the stock.

1 tablespoon ghee or olive oil
1 large brown onion, coarsely chopped
5 small–medium carrots, skin-on and
coarsely chopped
1 small–medium sweet potato,
scrubbed and coarsely chopped
2–3 celery stalks, coarsely chopped
5 small–medium dried shiitake
mushrooms, stems snapped off
and discarded

5 cm (2 in) piece kombu or wakame,
or 2 teaspoons agar flakes
3–4 parsley sprigs, with or without
leaves
1 bay leaf
2 thyme sprigs

Heat the ghee in a stockpot or large heavy-based saucepan over medium heat. Add the onion, carrots, sweet potato and celery and cook for 6–7 minutes or until lightly coloured. Add the remaining ingredients and 3 litres (105 fl oz/12 cups) water and bring to a gentle boil. Reduce the heat to low and simmer gently for 1–1½ hours.

Strain the stock through a colander placed over a bowl, then discard the solids. Either use the stock as is, or for a more concentrated flavour, place the stock in a clean pan and simmer over rapid heat for 10–15 minutes, until you have a richer and more concentrated stock.

Allow to cool, then place the stock in airtight containers (see Storage, page 38) and refrigerate for up to 1 week or freeze for up to 3 months.

KITCHEN NOTES
● Play around with the ingredients depending on the season. When onion is scarce, I will often use leek greens or spring onion (scallion) greens. When celery is unavailable, parsley stems (and especially roots) are a great alternative, as are celeriac ribs. Corncobs (with the kernels removed) and the outer leaves of lettuces are flavourful additions too.
● Avoid using vegetables from the cruciferous family such as broccoli, cabbage, cauliflower and brussels sprouts because they ruin the taste of the stock.
● For a stock with Asian flavours you can add ginger, lemongrass and/or kaffir lime leaves. For a stock with Mediterranean flavours, you can add garlic, sage and rosemary.

42

chicken or duck stock

Chicken or duck stock is what I keep as the base stock in my freezer. I prefer its slightly sweet flavour to the richer lamb or beef. As with any bone stock, it is best made with the cartilaginous bits – wings, feet, head – as this is where the best gelatine will come from. If you have access to a rooster or stewing hen (hens that no longer lay eggs), I would encourage you to use that, whole.

6–8 chicken or duck wings
2–3 chicken or duck carcasses
6–8 chicken feet
60 ml (2 fl oz/¼ cup) white wine or
  2 teaspoons apple cider vinegar
3 carrots, scrubbed and
  roughly chopped

3 celery stalks, roughly chopped
1 brown onion, quartered
4 thyme sprigs
4 bay leaves
4 parsley sprigs
2 sage leaves
4 black peppercorns

Place the wings in a stockpot or large heavy-based saucepan and cook over low heat for 20–30 minutes, or until light golden and with an aroma that is very OMG delicious. Add the remaining ingredients (including the carcasses and feet) along with 6–7 litres (210–245 fl oz/24–28 cups) water and bring to a gentle boil. As soon as the stock comes to the boil, reduce the heat to very low and simmer, partially covered for 8–24 hours, skimming any scum from the surface regularly and topping up with extra water when needed. During cooking you should be able to see just a blip of bubbles.

Strain through a colander placed over a bowl, then discard the solids. Either use the stock as is, or for a more concentrated flavour, place the stock in a clean pan and simmer over a fairly rapid heat for 15–20 minutes, until richer and more concentrated.

Allow the stock to cool, then place the stock in airtight containers (see Storage, page 38) and refrigerate for up to 1 week or freeze for up to 3 months.

KITCHEN NOTES

● Adding salt: Personally, I prefer to avoid salt in my stock as I don't know how I am going to be using it, but it's up to you.

● Developing a more complex flavour: Roasting the bones and/or vegetables in the oven first will not only deliver a deeper flavour, but also a darker colour of the stock. In the case of bones, this will render much of the fat, which can be stored for other uses. Bones and/or vegetables can also simply be browned over a gentle heat in the stockpot first before adding the other ingredients.

● The longer the stock cooks, the better. You will have a good stock after 6–8 hours of cooking, but for a deeply nourishing stock, this will take 12–24 hours. As it isn't always possible (and safe) to leave the stock bubbling away on the stovetop overnight, you can simmer it all day, remove from the heat, cool and refrigerate, then continue cooking the following day. If you do leave it overnight, a heat diffuser is a good option for ensuring a low, even heat.

● Never rapidly boil the stock because this can impart a bitter taste – keep the heat at a low simmer.

● Adding a small amount of acid (vinegar, wine) helps to break down the bone and release the nutrients from the bone stock.

KITCHEN NOTE

Take care to cook the butter over a slow, gentle heat. This way, the end result should smell insanely delicious, reminiscent of caramel and not too nutty. If you have a heat diffuser, this can help to keep the heat low.

ghee

DIETARY INFO GLUTEN FREE | VEGETARIAN | EGG FREE
MAKES ABOUT 200 G (7 OZ)

In the end, pure butterfat is what we are really after; Ayurveda considers this the most sacred and nourishing food. Ghee is the final stage in the process of concentrating the fat from milk, separating the watery whey, milk protein and lactose as we go. The process of making ghee is to evaporate off the water and remove the milk solids, giving you pure butterfat. Ghee will add glorious flavour to almost anything it touches and it's wonderful rubbed on your skin too. It is worth mentioning that people who are intolerant to dairy often find they can tolerate ghee so it's absolutely worth a try.

250 g (9 oz) unsalted butter

Melt the butter in a small saucepan over low heat. Once melted, increase the heat to a gentle simmer, taking care not to have the heat too high. As the water evaporates, the butter will gurgle and spit a bit and white foam will form on the surface. After 10–15 minutes the water will have evaporated and the butter will appear like yellow fat, with white bits in it – these are milk solids and they also form part of the foam on the surface of the butterfat. The time it takes for the water to evaporate off will be different depending on the kind of butter used (commercial butters often have more water content than organic ones). As the water evaporates, the foam on top will begin to look drier. Skim the foam off the top as it forms and discard.

When the foam on the top starts reducing and most of it has been skimmed away, check to see if any milk solids in the pan remain – some will have dropped to the bottom of the pan and be lightly browned. Remove the pan from the heat and stand until cool. Skim off any remaining foam and pour through muslin (cheesecloth) into a clean jar and refrigerate for up to 1 month (if the weather is cool it will keep at room temperature).

basic kefir milk

DIETARY INFO GLUTEN FREE | VEGETARIAN | EGG FREE
MAKES ABOUT 435 ML (15¼ FL OZ/1¾ CUPS)
YOU WILL NEED TO BEGIN THIS RECIPE ONE DAY AHEAD

Using dairy kefir 'grains', this culturing process can be applied to most dairy milks and their creams. You can also use them to culture coconut milk or non-dairy milks, but these milks don't have what the grains need to thrive. The grains tend to shrivel or flatten and must be cultured again in dairy milk or cream to keep them healthy.

1 tablespoon kefir grains
500 ml (17 fl oz/2 cups) organic full-cream (whole), non-homogenised milk

Step 1: Begin the process
Place the kefir grains in a clean jar and gently stir in the milk. Cover the top of the jar with a small piece of muslin (cheesecloth) or a lid – either is fine.

Step 2: How to tell when it's ready
Like all life, bacteria and yeasts require warmth to grow. Warmth is indeed a critical factor, with body temperature being the ideal temperature for them to grow. The rule here is: the warmer it is, the quicker it will culture and the more it cultures, the more sour the taste. I try to leave my kefir to culture over 24 hours, the time advocated by lacto-fermentation queen, Holly Davis. Thus, you may need to manipulate the environment to maintain optimal body temperature warmth over that time. If it is too hot in summer, leave it out at night and put it in the fridge during the day. In winter, leave it for a couple of days, but if you want to hurry it up to the 24-hour time frame, place it near a stove or wrap it with a hot-water bottle and rug.

WHY IS MY KEFIR MILK SOMETIMES STINKY AND AWFUL?

Invariably, your first kefir milk batch is made with a small amount of grain – about 2 teaspoons unless you have more. If you give it too much milk, it can't make enough lactic acid to preserve the milk and putrefying bacteria will proliferate more quickly. If you only have a small amount of grain, start with just a little milk. The grains grow extremely quickly and before you know it, you will have plenty. This problem is much more common with pasteurised milk and rarely happens with raw milk. Approximately 250 ml (9 fl oz/1 cup) milk to 2 teaspoons kefir grains is a good place to start.

If the kefir milk has been left for a long period of time, then the strong, cheesy smell is normal. Simply tip the whole thing into a colander and run filtered water through it. You need the larger holes of a colander as the milk becomes quite thick and cheesy. Wash with water until the grains are clear, then put them in a clean jar with milk. It may take a couple of goes with milk to clear the cheesy flavour.

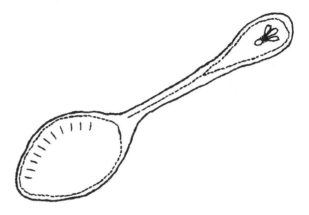

If left at too hot a temperature the milk may become incredibly sour in taste and almost cheesy, but it will still be fine and some people love it like that. As the culture develops, it will begin to separate into curds and whey. I prefer my kefir milk when the curds and whey are not too pronounced, but rather just beginning to separate and the texture is more like yoghurt. I find the taste a little too sour when it has fully separated.

Step 3: Straining

Place a sieve over a jug and tip the entire contents of the jar into it. Use a spatula to gently push the grains to the side, allowing the liquid to seep through the sieve, until you only have grains left in the sieve. What is in the jug is yours to drink or use. Wash out the jar, then add the kefir grains with some new milk – you are ready to go again.

Step 4: Storing

Transfer the strained cultured milk into a clean bottle and store in the fridge. At this stage the bacteria will continue to proliferate and consume lactose and protein, this is known as ripening. As the milk ripens, it will become increasingly sour, but it will still be delicious. It will keep for 3–4 days in the fridge. You will easily be able to tell when it is off, as it will smell nasty.

HOW DO I STORE MY KEFIR GRAINS IF I DON'T WANT TO MAKE KEFIR MILK REGULARLY?

As your grains grow, you can end up with a lot of them, all demanding to be fed and loved – just like your children – although one can only use so much cultured milk! Simply split the grains and keep your ratio of 1 tablespoon to 500 ml (17 fl oz/2 cups) milk. Either give the rest away or store in a jar of milk or cream, with the lid on, in the fridge. Another option is to make the most of them and use them to make cultured cream, butter and buttermilk (pages 48–50).

HOW DO I KEEP MY GRAINS ALIVE IF I'M GOING AWAY?

I place them in milk, cover and store in the fridge. It's all going to be a bit cheesy when you get back, but they're hard to kill. Many people also give them to a friend to look after and enjoy.

KITCHEN NOTE

This recipe makes a large amount of cultured cream, which you will need if you want to make cultured butter and cultured buttermilk. If you simply want to make a small amount of cultured cream, note that 2 teaspoons kefir grains or 1 tablespoon buttermilk or yoghurt is enough to culture 250 ml (9 fl oz/1 cup) cream. This will give you roughly 185 ml (6 fl oz/¾ cup) thick, cultured cream.

easy cultured (sour) cream, two ways

DIETARY INFO GLUTEN FREE | VEGETARIAN | EGG FREE
MAKES ABOUT 750 G (1 LB 10 OZ) SOUR CREAM, 285–370 G (10–13 OZ) CULTURED BUTTER OR 375–500 ML (13–17 FL OZ/ 1½ CUPS) BUTTERMILK
YOU WILL NEED TO BEGIN THIS RECIPE ONE OR TWO DAYS AHEAD

Cultured cream is naturally thick and has the most delicious flavour with a wonderful sour edge. To make it, good bacteria are introduced to the cream using kefir grains, yoghurt or cultured buttermilk. It's best to use runny thin (pouring) cream, not a thick (double/heavy) or thickened cream and certainly not ultra-pasteurised.

These are the two primary ways I culture cream and both are incredibly easy to do. The first – and this is my preference – involves culturing cream with kefir grains, which results in a stronger flavour and broader spectrum of good bacteria and yeasts. This method requires straining before use. The second involves inoculating the cream with yoghurt or cultured buttermilk (each will give a slightly different flavour) and doesn't need to be strained before use. You can either enjoy this delicious cream as is or use it in other recipes (see opposite page).

kefir method

2 tablespoons kefir grains
1 litre (35 fl oz/4 cups) thin (pouring) cream

Place both ingredients in a clean, dry jar, gently stir through and cover with muslin (cheesecloth) or a lid. Leave to culture in a warm place. The warmer it is, the quicker it will culture and the longer it cultures, the more sour the taste becomes. In summer, I look for a culturing time of approximately 24 hours, leaving it out at night and putting it in the fridge during the day. In winter, it may take 2–3 days. As the culture develops, the cream will begin to lighten and will resemble whipped cream and this is when it's ready to strain. When making cultured cream in this way, it won't separate into curds and whey as it does when making kefir milk (page 46).

Place a sieve with fairly large mesh (too fine and the cream won't go through) over a jug and tip the entire contents of the jar into it. Use a spatula to very gently lift up the grains, allowing the liquid to seep through, until there are only grains left in the sieve. Take care not to overwork the cream as you strain it as the agitation may cause the cream to separate into butter and cultured buttermilk in the sieve, and its takes ages to get all the grains out from the 'butter'. What is left in the jug is yours to use. And the grains in the sieve? You're ready to make another batch of cream or milk; simply add the grains to a clean jar with some more cream or milk, as desired.

Transfer the kefir cream into a clean jar with a lid and store in the fridge. The bacteria will proliferate and ripen. It will keep for at least 5–6 days.

yoghurt or cultured buttermilk method

1 litre (35 fl oz/4 cups) thin (pouring) cream
70 g (2½ oz/¼ cup) plain natural yoghurt or cultured buttermilk

Place both ingredients in a clean, dry jar, gently stir through and cover with muslin (cheesecloth) or a lid. (Either is fine but of late I prefer to use a lid and find I get a better end result.) Leave to culture in a warm place, in winter this may take a few days, and in summer you may prefer to leave it out overnight, and in the fridge during the day. Give it a stir through, every day, with a clean spoon. You will notice it thickening up – indeed it is ready once thick. Make sure that you lick the spoon; it is delicious. When ready, store in the fridge for up to 2 weeks.

cultured butter and buttermilk

DIETARY INFO GLUTEN FREE | VEGETARIAN | EGG FREE
MAKES BETWEEN 285-370 G (10-13 0Z) OF BUTTER AND
375-500 ML (13-17/1½-2 CUPS) OF BUTTERMILK PER LITRE
OF CREAM (DEPENDING ON THE FAT CONTENT OF THE CREAM)

Essentially, when the cultured cream is whipped it will concentrate the fat globules creating butter. The watery by-product, known as buttermilk, consists of the watery whey along with some protein and lactose, and is naturally low fat.

1 recipe Cultured Cream (page 48)
sea salt, to taste

finely chopped fresh herbs or garlic, optional, to taste

Place the cultured cream in a bowl and whisk either by hand or use a stand mixer fitted with the whisk attachment. If using a stand mixer, take care to whisk the cream slowly, keeping your eyes on it at all times because as the butter begins to form, buttermilk can go flying if the mixer is going too fast. It can take up to 5–10 minutes for the butter to form. Once you have a good ball of butter, remove any butter from the whisk and tip everything into a sieve placed over a bowl, making sure the bottom of the sieve is not touching the liquid – this will let the buttermilk fall through the sieve, giving you a lovely buttermilk. Removing the buttermilk will also help to keep the butter fresher for longer. Either use a butter pat, or get a large bowl filled with iced water. Put your hands into the iced water to cool them, making sure you flick off any extra water from your hands, then squeeze out as much buttermilk as possible over the sieve. Keep your hands cool throughout the process by dipping them into the iced water. Do the best you can but it doesn't need to be perfect. This is your primary buttermilk, thick and luscious, and the one I use for the recipes in this book. Pour it into a clean dry glass jar and place in the fridge. Continue to squeeze as much remaining buttermilk as possible. You can pour iced water over the butter to keep it cold while you squeeze, but the resulting buttermilk will be watered down and not as thick as the primary buttermilk above. But I would still keep it for soaking or drinking.

To salt the butter, place it in a bowl and use a fork to mash in the salt, to taste. Add herbs and/or garlic, if using, shape into a log and wrap in baking paper and foil then refrigerate for up to 2 weeks.

yoghurt

DIETARY INFO GLUTEN FREE | VEGETARIAN | EGG FREE
MAKES ABOUT 650 G (1 LB 7 OZ/2½ CUPS)
YOU WILL NEED TO BEGIN THIS RECIPE ONE DAY AHEAD

Making yoghurt is a slightly more time-intensive process than kefir as the milk must first be heated to create a 'blank slate' so that yoghurt cultures have no competition when they are introduced. You will notice that this is slightly thinner than many commercial yoghurts, which are often thickened with milk solids – something you don't want. This yoghurt can be thickened up, naturally, by making labne (page 52).

1 litre (35 fl oz/4 cups) organic
   full-cream (whole),
   non-homogenised milk

1 tablespoon plain natural yoghurt
   (it must say 'live cultures' on
   the label)

Place the milk in a saucepan and bring to just below the boil, or 82°C (180°F) on a thermometer, stirring occasionally. Remove from the heat and stand until cooled to 43°C (109°F), or until it is still quite warm, but you can put your finger in it and keep it there. Stir the milk a couple of times to prevent a skin forming.

Spoon the yoghurt into a sterilised Thermos or glass jar and pour in a little of the milk. (Don't be tempted to add a little extra yoghurt to the culture; the bacteria need lots of room to grow and develop.) Stir to combine well, then add the remaining milk and put the lid on.

Leave the Thermos or jar to sit overnight, or for at least 8 hours. If using a jar, leave it in a warm, but not hot place, approximately 20–25°C (68–77°F) will do. I wrap mine in a blanket and place it right up next to the fridge, where the motor keeps the side warm.

The next morning you should have lovely thick yoghurt. Allow it to cool a little, then refrigerate. It will keep for about 5–6 days in the fridge.

KITCHEN NOTES
● You can make this in a stainless-steel wide-mouthed Thermos (by far the easiest) or a clean preserving jar with a lid. Whichever you choose, sterilise it by washing the interior and lid well with hot soapy water, including any plastic bits of the Thermos, and then rinse with boiling water and drain to dry.
● A thermometer is handy, but not essential.

KITCHEN NOTE

If you prefer to roll the labne into balls, make sure you fold the muslin over the yoghurt when draining, then place a plate on top. Place a food tin or something heavy on top of the plate to put pressure on the yoghurt, this will give you a nice thick labne that will be easy to roll into balls.

labne

DIETARY INFO GLUTEN FREE | VEGETARIAN | EGG FREE
MAKES ABOUT 500 G (1 LB 2 OZ/2 CUPS) LABNE AND ABOUT 500 ML (17 FL OZ/2 CUPS) WHEY

It's incredibly easy and quick to thicken real yoghurt yourself by straining the yoghurt in muslin (cheesecloth) to drip off the whey. What you have left is labne, which is also known as yoghurt cheese. The whey that drips from the yoghurt into the bowl will keep for weeks in a sealed container (glass is best) in the fridge and is perfect for adding to the water used to soak grains, using in salad dressings and for culturing vegetables.

1 kg (2 lb 4 oz/4 cups) real, full-cream, non-homogenised plain natural yoghurt

Place a sieve lined with four layers of muslin (cheesecloth) over a bowl. Spoon the yoghurt into the sieve and allow it to drain in the fridge for 2–3 hours. When the weather is milder, you can leave it to drip at room temperature. The longer it sits, the firmer it will become. You can store the labne by itself in a jar in the fridge for 2–3 days. For longer storage, pour the whey into a clean glass jar, pick up the muslin and twist it around the labne, then place it into the whey (muslin and all). Seal and store in the fridge for up to 5–7 days.

54

savoury labne variations

HERBED LABNE Scoop the labne onto a serving plate, sprinkle with finely chopped fresh herbs (chives, fennel greens, rosemary, oregano, lemon thyme) and sea salt and drizzle with extra virgin olive oil.

LABNE BALLS WITH GARLIC AND HERBS Roll the labne into small balls, then gently roll in finely chopped herbs – you need about 3 teaspoons chopped herbs per ball of labne. Rosemary, lemon thyme, chives, garlic chives, marjoram, oregano and flat-leaf (Italian) parsley are all good. I tend not to use basil as it oxidises very quickly, so instead I use it to flavour the oil. Gently place the balls into a jar and cover with extra virgin olive oil. Add a couple of peeled garlic cloves (and basil if using), then seal. These will keep in the fridge for at least 2 months. When all the labne balls are finished, the herb and garlic-infused oil makes a wonderful dressing.

CRISTEL'S LEMONY LABNE Combine 250 g (9 oz) labne, the finely grated zest of 1 lemon, 1 tablespoon lemon juice, 2½ tablespoons extra virgin olive oil, or Rosemary-infused Olive Oil (page 72), and sea salt to taste in a bowl.

sweet labne variations

LABNE CREAM Labne takes on sweet flavours with delight and makes a wonderful alternative to cream. Maple syrup and honey are my favourite sweeteners, while vanilla seeds or extract and cinnamon are excellent flavouring agents. Simply stir them into the labne.

SWEET LABNE DIP Similar to the Herbed Labne (left), and delicious served with a fresh fruit platter. Scoop the labne onto a serving plate, drizzle with maple syrup or honey, natural vanilla extract and finely chopped Maple and Cinnamon Almonds (page 82).

almond milk

DIETARY INFO GLUTEN FREE | DAIRY FREE
VEGAN | EGG FREE
MAKES ABOUT 750 ML (26 FL OZ/3 CUPS)
**YOU WILL NEED TO SOAK THE NUTS THE
NIGHT BEFORE**

*Freshly made almond milk is easy to make and
incredibly delicious and bears no comparison to its
tetra-packed cousins. I prefer to use raw almonds
with their skins on as opposed to blanched. I
absolutely love this as its own almond self, but
if you'd like to add a date or two, and a teaspoon
of natural vanilla extract, please do.*

240 g (8½ oz/1½ cups) raw almonds
750 ml (26 fl oz/3 cups) filtered water

The night before, place the almonds in a
medium bowl with a tiny pinch of salt and
cover well with water. Stand overnight at
room temperature.

The following day, slip the almonds out of their
skins, which should come off easily. If they
don't, place them in a heatproof bowl, cover
with boiling water and let stand for 5 minutes
before draining. The skins should now slip off
easily. You now have blanched almonds.

Place the blanched almonds and filtered
water into a blender or food processor and
process very well, until very smooth. Blending
is the most important factor in this recipe.
Pour the mixture into a nut milk bag (this is
best) or through at least four layers of muslin
(cheesecloth), into a bowl, and squeeze by hand
to extract as much nut milk as possible. Transfer
to a glass bottle and refrigerate for up to 3 days.

almond and coconut milk

DIETARY INFO GLUTEN FREE | DAIRY FREE
VEGAN | EGG FREE
MAKES ABOUT 750 ML (26 FL OZ/3 CUPS)
**YOU WILL NEED TO SOAK THE NUTS THE
NIGHT BEFORE**

160 g (5¾ oz/1 cup) raw almonds
90 g (3¼ oz/1 cup) desiccated coconut
750 ml (26 fl oz/3 cups) filtered water

The night before, place the almonds in a
medium-size bowl with a tiny pinch of salt
and cover well with water. Stand overnight
at room temperature.

The following day, slip the almonds out of their
skins, which should come off easily. If they
don't, place them in a heatproof bowl, cover
with boiling water and let stand for 5 minutes
before draining. The skins should now slip off
easily. You now have blanched almonds.

Place the blanched almonds, coconut and
filtered water into a blender or food processor
and process until very, very smooth. Blending
is the most important factor in this recipe.
Pour the mixture into a nut milk bag (this is
best) or through at least four layers of muslin
(cheesecloth), into a bowl, and squeeze by hand
to extract as much nut milk as possible. Transfer
to a glass bottle and refrigerate for up to 3 days.

nature's seeds

Grains, legumes, nuts and seeds are all seeds that store food for the growing plant and enzymes to process this food. Nature packs the seed with a range of protective mechanisms against spoiling and damage from bacteria, moulds, fungi or animals, or that stop them from germinating until the conditions are right. These mechanisms include enzyme inhibitors that prevent germination, those that can inhibit digestive enzymes and anti-nutrients such as oxalates, tannins, lectins and phytic acid. All of these anti-nutrients can impact on the mineral and nutrient bio-availability of the food; phytic acid, for example, loves to bind to other minerals such as magnesium, iron and zinc. Because of the complexity of the carbohydrates, and the enzyme inhibitors present, you may also find the carbohydrate in grains and legumes difficult to digest. Soaking (which may involve some or a lot of sprouting) and/or fermenting, however, tells that seed that the conditions are perfect for germination, and increases seed digestibility hugely.

In all cases, moisture (preferably warm) is the first requirement for germination. It initiates a biochemical reaction in the seed that releases enzymes; growth is no longer inhibited, and the complex starch of the endosperm in a grain or legume can transform to the simpler sugars to feed a young plant embryo, also making them easier for us to digest. The second requirement is for warmth. All unsprayed seeds will have a wealth of bacteria coating them and when they meet with a moist and warm environment (along with food), they will feed and multiply – this is the process of lacto-fermentation, and the lactobacilli will help to break down and neutralise enzymes, phytic acid and other anti-nutrients, even gluten. Soaking over a longer period of time (such as 24 hours rather than six) allows fermentation to do more of its work.

phytic acid and anti-nutrients

Adding acid to the water you soak grains in activates the enzyme phytase that frees the phosphorus. Some grains have more phytase than others: wheat, rye, spelt, barley and buckwheat contain high levels; quinoa and amaranth contain medium levels; and brown rice, corn (maize), millet, oats and teff have very low levels.

Soaking low-phytase grains in an acid medium won't do that much, but adding about 10 per cent of freshly ground rye grain (or buckwheat for a gluten-free version) to the soaking mix will increase the phytase levels. When acid is called for, I prefer lactic acid from a cultured product such as yoghurt, cultured buttermilk, kefir or their whey, as the good bugs they contain will bump up the fermentation process, dairy-free cultured options include kombucha, water kefir or sourdough leavener. Apple cider vinegar or lemon juice are also great options.

For legumes, slightly alkaline water (created by adding a pinch of bicarbonate of soda/baking soda) is now considered to give the best end results for high oligosaccharide beans rather than acidulated water, with acid being fine for most lentils, peas and some beans. I prefer using the sea vegetable kombu, which contains an enzyme needed to break those long chain sugars down, for soaking and for cooking. A 5 cm (2 in) piece is adequate for up to 2 cups (400 g/14 oz) raw beans. This also helps to slightly alkalinise the water and reduce the phytic acid. If you can't get kombu, wakame is the next best thing.

Sprouting grains and legumes continues the germination process and neutralises more of the complex carbohydrates, oligosaccharides and some phytic acid. If eating these raw (fresh), they should be well-sprouted to ensure optimal digestion. Cooking helps to neutralise a little more of the remaining phytic acid. Sprouted and dehydrated grains and legumes are great options to cook when you haven't had time to soak.

Fermentation also delivers many benefits: it breaks down long chain sugars in beans and grains, along with many other anti-nutrients. We typically see this in legume products such as tempeh, miso and brewed soy sauces (tamari and shoyu); grains such as wild rice; and seeds such as chocolate and coffee.

In summary, all grains and legumes are best soaked; the germination and lacto-fermentation process alone delivers a more digestible end result. If life gets in the way, cooking grains in a bone stock provides plenty of bio-available minerals and buffers some of the effects of the phytic acid and other anti-nutrients. Adding fat-soluble vitamins for optimal mineral absorption also helps (toasting the grain in butter or ghee for example, or serving it with cream, butter or cheese). If you are dairy free, bone stock becomes paramount, but serving with an egg yolk or meat fat also works.

nuts and seeds

Nuts and seeds are soaked with salt rather than an acid, about 1 tablespoon salt to 4 cups nuts or seeds. Warmth is always best for between 12 and 24 hours. Once drained and slowly dried out in a dehydrator or slow oven, these are known as 'activated' nuts or seeds. I don't always soak nuts and seeds as I don't eat many of them. Instead, I do a couple of simpler things to reduce those anti-nutrients.

- Roasting or toasting the seeds or rolled grains (i.e. oats), before using them in baking.
- Removing the papery skin where the bulk of the problems lie (i.e. removing the skin from almonds when making almond milk).

preparing and cooking beans and lentils

When we prepare legumes we have two goals: to hydrate and to reduce the anti-nutrients the seed carries, such as enzyme inhibitors and phytic acid. In the case of hearty beans, we also want to leach out and break down some of the long chain sugars. Pick out any stones that may be mixed in with your legumes. Cover them with plenty of water (warm to encourage fermentation is best). Add the acid or alkaline as directed below and soak them from anywhere between 12 and 24 hours (hearty beans for the longer period of time), preferably in a warm place, and, if possible, change the soaking water at least once. If the legumes have begun to sprout, all the better. Cooking legumes in a bone stock will add a rich bounty of highly bio-available minerals, helping to buffer the effects of any anti-nutrients. Calmative herbs such as asafoetida, cumin, epazote, fennel and ginger can also make digesting legumes a little easier.

HEARTY BEANS (ALKALINE SOAKING)

Adzuki, borlotti (cranberry), cannellini, Christmas lima, great northern, kidney, lima, navy, pinto.

For each ½–1 cup dried beans add a pinch of bicorbonate of soda (baking soda) or a 2 cm (¾ in) piece of kombu or wakame sea vegetable to the soaking water (I prefer using kombu).

Once soaked, drain and rinse well, reserving the sea vegetable. Place the beans in a saucepan and cover well with water or bone stock, adding the reserved soaking kombu or wakame, or a fresh piece and aromatics, as desired. Beans can take anywhere from 1 to 5 hours to cook; the fresher a bean is (under 1 year), the less time it will take to cook. To be digestible, beans must be well cooked, that is when they yield their soft and creamy centre when pressed gently. Remove any scum that forms during cooking, and ensure the beans are well covered with liquid throughout cooking. Don't add salt or acid until the beans are nearly cooked as this will toughen them.

Once cooked, store the legume in their cooking liquid in the fridge for 2–3 days, or in the freezer.

LESS-HEARTY BEANS, LENTILS AND PEAS (ACID SOAKING)

Black (turtle) beans, dried broad beans (fava), chickpeas (garbanzo beans), chana dal, mung beans. All whole lentils with their skins on: Black beluga, whole red, French, green and brown. Black-eyed peas, split yellow and green peas, entire family of dal.

For each ½–1 cup dry legume add 1 tablespoon cultured product such as whey, yoghurt, kefir, cultured buttermilk or the like. For dairy-free options, use water kefir (see page 39) or kombucha drink, 2 teaspoons lemon juice or apple cider vinegar.

Once soaked, drain and rinse well, place in a saucepan and cover with 4 cm (1½ in) water or bone stock. Add aromatics (such as herbs, ginger or garlic) as desired, or a 2 cm (¾ in) piece of kombu or wakame sea vegetable for extra flavour. Bring to a simmer and cook gently until tender to the bite.

Once cooked, store the legumes in their cooking liquid in the fridge for 2–3 days, or in the freezer.

KITCHEN NOTES

● If eating as is, you may like to add more flavour and season them. Try a little tamari, mirin and freshly ground black pepper, or brighten them up with lemon zest and juice, freshly ground black pepper, salt and olive oil.

● Kombu isn't necessary but will add more depth and complexity to the lentils, especially if they are to be cooked in vegetable stock or water.

green lentils, two ways

DIETARY INFO GLUTEN FREE | DAIRY-FREE OPTION | VEGAN OPTION
EGG FREE
MAKES 300 G (10½ OZ/1¼ CUPS) COOKED LENTILS
YOU WILL NEED TO SOAK THE LENTILS THE NIGHT BEFORE

These two ways of cooking French green lentils are equally good. The benefit of the first version is the nourishment that a bone stock such as chicken stock lends to lentils, helping to buffer their astringency and aid their digestibility, however the second version that uses vegetable stock with olive oil is an entirely delicious alternative for vegans or vegetarians.

1. USING CHICKEN OR DUCK STOCK

100 g (3½ oz/½ cup) French
   green lentils
1 tablespoon whey or choice of acid
   (page 59)
310 ml (10¾ fl oz/1¼ cups) chicken
   or duck stock
1 thyme sprig
1 bay leaf

2. USING VEGETABLE STOCK

100 g (3½ oz/½ cup) French
   green lentils
1 tablespoon whey or choice of acid
   (see page 59)
310 ml (10¾/1¼ cups) vegetable stock
   (page 41)
2 cm (¾ in) piece kombu, optional
1 thyme sprig
1 bay leaf
2 teaspoons extra virgin olive oil

The night before, soak the lentils with your chosen acid overnight, following the instructions on page 59.

The following day, drain the lentils and place in a saucepan with the remaining ingredients. Bring to the boil, then simmer over medium heat for 15–25 minutes or until the lentils are cooked, but still a bit toothsome. You will need to test them from time to time. Stir gently during the cooking process to ensure that any lentils on the top don't dry out. Remove from the heat and store the lentils in their cooking liquid until ready to use.

black beluga lentils

DIETARY INFO GLUTEN FREE | DAIRY-FREE
OPTION | VEGAN OPTION | EGG FREE
MAKES 300 G (10½ OZ/1¼ CUPS) COOKED LENTILS
**YOU WILL NEED TO SOAK THE LENTILS THE
NIGHT BEFORE**

Black beluga lentils have a delicious subtle flavour, and in this basic recipe I've cooked them without a bone stock so I can use them for vegetarian dishes. If you would prefer to use a bone stock, please do, it will only add to their digestibility and nutrient density. If you would like more flavour, you can most certainly cook them in a vegetable stock as well.

110 g (3¾ oz/½ cup) black beluga lentils
1 tablespoon whey or choice of acid
  (page 59)
1 thin slice fresh ginger, unpeeled
2 cm (¾ in) piece kombu, optional

The night before, soak the lentils with your chosen acid overnight, following the instructions on page 59.

The following day, drain the lentils and place in a saucepan with the ginger, kombu, if using, and 310 ml (10¾ fl oz/1¼ cups) water or stock. Bring to the boil, then simmer over medium heat for 15–25 minutes, until the lentils are cooked, but still a bit toothsome. You will need to test them from time to time. Stir gently during the cooking process to ensure that any lentils on the top don't dry out. Remove from the heat and store the lentils in their cooking liquid with the ginger, and kombu, if used, until needed.

black beans

DIETARY INFO GLUTEN FREE | DAIRY-FREE
OPTION | VEGAN OPTION | EGG FREE
MAKES 250-300 G (9-10½ OZ/1¼-1½ CUPS)
COOKED BEANS
**YOU WILL NEED TO SOAK THE BEANS THE
NIGHT BEFORE**

Cooked black beans are one of my favourite beans to have on hand. With very little effort and time, the beans can be transformed into refried beans, or something a little more complex.

110 g (3¾ oz/½ cup) dried black (turtle) beans
1 tablespoon whey or choice of acid
  (page 59)
2 cm (¾ in) piece kombu

The night before, soak the lentils with your chosen acid and the piece of kombu overnight, following the instructions on page 59.

The following day, drain and rinse well, reserving the sea vegetable. Place the beans in a medium-size saucepan with enough water to cover by 3 cm (1¼ in), adding the reserved soaking kombu, or a fresh piece. Bring to the boil over medium heat, then reduce the heat to low and simmer for 1–1½ hours, or until tender and the beans yield their soft starchy centres to light pressure. Remember that beans that are not as old will take far less time and it is best to check them after 50 minutes. Remove from the heat and store the beans in their cooking liquid with the kombu until ready to use.

refried black beans

DIETARY INFO GLUTEN FREE | DAIRY FREE
EGG FREE | VEGAN OPTION
MAKES 1¼–1½ CUPS

This is such a versatile dish. For a quick and truly delicious meal, serve it topped with avocado and a dollop of Sweet Sultana and Chilli Sauce (page 76) and cultured cream (page 48).

1 quantity cooked Black Beans (page 61)
1 tablespoon extra virgin olive oil, lard or bacon fat
1 small–medium brown onion, finely chopped
2 garlic cloves, finely chopped
½–1 red capsicum (pepper), seeds and membrane
  removed, cut into small dice
1 charred jalapeño chilli (page 142), seeded and
  cut into thin strips
1–2 teaspoons apple cider vinegar
freshly ground black pepper, to taste
20–30 g (¾–1 oz/⅓–⅔ cup) coarsely chopped coriander
  (cilantro) roots, stems and leaves
sea salt, to taste

Place the beans into a sieve placed over a bowl and discard the kombu. Reserve 250 ml (9 fl oz/ 1 cup) of the cooking liquid. If you don't have that much cooking liquid, add stock or water to make up the difference.

Heat the olive oil, onion, garlic and capsicum in a medium-size frying pan over low heat for 10– 15 minutes, until translucent. Stir in the drained beans, reserved cooking liquid, chilli, 1 teaspoon vinegar, pepper and coriander, then simmer gently for 15 minutes. To thicken the beans you can either mash some of them into the liquid or simmer over high heat until reduced to your liking. Taste and season with salt.

a pot of beans

DIETARY INFO GLUTEN FREE | DAIRY FREE
EGG FREE | VEGAN
MAKES 250–300 G (9–10½ OZ/1¼–1½ CUPS)
COOKED BEANS (DEPENDING ON BEAN TYPE)
**YOU WILL NEED TO SOAK THE BEANS 12–24 HOURS
BEFORE COOKING**

A basic technique for cooking beans.

95–100 g (3¼–3½ oz/½ cup) dried beans
2 cm (¾ in) piece kombu

The day before, soak the beans with one piece of kombu for 12–24 hours following the instructions on page 59.

The following day, drain and rinse well, reserving the sea vegetable. Place the beans in a medium-size saucepan with enough water to cover by 3 cm (1¼ in), adding the reserved soaking kombu or wakame, or a fresh piece. Bring to the boil over medium heat, then reduce the heat to low and simmer for 1–1½ hours, or until tender and the beans yield their soft starchy centres to light pressure — chickpeas and pinto beans will take longer, up to 5 hours. Beans that are not as old (under 1 year) will take far less time and it is best to check them after 45 minutes. Remove from the heat and store the beans in their cooking liquid with the kombu and other aromatics (see Kitchen Note).

KITCHEN NOTE

Adding aromatics to the cooking beans can help develop great flavour – broad (fava), borlotti (cranberry) and cannellini work well with Mediterranean herbs such as bay, fennel, rosemary, sage and garlic. Adzuki with Asian flavours such as ginger, pinto and black (turtle) beans with cumin and coriander (cilantro), or southern flavours such as smoked ham. Christmas lima beans work well with bay, thyme, pepper and juniper berries.

preparing and cooking grains

Grains must be well cooked – this means they may not look perfect, some grains may have burst, but the carbohydrate will be optimally digestible – they should not be al dente.

We begin the path to deliciously digestible grains by soaking them, for all the reasons discussed on pages 58–59. Add water to cover the grains by at least 5 cm (2 in) — enough so they will still be covered when they swell. For every ½ cup of grain add 2 teaspoons of a cultured product such as whey, yoghurt, kefir, cultured buttermilk or the like. For dairy-free options use water kefir or kombucha drink, 1 teaspoon lemon juice or apple cider vinegar. Soak from 8 to 24 hours; a longer soaking time and warmth will encourage good lacto-fermentation.

Some grains, buckwheat and millet in particular, respond well to dry-roasting after soaking and before cooking —this develops great flavour. Place the grains in a dry saucepan over gentle heat for 5–10 minutes, stirring frequently or until fragrant and lightly coloured. Grains can also be toasted in a fat such as ghee or coconut oil. Grains that are toasted before cooking, and especially toasted in a fat, will take much longer to cook as the liquid has to penetrate the fat barrier, and then the tighter bran.

After soaking, tip the grains into a sieve, drain well and, if you have added ground rye or buckwheat flour (as discussed on page 66), rinse well to remove the flour as much as possible. Pat the top of the grains and bottom of the sieve with a tea towel (dish towel) absorbing as much water as you can and place the grains and required liquid in a saucepan with a pinch of sea salt. If unsoaked, rinse the grains well, and continue as above. Cover with a lid, preferably glass, so you can see what is happening without having to take the lid off. Place the pan over medium heat and bring to the boil (cooking time commences when it comes to the boil), then immediately turn the heat down as far as it will go (a heat diffuser would be ideal). Too high a heat can result in loss of liquid through the escaping steam. Don't remove the lid, this allows steam to escape, and try to avoid stirring them as this will result in sticky, mushy grains. At the end of the cooking time, take off the lid and gently tip the pan on an angle. If any water remains, put the lid back on and cook for another 5–10 minutes. It is ready when there is no water pooling, small steam holes appear on the surface and the grains look cooked. If it is still uncooked, but no liquid remains, add more boiling liquid to the grains — they cannot cook if there is no liquid for them to absorb. Add it in small increments — this will depend on how dry and uncooked the grains are and which grain it is: millet may only need 1 tablespoon increments to the original ½ cup of raw grain whereas the denser barley or wheat will need 2 tablespoon increments.

When ready, take the pan off the heat with the lid still on. Leave to sit for about 5–20 minutes. Placing a clean tea towel or sheet of paper towel on the grains, under the lid, will help to absorb steam, resulting in a drier, fluffier and less 'wet' grain, perfect for salads. As a general rule, if requiring a grain with more binding capacity (for example as a binder in a patty) they are best without the paper towel trick and used warm, they will be stickier this way.

my favourite grains

DIETARY INFO GLUTEN FREE | DAIRY-FREE OPTIONS | VEGAN OPTIONS | EGG FREE
YOU WILL NEED TO SOAK THE GRAINS 8-24 HOURS AHEAD OF USING

SOAKED Wheat, including emmer and einkhorn, spelt, rye and buckwheat are all high-phytase grains; amaranth and quinoa are medium-phytase grains, and are at their best after being soaked in acidulated water. Bone stock is not necessary for these grains, water or vegetable stock is fine. Buckwheat will have the best flavour when toasted, preferably in a fat. You can still add butter or ghee for flavour and extra nourishment after, if desired, but consider how you will be using the grain; in a salad, for example.

UNSOAKED If you don't have the time or the desire to soak the grains, the next best thing is to cook them in a bone stock. If not using bone stock, ensure you serve the grain with animal fat such as butter, ghee, cheese, egg or meat fat.

amaranth

MAKES 100 G (3½ OZ/½ CUP) COOKED

Whilst this may at first appearance seem like a bit of trouble, it's the best way I've found to get a dryer, more usable end result. I only suggest cooking a small amount here as a little bit of cooked amaranth goes a very long way.

50 g (1¾ oz/¼ cup) amaranth, soaked overnight
1 teaspoon whey or other acid as desired (page 59)
pinch of sea salt

Soak the grains overnight as discussed on page 59. The next morning you will need:

80 ml (2½ fl oz/⅓ cup) hot water or stock
pinch of sea salt

Using a very fine sieve, drain the amaranth and pat dry with a tea towel (dish towel).

Place a small saucepan over medium heat, allow to heat a little before adding half the grains. Stir frequently, or shake the pan – the amaranth will become sandier and less clumpy as it dries out. Cook for 2–3 minutes or until lightly golden – reduce the heat if it is colouring too quickly, and has not yet dried out. Turn out into a small bowl and toast the remaining grains.

Meanwhile, heat your liquid. When ready, return the first batch of grains to the pan along with a pinch of salt and the hot water – stand back as this will splutter a little. Reduce the heat and cover the pan with the lid so no steam can escape. Cook for 10–15 minutes, or until the liquid is absorbed and the amaranth is cooked.

Turn off the heat, remove the lid and place a clean tea towel on the amaranth, then replace the lid. Leave to steam for 15 minutes. It will still be sticky, but it should not be too wet or porridge-like in consistency.

64

spelt berries

MAKES 250 G (9 OZ/1¼–1½ CUPS) COOKED

SOAKED

100 g (3½ oz/½ cup) spelt berries
2 teaspoons whey or other acid as desired (page 59)
200 ml (7 fl oz) water, bone or vegetable stock
pinch of sea salt

Soak the spelt overnight as discussed on page 59. The next morning, strain the soaked spelt and pat dry with a tea towel (dish towel).

Add to a medium-size saucepan with water and salt, cover and gently bring to the boil. Reduce the heat so no steam escapes the lid. Cook for 50–60 minutes, or until the liquid is absorbed and the spelt is cooked.

Turn off the heat, remove the lid and place a clean tea towel on the spelt then replace the lid. Leave to sit and steam for 10 minutes. If you want to use butter for flavour, add this now.

UNSOAKED

100 g (3½ oz/½ cup) spelt berries
250 ml (9 fl oz/1 cup) water, bone or vegetable stock
pinch of sea salt

Add the spelt to a sieve and briefly rinse under the tap, pat dry with a tea towel (dish towel). Add to a medium-size saucepan with the stock and salt, cover and gently bring to the boil. Reduce the heat so no steam escapes the lid. Cook for 50–60 minutes, or until the liquid is absorbed and the spelt is cooked.

Turn off the heat, remove the lid and place a clean tea towel on the spelt then replace the lid. Leave to sit and steam for 10 minutes before removing the lid, then fluff with a fork to serve.

quinoa

MAKES 300 G (10½ OZ/1¾ CUPS) COOKED

SOAKED

100 g (3½ oz/½ cup) quinoa
2 teaspoons whey or other acid as desired (page 59)
185 ml (6 fl oz/¾ cup) water, bone or vegetable stock
pinch of sea salt

Soak the quinoa overnight as discussed on page 59. The next morning, strain the soaked quinoa and pat dry with a tea towel (dish towel).

Add to a medium-size saucepan with water and salt, cover and gently bring to the boil. Reduce the heat so no steam escapes the lid. Cook for 25 minutes, or until the liquid is absorbed and the quinoa is cooked.

Turn off the heat, remove the lid and place a clean tea towel on the quinoa then replace the lid. Leave to sit and steam for 10 minutes before removing the lid. If you want to use butter for flavour, add this now.

UNSOAKED

100 g (3½ oz/½ cup) quinoa
220 ml (7½ fl oz) water, bone or vegetable stock
pinch of sea salt

Add the quinoa to a sieve and briefly rinse under the tap and pat dry with a tea towel (dish towel).

Add to a medium-size saucepan with water and salt, cover and gently bring to the boil. Reduce the heat so no steam escapes the lid. Cook for 25 minutes, or until the liquid is absorbed and the quinoa is cooked.

Turn off the heat, remove the lid and place a clean tea towel on the quinoa then replace the lid. Leave to sit and steam for 10 minutes before removing the lid, then fluff with a fork to serve.

rice and millet

DIETARY INFO GLUTEN FREE | DAIRY-FREE OPTIONS | VEGAN OPTIONS | EGG FREE
YOU WILL NEED TO SOAK THE GRAINS 8-24 HOURS AHEAD OF USING

SOAKED Both millet and rice have low levels of phytase so these are best soaked with high phytase buckwheat – freshly ground (if possible) wholegrain buckwheat flour. If you are vegetarian or vegan, this is an excellent option.

UNSOAKED It is worth remembering that soaking the grain, even without optimal phytase from the buckwheat will deliver some benefits from the germination and fermentation process. That said, if you don't have the time, or desire, to do that, cooking in bone stock is the best path for millet and rice (either soaked without buckwheat, or unsoaked). If not using bone stock, ensure the addition of an animal fat as discussed on page 65.

medium or long grain brown rice

MAKES 225 G (8 OZ/1½ CUPS) COOKED

SOAKED If soaking without buckwheat, ensure you use a bone stock.

100 g (3½ oz/½ cup) medium- or long-grain brown rice
1 tablespoon buckwheat grain, freshly ground or
  1½ tablespoons buckwheat flour
2 teaspoons whey – or other acid as desired (see page 59)
220 ml (7½ fl oz) water, bone or vegetable stock for
  medium-grain, or 190 ml (6½ fl oz) for long-grain
pinch of sea salt

Soak the rice and buckwheat overnight as discussed on page 59. The next morning, using a larger-mesh sieve, strain the rice allowing the buckwheat meal to fall through the sieve and pat the rice dry with a tea towel (dish towel).

Add the rice to a medium-size saucepan with the liquid and salt, and cover with a lid. Reduce the heat so no steam escapes the lid; cook for 40–45 minutes, until the liquid is absorbed and the rice is cooked.

Turn off the heat, remove the lid, place a clean tea towel on the rice and replace the lid. Leave to sit and steam for 10 minutes before removing, then fluff with a fork to serve. If you want to use butter for flavour, add this now.

UNSOAKED

100 g (3½ oz/½ cup) medium- or long-grain brown rice
250 ml (9 fl oz/1 cup) water, bone or vegetable stock for
  medium-grain, or 220ml (7½ fl oz) for long-grain

Add the rice to a sieve and briefly rinse under the tap. Pat dry with a tea towel (dish towel) and follow the same instructions for cooking the soaked rice.

millet

MAKES 250-280 G (9-10 OZ/2 CUPS) COOKED

Millet is a dry, astringent grain which is best balanced with some fat, either by toasting in ghee or butter before cooking, or adding it once cooked. The flavour and texture of millet is also enhanced by toasting. It's very important to leave it to cool down a fair bit once cooked (on a tea towel or paper towel) before fluffing it with a fork or spoon. If using for a salad, I recommend leaving it to cool completely before touching it.

SOAKED If soaking without buckwheat, use a bone stock. If you prefer not to toast the grain in the fat, reduce the liquid by 30 ml (1 fl oz), and add your choice of fat once the grain is cooked.

100 g (3½ oz /½ cup) hulled millet
1 tablespoon buckwheat grain, freshly ground or
  1½ tablespoons buckwheat flour
2 teaspoons whey or other acid, as desired (page 59)
2 teaspoons ghee, chicken or duck fat, or olive oil
280 ml (10 fl oz) very hot stock (any) or water
pinch of sea salt

Soak the millet and buckwheat flour overnight as discussed on page 59. The next morning, using a larger-mesh sieve, strain the soaked millet well, ensuring as much of the buckwheat flour is removed and pat the millet dry with a tea towel (dish towel). Melt the ghee in a small saucepan and add the millet. Cook over medium heat, stirring frequently until the millet becomes fragrant — about 2–3 minutes. Soaked millet won't toast as beautifully as when unsoaked. Immediately pour the hot liquid in; be careful as this will splutter so stand back a little. Add the salt and cover. Reduce the heat so no steam escapes the lid. Cook for 40–50 minutes or 30–35 minutes if not toasted in fat.

Turn off the heat, remove the lid and place a clean tea towel on the millet then replace the lid. Leave to cool for 15 minutes before removing then fluff with a fork to serve.

UNSOAKED If you prefer not to toast the grain in the fat, reduce the liquid by 30 ml (1 fl oz), and add your choice of fat once the grain is cooked as desired.

1 teaspoon ghee, chicken or duck fat, or olive oil
100 g (3½ oz/½ cup) hulled millet
310 ml (10¾ fl oz/1¼ cups) very hot bone or
  vegetable stock, or water
pinch of sea salt

Melt the ghee in a small saucepan and add the millet. Cook over medium heat, stirring only every now and then, until the millet begins to smell fragrant – about 3 minutes. Immediately pour the hot stock in; be careful as this will splutter, so stand back a little. Add the salt and cover. Reduce the heat so no steam escapes the lid. Cook for 40–50 minutes, or until the liquid is absorbed and the millet is cooked, or 30–35 minutes if not toasted in fat.

Turn off the heat, remove the lid and place a clean tea towel on the millet then replace the lid. Leave to sit and steam for 15 minutes before removing then fluff with a fork to serve.

67

THE LITTLE SPOONFULS THAT CAN MAKE A MEAL SING

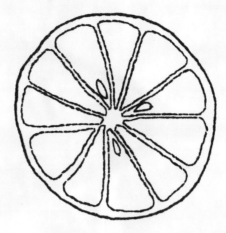

sauces, dressings
AND EXTRAS

mayonnaise

DIETARY INFO GLUTEN FREE | DAIRY FREE
VEGETARIAN
MAKES ABOUT 85 G (3 OZ/⅓ CUP)

Homemade mayonnaise is one of the most flexible foods to have on hand and is perhaps the best alternative to butter for those who are dairy free; it is also a profoundly rich source of quality fats and antioxidants. Using this mayonnaise as is, or as a base upon which to build a dressing, will provide all the fat-soluble vitamins to help make those minerals in the salad bio-available.

1 egg yolk, at room temperature
1 garlic clove, crushed
½ teaspoon white wine vinegar or lemon juice
½ teaspoon wholegrain mustard
80 ml (2½ fl oz/⅓ cup) extra virgin olive oil
pinch of sea salt

Place a damp tea towel (dish towel) on your work surface, then place a small mixing bowl on top of this. (The cloth will keep the bowl steady while you whisk.) Place the egg yolk, crushed garlic, vinegar and mustard in the bowl and whisk together. Whisking continuously, gradually add the oil, drop by drop at first, making sure it is well emulsified before adding more, then slowly build up to a slow steady drizzle. If using organic olive oil, you may not be able to incorporate all the oil as it can be far denser than its conventional counterpart. If there is a minute trail of oil in the mix, rather than a homogenous colour, the mayonnaise may be splitting so continue whisking well, without adding any more oil. Whisk in the salt, taste and adjust with more vinegar if desired. Store in a clean glass jar in the fridge for up to 2 weeks.

mayonnaise and yoghurt dressing

DIETARY INFO GLUTEN FREE| VEGETARIAN
MAKES ABOUT 185 ML (6 FL OZ/¾ CUP)

Similar to the Buttermilk Dressing (opposite page), this is also nutrient dense and rich in good bugs. It will be delicious as is, but there is no reason you can't use a mayonnaise made with either rosemary oil or preserved lemon, or indeed both. If doing so, you would need to consider the herbs you add – fennel, dill, chives, parsley, tarragon, mint and basil are all good.

85 g (3 fl oz/⅓ cup) Mayonnaise (see left)
95 g (3¼ oz/⅓ cup) plain natural yoghurt
sea salt, to taste
1 tablespoon lemon juice, or to taste
finely chopped fresh herbs of choice, to taste
¼–½ teaspoon honey, or to taste

Whisk all the ingredients in a bowl to combine well. Taste and adjust the flavours as needed. Store in a clean glass jar in the fridge for up to 2 weeks.

KITCHEN NOTES ON MAYONNAISE

● Use organic, free-range eggs for this recipe and know their source.
● You can make this by hand or use a stand mixer with a whisk attachment – either method is preferable to a blender or food processor. If making by hand, use 1 or 2 egg yolks. If using an electric mixer, use 3, which will give you a lighter texture and more mayonnaise.
● To make Rosemary and Preserved Lemon Mayonnaise, replace the oil with Rosemary-infused Olive Oil (page 72) and stir 1–2 tablespoons finely chopped preserved lemon into the mayonnaise when finished.

tartare sauce

DIETARY INFO GLUTEN FREE | VEGETARIAN
DAIRY FREE
MAKES ABOUT 125 ML (4 FL OZ/½ CUP)

*When made with real mayonnaise, tartare sauce
is a wondrous thing. I like mine sharp with citrus,
and I have a great weakness for gherkins. Try
this with the Best Fish Cakes Ever (page 173) and
you will never, ever buy the versions built on fake
mayonnaise again.*

85 g (3 oz/⅓ cup) Mayonnaise (opposite page)
sea salt, to taste
2 teaspoons finely chopped gherkins or cornichons
2 teaspoons finely chopped capers (see Kitchen Note)
1–1½ tablespoons lemon or lime juice
1–2 tablespoons finely chopped herbs (such as parsley,
    coriander/cilantro, mint, dill)
¼ teaspoon honey

Whisk all the ingredients in a bowl to combine
well. Taste and adjust the flavours as needed.
Store in a clean glass jar in the fridge for up to
2 weeks.

KITCHEN NOTE
When seasoning this sauce with salt, take into account the capers
you're using and leave it out altogether if using salted capers.

buttermilk dressing

DIETARY INFO GLUTEN FREE | VEGETARIAN
EGG FREE
MAKES 310 ML (11 FL OZ/1¼ CUPS)

*If you have mayonnaise, cultured buttermilk or
yoghurt in the fridge, you have the beginning of
a brilliant dressing that will be nutrient dense
and rich in good bugs. Toss this dressing through
easily digestible greens (lettuce, celery, fennel,
herbs) and you not only extend the fuel available
to you, but ensure all those wonderful minerals
are fully bio-available. It is both simply delicious,
nourishing and incredibly easy.*

2–4 tablespoons Green Drizzle Sauce (page 75)
250 ml (9 fl oz/1 cup) Cultured Buttermilk (page 50)

In a bowl, combine the green drizzle sauce and
buttermilk, then taste and add more sauce if
desired. Store in a clean glass jar in the fridge
for up to 1 week.

rosemary-infused olive oil

DIETARY INFO GLUTEN FREE | DAIRY FREE | VEGAN | EGG FREE
MAKES 60 ML (2 FL OZ/¼ CUP)

Make this because it's so easy and so yummy. It has a multitude of applications and is one of the quickest ways to add instant flavour to a dish. I would most definitely recommend doubling the recipe to always have rosemary-infused olive oil on hand.

60 ml (2 fl oz/¼ cup) extra virgin olive oil
6 small rosemary sprigs (about 2 cm (¾ in) in length)

Place the oil and rosemary in a small saucepan over low heat – you are simply warming the oil, so in no way should it ripple or smoke. You will need enough heat to hear a bit of a sizzle. Use a wooden spoon to press the rosemary down into the oil, from time to time, and cook on a very gentle heat for 5 minutes. Remove from the heat and stand to infuse for 30 minutes. Drain the oil into a bowl and discard the rosemary. Store in a clean glass jar or bottle in a cool dark place for up to 4 weeks. You may want to add a small sprig of fresh rosemary to the jar or bottle.

KITCHEN NOTE

Here, ripe tomatoes will give you the flavour that you are after. Any leftover tomato flesh can be used in a tomato sauce. Both the tomato and lemon will add acidity to this dressing and this will vary enormously depending on your ingredients. Taste and add more lemon juice to balance the acidity level as needed. For a vegan option, use vincotto or rapadura sugar to sweeten.

rosemary, preserved lemon and tomato dressing

DIETARY INFO GLUTEN FREE | DAIRY FREE | VEGAN OPTION
EGG FREE
MAKES ABOUT 185 ML (6 FL OZ/¾ CUP)

This is the perfect go-to dressing in summer. You can marinate one quantity of the borlotti (cranberry) beans on page 62 in this quantity of dressing, and the addition of finely chopped fresh rosemary or basil leaves is simply divine.

60 ml (2 fl oz/¼ cup) Rosemary-
  infused Olive Oil (page 72)
1–2 teaspoons finely chopped
  preserved lemon, pith removed
1 teaspoon lemon juice
1 teaspoon wholegrain mustard

½ teaspoon honey, optional
1 garlic clove, crushed
pinch of sea salt
14 medium basil leaves, thinly sliced,
  optional
2–3 ripe tomatoes

Place all the ingredients. except the tomatoes, in a small clean glass jar. Take care to use just the preserved lemon skin, discarding the pith and centre fruit.

Cut the tomatoes in half crossways, then rub them, cut side down through a sieve placed over a bowl to catch the juices, flattening the tomatoes as you go. You might find yourself grating the tomato just a little, but try not to. You will need 80 ml (2½ fl oz/⅓ cup) juice. Reserve the flesh for another use, then add the juice to the jar, seal and shake to combine well. Taste and adjust as needed; I like this to be quite sharp with a noticeable preserved lemon tone. This will keep in the fridge for up to 2 weeks.

lime, cumin and honey dressing

DIETARY INFO GLUTEN FREE | DAIRY FREE
VEGAN OPTION | EGG FREE
MAKES A GENEROUS 125 ML (4 FL OZ/½ CUP)

This dressing will keep well in the fridge for about one week, but it really is best used soon after making, while the coriander (cilantro) still has its vibrant colour and flavour.

60 ml (2 fl oz /¼ cup) extra virgin olive oil
60 ml (2 fl oz /¼ cup) lime juice
25 g (1 oz/½ cup) finely chopped coriander (cilantro) leaves
1–1¼ tablespoons honey, or maple syrup for a vegan option, to taste
½ teaspoon ground cumin, plus extra to taste

Place all the ingredients in a small clean glass jar, starting with just 1 tablespoon of honey. Seal the jar, shake well, then taste and add extra honey, cumin or lime if needed.

green drizzle sauce

DIETARY INFO GLUTEN FREE | DAIRY FREE
VEGAN | EGG FREE
MAKES A GENEROUS 185 ML (6 FL OZ/¾ CUP)

Lighter and brighter than a pesto, but with more body than a chimichurri, this is a multi-purpose sauce to add flavour.

20 g (¾ oz) parsley, tough stems removed, rinsed
20 g (¾ oz) basil, tough stems removed, rinsed
20 g (¾ oz) coriander (cilantro), tough stems and roots removed, rinsed
40 g (1½ oz/¼ cup) pine nuts
125 ml (4 fl oz/½ cup) Rosemary-infused Olive Oil (page 72) or extra virgin olive oil
¼ teaspoon sweet white miso (shiro)
2 tablespoons lemon juice
½–1 teaspoon rapadura sugar or raw sugar
1 garlic clove
1 tablespoon capers in salt, rinsed
good pinch of sea salt

Place all the ingredients in a blender and process until well combined but still a bit chunky. Taste and add a bit more lemon juice as required. Store in a clean glass jar in the fridge for up to 1 week.

KITCHEN NOTE
The amount of salt you need to add will depend on how salty your capers are, so just start with a bit and add more if needed.

KITCHEN NOTE

It's important to slice the onions as thinly and uniformly as you can; this will ensure even cooking.

fig, balsamic and onion jam

DIETARY INFO GLUTEN FREE | DAIRY FREE | VEGAN | EGG FREE
MAKES ABOUT 500 G (1 LB 2 OZ)

Sweet and sour and intensely flavoured, I find many uses for this delicious jam. It will store for up to two months in the fridge. I like it in the Christmas Lima Bean Terrine (page 148), on the Roast Plum, Goat's Curd and Basil Tart (page 156), or in the Pocket Pie (page 160). It also pairs beautifully with feta or goat's cheese in a quiche.

2 large red onions, halved and
  very thinly sliced
2 tablespoons extra virgin olive oil
pinch of sea salt
6 dried figs, thinly sliced

60 ml (2 fl oz/¼ cup) balsamic
  vinegar
1 tablespoon rapadura sugar or
  raw sugar

Place the onions, olive oil and salt in a medium-size frying pan. Cook over low–medium heat, stirring frequently, for about 10–15 minutes, until the onions are beginning to look a little translucent and soft. Stir in the figs, vinegar and sugar and reduce the heat to low; just enough so that the liquid is bubbling very gently. Continue to cook, stirring frequently, for 30–40 minutes or until dark and sticky. At this stage, the onions should still be soft and pliable. Take care not to overcook as the jam can become too dry, especially as it sits in the fridge over time. Remove from the heat and allow to cool. Store in a sterilised glass jar in the fridge for up to 4 months.

sweet sultana and chilli sauce

DIETARY INFO GLUTEN FREE | DAIRY FREE | VEGAN | EGG FREE
MAKES 500 ML (17 FL OZ/2 CUPS)

I buy a delicious sweet chilli sauce, and this is my attempt to replicate it. Made with rapadura sugar and sultanas to sweeten the sauce, it is deeply flavoured and goes with just about everything. To add a smoky dimension to this, add a little chipotle chilli or smoked paprika to taste.

125 g (4½ oz) red chillies (I like a mixture of long red and jalapeño), seeds and stems discarded
4 garlic cloves
25 g (1 oz) fresh ginger, peeled and coarsely chopped
170 g (6 oz/1 cup) sultanas (golden raisins)

250 ml (9 fl oz/1 cup) apple cider vinegar
440 g (15½ oz/2 cups) rapadura sugar or raw sugar
1 teaspoon sea salt
½ teaspoon ground turmeric

Place all the ingredients in a food processor or blender with 250 ml (9 fl oz/1 cup) water and process until the sultanas and chilli are very, very finely chopped. Transfer to a medium-size saucepan and simmer over low heat, stirring occasionally for 1–1½ hours, until thick and the consistency of soft jam. Keep in mind that the sauce will thicken and 'sticky up' a bit as it cools. Transfer to a clean glass jar and store in the fridge for up to 6 months.

KITCHEN NOTE
Use a good-quality gelatine for this recipe. Read more on page 22.

rosemary and raspberry jelly

DIETARY INFO GLUTEN FREE | DAIRY FREE | EGG FREE
MAKES 250 G (9 OZ/1 CUP)
YOU WILL NEED TO BEGIN THIS RECIPE ONE DAY AHEAD

Gelatine is a wonderful aid to digestion, especially protein. This is a delicious, gelatine-rich savoury jelly that pairs brilliantly with lamb, be it sausages, chops or a roast. I've paired it with the crumbed cutlets on page 212.

125 ml (4 fl oz/½ cup) apple cider vinegar
185 g (6½ oz/1½ cups) fresh or frozen raspberries

3 rosemary sprigs, 5 cm (2 in) long
55 g (2 oz/¼ cup) golden caster (superfine) sugar
3 teaspoons powdered gelatine

The day before, place the vinegar and raspberries in a small saucepan, cover and stand overnight or for 8–12 hours.

The following day, add 2 rosemary sprigs to the pan and bring to just below the boil. Remove from the heat and stand for 1 hour. Strain the mixture through a sieve into a bowl, gently moving the berries in the sieve, helping the juice drain through, but not so firmly that you press the flesh into the liquid. Return the juice to the pan – there should be a generous 185 ml (6 fl oz/¾ cup) – and leave the berries and rosemary sitting in the sieve over the bowl as they will continue to drip a little more juice. Add the sugar to the juice in the pan, then cook over medium heat, stirring every now and then, and bring to just below the boil, ensuring the sugar is dissolved. Remove from the heat, add the gelatine and stir until dissolved. Add any extra juice that has dripped into the bowl. Let cool a little before pouring into a clean glass jar. Add the remaining rosemary sprig to the jar, put the lid on and refrigerate overnight or until set. Store for up to 2 months in the fridge.

date, cinnamon and honey cultured butter

DIETARY INFO GLUTEN FREE | VEGETARIAN | EGG FREE
MAKES ABOUT 150 G (5½ OZ/¾ CUP)

*This recipe is great to have in the fridge and can be served with the
Sweet Potato, Cinnamon Bread (page 120), Best-ever Buttermilk
Pancakes (page 118) or added to porridge. It not only adds delicious
flavour and wholesome sweetness, but a serving of good bacteria
as well.*

125 g (4½ oz) unsalted Cultured
   Butter (page 50), softened
3 fresh dates, seeded and cut into
   small pieces

sea salt, to taste
1 teaspoon ground cinnamon,
   or to taste
1–1½ tablespoons well-flavoured honey

Using a fork, spread the softened butter out onto a dinner plate.
Sprinkle the butter with the dates, cinnamon and salt, then drizzle
evenly with the honey. Mash together, taste and adjust the flavour
as desired.

Using a spatula, transfer the butter mix to a sheet of baking paper,
then using the paper as a guide, roll the paper into a log. Wrap and
seal both ends and refrigerate until needed. The butter will keep
for 1–2 weeks. It also freezes well if wrapped tightly for up to
3 months.

wakame gomasio

DIETARY INFO GLUTEN FREE | DAIRY FREE
VEGAN | EGG FREE
MAKES 75 G (2½ OZ/½ CUP)

*Wakame gomasio is a powerhouse of minerals –
especially calcium. This salty condiment can be
used instead of salt to sprinkle on just about any
savoury thing you can imagine. I especially like
this sprinkled into a cooked grain-based salad
or served with vegetables. It is also great in the
dairy-free pastry on page 86.*

3 g (⅛ oz) wakame sea vegetable
75 g (2½ oz/½ cup) sesame seeds, lightly toasted
½–1 teaspoon sea salt

Preheat the oven to 165°C (320°F).

Place the wakame on a baking tray and bake
for 5–10 minutes, until crisp and completely
dried out. Using a mortar and pestle, pound
the wakame until it becomes a fine powder,
discarding any stems that may be left. Add the
sesame seeds to the wakame and continue to
grind until they begin to glisten and take on a
fragrant aroma. Stir in the salt, then store in
a clean glass jar in the fridge for up to 4 weeks.

coconut palm sugar syrup

DIETARY INFO GLUTEN FREE | DAIRY FREE
VEGAN | EGG FREE
MAKES ABOUT 170 ML (5¼ FL OZ)

*This syrup is lovely drizzled over porridge,
pancakes, panna cotta or the Amaranth and
Tapioca Coconut Porridge (page 127).*

100 g (3½ oz) granulated coconut palm sugar (jaggery)

Place the sugar in a small saucepan with
125 ml (4 fl oz/½ cup) water. Use a pastry brush
to brush down any granules on the side of the
pan. Cook over low heat, stirring occasionally
until the sugar has dissolved. Increase the heat
to medium and simmer for 5 minutes or until
a light syrup forms. Remove from the heat and
allow to cool. If you find that the syrup solidifies
when cool, just add a tiny bit of hot water to
loosen it up. Pour into a clean glass bottle and
refrigerate for up to 2 weeks.

tamari almonds

DIETARY INFO GLUTEN-FREE OPTION | DAIRY FREE | VEGAN | EGG FREE
MAKES 160 G (5¾ OZ/1 CUP)

Salty, tangy tamari almonds are a little addictive, but make a wonderful addition to a salad or meal, helping to add protein and fat for nutrient density. You can make them using soaked or unsoaked nuts – soaked nuts will be more nourishing, but the drying process is considerably longer. Both will store in an airtight container in a cool dark place for up to four weeks.

OPTION 1: UNSOAKED

160 g (5¾ oz/1 cup) almonds, with skin on
1 tablespoon tamari (or wheat-free tamari for
  a gluten-free option)
½ teaspoon sea salt

Choose a small jar with a lid into which the almonds will fit snugly. Add the almonds and tamari to the jar, then screw the lid on tightly and stand for 2–4 hours, turning the jar on its lid from time to time.

When ready to cook, preheat the oven to 120°C (235°F). Scatter the almonds on a baking tray and sprinkle with the salt. Bake, stirring occasionally, for 20–30 minutes, until lightly toasted.

OPTION 2: SOAKED

160 g (5¾ oz/1 cup) almonds, with skin on
½ teaspoon sea salt
1 tablespoon tamari (or wheat-free tamari for
  a gluten-free option)

The day before, place the almonds and salt in a bowl, cover with water and stand overnight.

The following day, drain the nuts and pat dry with paper towel. Place in a jar that will fit the nuts snugly with the tamari, then screw the lid on tightly and stand for 1–2 hours, turning the jar on its lid from time to time.

When ready to cook, preheat the oven to its lowest setting. Scatter the almonds on a baking tray and cook for 6–20 hours or until the nuts are absolutely dry and crisp. (Test them from time to time, but they take longer than you think.) Hotter is not necessarily better in this case, as the nuts will toast on the outside, and remain damp on the inside.

KITCHEN NOTE

These take longer than you think, but your heat should be medium and slow, not hot and fast. When you cut through one to check after the first 20 minutes, it should only just be beginning to toast.

maple and cinnamon almonds

DIETARY INFO GLUTEN FREE | DAIRY FREE | VEGAN | EGG FREE
MAKES 80 G (2¾ OZ/½ CUP)

Subtly sweet and with a definite cinnamon flavour, these are a wonderful addition for a porridge, pancake or salad.

80 g (2¾ oz/½ cup) natural almonds with skin on
¼–½ teaspoon ground cinnamon, or to taste
1 tablespoon maple syrup

Preheat the oven to 180°C (350°F).

Place the almonds on a baking tray and bake for 20 minutes or until just toasted through when cut. Remove from the oven and add the cinnamon and maple syrup, mixing the almonds well.

Reduce the heat to 150°C (300°F) and bake for 10–15 minutes, until dry and crispy. Leave to cool before using, and store any leftovers in a clean glass jar. Store in a cool, dark place for up to 4 weeks.

almond, honey and olive oil brittle

DIETARY INFO GLUTEN FREE | DAIRY FREE
VEGAN OPTION | EGG FREE
MAKES 270 G (9½ OZ/1 GENEROUS CUP)

Other than fruit, serving a little nut and seed mix with panna cotta, cultured cream, pancakes or porridge will help extend the nutrient density.

2 teaspoons extra virgin olive oil
1 tablespoon vincotto (or brown rice syrup)
1 tablespoon honey (swap for 1 tablespoon of maple syrup if you want a vegan option)
1 tablespoon brown rice syrup
1 teaspoon natural vanilla extract
40 g (1½ oz/¼ cup) blanched almonds, cut lengthways into 3–4 slices
40 g (1½ oz/¼ cup) sunflower seeds
40 g (1½ oz/¼ cup) pumpkin seeds (pepitas)
½ teaspoon ground cinnamon, optional

Preheat the oven to 180°C (350°F) and line a baking tray with baking paper.

Combine the olive oil, vincotto, honey, brown rice syrup and vanilla extract in a bowl. Add the remaining ingredients and combine well, then spread out over the lined tray. Bake for 10–15 minutes, or until the nuts and seeds are well toasted, but most importantly, the syrup must be gently bubbling. This ensures the brittle will have a desirable crunch. Remove from the oven and stand until completely cooled, then break up and store in a clean airtight glass jar for up to 2 weeks. Because of the honey and vincotto, this brittle may soften a little as it sits in the jar, but it should still have crunch.

macadamia, sesame and coconut brittle

DIETARY INFO GLUTEN FREE | DAIRY FREE
VEGAN | EGG FREE
MAKES 270 G (9½ OZ/1 GENEROUS CUP)

2 teaspoons coconut oil, melted
1 tablespoon maple syrup
2 tablespoons brown rice syrup
1 teaspoon natural vanilla extract
75 g (2½ oz/½ cup) macadamia nuts, coarsely chopped, but so you still have nice big chunks
40 g (1½ oz/¼ cup) hulled sesame seeds
20 g (¾ oz/¼ cup) shredded coconut

Preheat the oven to 180°C (350°F) and line a baking tray with baking paper.

Combine the coconut oil, maple syrup, brown rice syrup and vanilla in a bowl. Add the remaining ingredients and combine well, then spread out over the lined tray. Bake for 10–15 minutes, or until the nuts and seeds are well toasted, but most importantly, the syrup must be gently bubbling. This will ensure the brittle will have crunch. Remove from the oven and leave to cool for a few minutes, then use a spatula to move it off the tray before it sets. Leave to cool, then store in a clean airtight glass jar in a cool place for up to 2 weeks.

barley and spelt shortcrust pastry

DIETARY INFO WHEAT FREE | VEGETARIAN
MAKES ENOUGH TO LINE A 24-26 CM × 2.5-3.5 CM DEEP (9½-10½ × 1-1¼ IN) TART TIN, OR TWO 24 CM (9½ IN) FREE-FORM TARTS OR 8 POCKET PIES

I know that for many people pastry is a scary thing, and trust me, the pastry will smell your fear. Making good pastry is very easy, you just need to follow some basic rules. This is a pastry with a great depth of flavour. Because it has low-gluten barley, it can't take too much more butter – it will just crumble.

130 g (4¾ oz/1 cup) white spelt flour
110 g (3¾ oz/1 cup) barley flour
pinch of sea salt
150 g (5½ oz) cold unsalted butter
1 egg
1–2 tablespoons ice-cold water (for sweet pastry, add 1½ tablespoons rapadura sugar or golden caster/superfine sugar and 1 teaspoon natural vanilla extract to the water)

To make using a food processor: Place the flours, salt, butter (and sugar if using) in a food processor and pulse 1–2 times or just until the mixture resembles very coarse breadcrumbs. The size of the butter should range from small breadcrumbs to small lentils. Don't be tempted to add the egg and water to the food processor as it is too easy to overwork the pastry, but rather turn it into a bowl.

To make by hand: Place the dry ingredients in a bowl and using your fingertips and thumb, rub the butter into the flour mixture. The aim is to press the butter into flat chips ranging from the size of breadcrumbs to small lentils. I tend to lift the butter and flour that I am working on and let it fall back into the bowl. This helps to aerate and keep the flour and butter cool. Working quickly and lightly will also keep the butter cool.

Place the egg and 1 tablespoon ice-cold water in a small bowl and beat with a fork until well combined. Add to the flour mix and use a butter knife to cut the liquid into the dry ingredients. Add the remaining water if needed, but be very careful not to use too much. (If making sweet pastry, 1 tablespoon of water should be enough.) Once the mixture looks evenly moist but not at all wet, bring it together into a ball – do not knead or play with it. Depending on how you will be using the pastry, divide it into portions if necessary, then cover in plastic wrap or in a resealable plastic bag and refrigerate for at least 1 hour or overnight. The dough can be frozen for up to 4 weeks at this point.

To roll the pastry: Ensure your rolling pin and work surface are lightly coated with flour. Roll the pastry out once or twice to assess it. If the pastry is very cold, pressing too hard may result in it cracking. Run a palette knife underneath and move the pastry firmly and quickly, then dust the rolling area and rolling pin again with a little flour, if necessary, and turn the dough over. Repeat this process, though as the dough gets bigger you will probably be able to give it 2–3 rolls each time. If you do too many rolls without moving it, the pastry has a tendency to stick to both the surface and the rolling pin. Also remember that it should feel well chilled at all stages – if it starts to warm up, place it on a baking paper-lined tray and place it in the freezer for 1–2 minutes.

dairy-free coconut oil and sesame pastry

DIETARY INFO DAIRY FREE | VEGAN | EGG FREE | WHEAT FREE
MAKES ENOUGH TO LINE A 24-26 CM × 2.5-3.5 CM DEEP (9½-10½ × 1-1¼ IN) TART
TIN, OR TWO 24 CM (9½ IN) FREE-FORM TARTS OR 8 POCKET PIES

It is best to use a food processor to make this delicous pastry as it will break down the coconut oil before it has a chance to melt – giving you the most desirable result.

260 g (9¼ oz/2 cups) white spelt flour
100 g (3½ oz/½ cup) well-chilled coconut oil
125 ml (4 fl oz/½ cup) ice-cold water
1½ teaspoons apple cider vinegar
75 g (2½ oz/½ cup) Wakame Gomasio (page 80),
   or lightly toasted sesame seeds

To make using a food processor: Place the flour in a food processor and, using a butter knife, break up the very cold and hard coconut oil into chunks as best you can, then add to the processor. Pulse 1 or 2 times, or until the mixture resembles very fine breadcrumbs. Mix 100 ml (3½ fl oz) ice-cold water and the vinegar together and add to the processor with the wakame gomasio or sesame seeds. Pulse 1 or 2 times just to bring the pastry together, taking care not to overwork the dough. You may need to add the remaining water if it looks dry as some white spelt flours absorb more liquid than others. Bring the dough together into a ball, without kneading or handling it too much.

To make by hand: Place the flour in a mixing bowl. Grate the very hard and cold coconut oil into the flour. Using your fingertips or pastry cutter, rub the oil into the flour as quickly as possible (body temperature will melt it) until the mixture looks like small breadcrumbs. Mix 100 ml (3½ fl oz) ice-cold water and the vinegar together and add to the bowl with the wakame gomasio or sesame seeds. Using a bread and butter knife, begin to cut the water into the flour mixture until the mixture looks evenly moist but not at all wet. Bring the mixture together into a ball, without kneading or playing with it. You may need the remaining water as some white spelt flours absorb more liquid than others.

Depending on how you will be using the pastry, divide it into portions if necessary, then wrap in plastic wrap or in a resealable plastic bag and refrigerate for at least 20 minutes, or until cold to the touch. The dough can be frozen for up to 4 weeks at this point.

To roll the pastry: Lightly dust your work surface and a heavy, decent-size rolling pin with flour, using as little flour as possible. If your pastry has been divided into portions, work with one piece of pastry at a time, leaving the other piece(s) in the fridge to keep cool. Roll the pastry once or twice – coconut oil sets harder and has less give than butter, so when it is very cold it may crack. If it does crack, just let it warm up and soften a little at room temperature before continuing. Run a palette knife under-neath, move the pastry firmly and quickly, lightly dusting the rolling area with a little more flour, and turn the dough over. Lightly sprinkle the surface of the pastry with flour and you are ready to roll again.

dairy-free sweet vanilla and coconut pastry

DIETARY INFO DAIRY FREE | VEGAN | EGG FREE | WHEAT FREE
MAKES 8 POCKET PIES

It is best to use a food processor to make this delicious pastry as it breaks down the coconut oil before it has a chance to melt – giving you the most desirable result.

195 g (7 oz/1½ cups) white spelt flour
1 tablespoon coconut palm sugar (jaggery)
¼ teaspoon baking powder
100 g (3½ oz/½ cup) well-chilled coconut oil
60 ml (2 fl oz/¼ cup) ice-cold water, plus extra if needed
1 teaspoon apple cider vinegar
1 teaspoon natural vanilla extract
25 g (1 oz/¼ cup) desiccated coconut

To make using a food processor: Place the flour, sugar, baking powder into a food processor. Using a butter knife, break up the cold and hard coconut oil into chunks as best you can, then add to the processor. Pulse 1 or 2 times, until the mixture resembles very fine breadcrumbs. In a bowl, combine the ice-cold water, vinegar and vanilla, and add to the processor with the desiccated coconut. Pulse 1 or 2 times just to bring the pastry together, taking care not to overwork the dough. Add a little more water if absolutely necessary – the mixture should be moist but not at all wet. Bring the dough together into a ball, without kneading or handling it too much.

To make by hand: Place the flour, sugar and baking powder into a mixing bowl. Grate the hard and cold coconut oil and add to the flour. Using your fingertips or a pastry cutter, rub the oil into the flour as quickly as possible, until the mixture resembles breadcrumbs. Stir through

the coconut. In a separate bowl, combine the ice-cold water, vinegar and vanilla and add this to the coconut-flour mixture. Using a bread and butter knife, cut the water into the flour mixture. Add a little extra water if absolutely necessary – the mixture should be moist but not at all wet. Bring the dough together into a ball, without kneading or handling it too much.

Depending on how you will be using the pastry, divide it into portions if necessary, then wrap in plastic wrap or in a resealable plastic bag and refrigerate for at least 20 minutes, or until cold to the touch. The dough can be frozen for up to 4 weeks at this point.

To roll the pastry: Ensure your rolling pin and work surface are lightly coated with flour. If your pastry has been divided into portions, work with one piece of pastry at a time, leaving the other piece(s) in the fridge to keep cool. Roll out the pastry once or twice to introduce yourself to it and assess it – coconut oil sets hard and has less give than butter so if the pastry is very cold, it may crack. If it does crack, just let it warm up and soften a little at room temperature before continuing. Run a palette knife underneath, move the pastry firmly and quickly, lightly dusting the rolling area with a little more flour, and turn the dough over. Lightly sprinkle the surface of the pastry with flour and roll again.

A GOOD MORNING, A GOOD MONTH, A GOOD YEAR

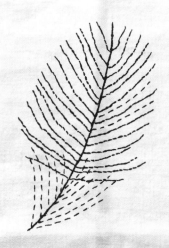

a NOURISHING START to the day

fruit-based breakfasts

Fruit is a wonderful way to start the day, especially in summer. But fruit alone, while delicious when ripe and in season, doesn't have the available fuel to keep us going very long. Adding nutrient density can help to extend the fuel and nourishment available to us. From a delicious breakfast salad highlighting the best of summer fruits, to roasted and stewed fruits, butters and syrups, this section showcases fruit alone, and fruit as a partner to many nutrient-dense options.

STEWED FRUIT Stewing is, fundamentally, adding fruit to an enclosed area (a saucepan with a lid) and using a low heat to encourage the juices to seep out. I find this pure fruit essence to be so much more fragrant and delicious than when the fruit is simply poached in a large amount of liquid.

The basics
- Add as little water as possible. Use a lidded saucepan and very gentle heat to sweat the juices out. This takes a bit of time, but it will result in intense flavour.
- I prefer using semi-refined sugar in small amounts, allowing the pure flavour of the fruit to shine through. Use a rapadura sugar when you want a deeper, earthier flavour.

ROASTED FRUIT While stewing allows you to concentrate flavour by sweating out the juices, roasting fruit allows you to concentrate the flavours and encourage caramelisation.

The basics
- Ensure your oven is hot and use a heavy-based ovenproof dish that can contain that heat. Cast iron is perfect.
- Choose a shallow dish that will allow the fruit to fit snugly.
- Add some fat to the fruit such as ghee, macadamia or olive oil, or duck fat. Duck fat is ideal for a savoury application. If the fat is solid, melt it first before tossing with the fruit.
- You can sprinkle the fruit with a little sweetness such as sugar, maple syrup or honey to add more caramelisation, although it's wise to taste the fruit first.
- Try adding other flavourings to the fruit – thyme, rosemary, vanilla bean and cinnamon are particularly delicious.

Add nutrient density to fruit-based breakfasts

FAT: Dairy, egg yolk, coconut milk or cream, seeds and nuts.
PROTEIN: Dairy, nuts and seeds, spirulina, sea vegetables, egg white.
CARBOHYDRATE: Whole grain porridges or pancakes.
BENEFICIAL BACTERIA: Kefir cultured milk or cream, or cultured butter.

Other than perfectly ripe, seasonal fruits eaten fresh and as close as possible to harvest, I love to roast and stew my fruit to concentrate their luscious flavour – resulting in what I think of as their essence.

apricot essence

DIETARY INFO GLUTEN FREE | EGG FREE
DAIRY FREE | VEGAN
MAKES ABOUT 310 ML (10¾ FL OZ/1¼ CUPS)

Long live the apricot – especially the Royal Blenheim or Moorpark. This recipe showcases the concentrated flavour of apricots, and is utterly divine. I've been known to add sparkling water to it on a very hot day.

10 apricots (about 520 g/1 lb 2 oz), halved and
    stones removed
½ vanilla bean, halved lengthways, seeds scraped
1–2 teaspoons golden caster (superfine) sugar, or to taste

Choose a saucepan that will allow the apricots to cover the base of the pan but still remain just a little crowded. Place the apricots, vanilla bean seeds and bean, 1 teaspoon sugar and 1 tablespoon water in the pan. Cover with a lid and cook over very low heat for 20 minutes. Remove the lid and taste, then add extra sugar if needed. Add a tablespoon more of water if needed. It can take some time for the juices to weep and cover the fruit. Replace the lid and cook for a further 10 minutes, until the apricots are cooked and juicy. Remove from the heat and set aside to cool a little.

Place a sieve over a bowl, making sure it doesn't sit too low in the bowl. Remove the vanilla bean (see Kitchen Note on page 104 on how to make vanilla sugar using the bean), then pour the apricots and their juice into the sieve. Using a spatula, push the apricots through the sieve until all but the skins remain. Store the apricot essence in an airtight container in the fridge for up to 1 week or freeze for up to 3 months in a tempered glass jar.

blueberry and lime sauce

DIETARY INFO GLUTEN FREE | DAIRY FREE
EGG FREE | VEGAN
MAKES ABOUT 625 ML (21½ FL OZ/2½–3 CUPS)

Lime is a wonderful partner for blueberry, and this recipe will work with fresh or frozen berries. This is a delicious match for the Amaranth and Tapioca Coconut Porridge (page 127).

425 g (15 oz/2¾ cups) fresh or frozen blueberries
60–125 ml (2–4 fl oz/¼–½ cup) brown rice syrup
3 teaspoons finely grated lime zest, or to taste

Place the blueberries, 60 ml (2 fl oz/¼ cup) brown rice syrup and the lime zest in a saucepan. Cover with a lid and cook over very low heat for 10–15 minutes, until the berries start to release their juices. Remove the lid, then taste and add extra lime zest, or brown rice syrup as desired. Increase the heat to medium and simmer the blueberries for 2–3 minutes, until the liquid has reduced to a thick syrup. Remove from the heat, stand until cool, then store in an airtight container in the fridge for up to 2 weeks, or freeze for up to 3 months.

500 g (1 lb 2 oz) Santa Rosa plums,
  halved and stones removed
½ vanilla bean, halved lengthways
  and seeds scraped
1–2 tablespoons golden caster
  (superfine) sugar, or to taste

*Although I have called for a Santa Rosa plum, you can really use
any plum here. If you have the chance, do search out this delicious
heirloom variety – it is so fragrant and something quite special.
This puree would also welcome a drop of rose water, which helps
make the flavour of this plum bloom.*

santa rosa plum puree

Choose a saucepan that will allow the plums to cover the base
of the pan but remain just a little crowded.

Place the plums, vanilla bean seeds and the bean in the pan. Add
1 tablespoon sugar and 1 tablespoon water. Cover with a lid and
cook over very low heat for 20 minutes. Remove the lid and taste,
then add extra sugar, if needed, and check there is enough liquid.
It can take some time for the juices to seep and cover the fruit. Put
the lid on and cook for another 10 minutes or until the plums are
cooked and juicy. Remove from the heat and stand to cool a little.

At this point, you can either serve or store as they are for stewed
plums. For the puree, place a sieve over a bowl, making sure it
doesn't sit too low in the bowl. Remove the vanilla bean (see
Kitchen Note on page 104 on how to make vanilla sugar using the
bean), then tip the plums and their juice into the sieve. Using a
spatula or large spoon, press on the plums until all but the skins
remain. Store the stewed plums or plum puree in an airtight jar
in the fridge for up to 1 week, or freeze for up to 3 months.

93

DIETARY INFO GLUTEN FREE | VEGETARIAN | DAIRY-FREE OPTION | VEGAN OPTION | EGG FREE
SERVES 2

94

70–80 g (2½–2¾ oz) mixture small
   lettuce leaves (mixture of
   rocket/arugula, radicchio
   and buttercrunch, or
   cos/romaine lettuce)
1 peach, peeled if desired and
   sliced into wedges, or seasonal fruit
   to equal quantity
6 strawberries, hulled and halved
50 g (1¾ oz) soft goat's cheese,
   crumbled, optional
handful of fresh herbs such as basil,
   mint, fennel fronds, or sunflower
   or quinoa sprouts
half quantity Maple and Cinnamon
   Almonds (page 82), optional

RASPBERRY VINAIGRETTE
2 tablespoons extra virgin olive oil
1 tablespoon raspberry vinegar
½ teaspoon dijon mustard

KITCHEN NOTES
● For the dressing, balsamic or
even a raspberry vincotto vinegar
are also wonderful.
● Choose a variety of greens and
consider the sweetness of the fruit.
Peaches are often very sweet and
are well balanced with some radicchio
and a bit of tart rocket. Tarter fruit
such as strawberries will do well with
a sweeter butter-crunch lettuce.
● Ripe seasonal fruit is what this salad
is all about. Berries and stone fruit such
as apricots, nectarines and cherries are
especially good.

I was first introduced to the idea of a 'breakfast salad' by Frog Hollow Farm in San Francisco. It is quite a perfect thing for a hot summer morning, as it's quick and easy to digest. Micro greens, sprouts or well-sprouted seeds would all be welcome. The addition of goat's cheese and nuts to the salad extend the nutrient density. This is more a template than a recipe, but there are some basics.

summer peach, greens and almond breakfast salad

Firstly, make the vinaigrette. Place all the ingredients in a small jar, then seal and shake until well combined.

Arrange the lettuce leaves on a platter, scatter with the peach wedges, strawberries and crumbled goat's cheese, if using. Drizzle with the vinaigrette, then scatter with the herbs and the maple and cinnamon almonds, if using, and serve.

DIETARY INFO GLUTEN FREE | DAIRY FREE | VEGAN | EGG FREE
MAKES 500 ML (17 FL OZ/2 CUPS)

360 g (12¾ oz) cherries,
   halved and stones removed
1–2 teaspoons golden caster
   (superfine) sugar
1 drop almond extract
1 teaspoon natural vanilla extract

I'm always looking for ways to mimic the intense marzipan flavour of sour cherries. I adore them, but have little access to good ones. I ended up adding a tiny drop of almond extract (I like Nielsen-Massey brand), and it works a treat. This is a delicious match for the Almond Milk Panna Cotta (page 106).

sweet cherry almond compote

Choose a small saucepan that will allow the cherries to cover the base of the pan but still be very crowded with some depth.

Place the cherries in the saucepan with 1 teaspoon sugar and the almond extract. (Cherries have quite a lot of juice and should not need any water.) Cover with a lid and cook over very low heat for 20 minutes. Remove the lid and taste, then add the vanilla extract, and extra sugar if needed. Check that there is enough liquid – it can take some time for the juices to seep out and cover the fruit. (If there isn't enough juice, return the lid and cook for a further 10 minutes – but avoid doing this if possible.) Cook for a few minutes over high heat to reduce the juice to a syrup. Remove from the heat, stand until cool, then store in an airtight container in the fridge for up to 1 week.

KITCHEN NOTE

If you have sour cherries, by all means use them here and simply omit the almond extract.

DIETARY INFO DAIRY FREE | GLUTEN FREE | VEGAN | EGG FREE
MAKES ABOUT 250 G (9 OZ/1 CUP)

4 ripe pears (about 800 g/
    1 lb 12 oz), Packham or Bartlett are
    best, peeled, cored and cut into
    2–3 cm (¾–1¼ in) pieces
½ vanilla bean, halved lengthways
1–2 teaspoons maple syrup, to taste
pinch of ground allspice
pinch of ground cinnamon

Many pear butter recipes are strongly scented with spices, however I prefer mine to showcase the true beauty that is the pear in partnership with vanilla. I also prefer to sweeten the butter with maple syrup, rather than rapadura sugar, as it matches the strong fragrance of pear. Small amounts of allspice and cinnamon support rather than overpower this. The butter is a perfect partner for the Best-ever Buttermilk Pancakes (page 118), or the Oat Kernel and Spelt Berry Porridge (page 124).

pear 'butter'

Choose a small saucepan that will allow the pears to crowd about halfway up the side of the pan.

Place the pears, vanilla bean halves, maple syrup and 2 teaspoons water in the pan. Cover and cook over very low heat for 15–25 minutes, until the juices have all been released. Continue to cook for another 10–15 minutes, until the pears are cooked through and tender when pierced with a knife. The pears will noticeably change in colour, appearing translucent when they are done. Remove the vanilla bean halves and set aside.

Tip the cooked pears into a sieve placed over a bowl and use a spatula or large spoon to work and press the pears through as much as possible. Return the sieved pear mix to the pan. Lay the reserved vanilla bean halves on a chopping board, and, using a small knife, scrape out the seeds and put them into the pan with the pears. (see Kitchen Note on page 104 on how to make vanilla sugar using the bean.) Add the spices, then cook over very low heat, stirring frequently for 15–30 minutes, until very thick and not at all watery. Remove from the heat and stand until cool, then store in a clean airtight container in the fridge for up to 2 weeks.

KITCHEN NOTES
● Make sure you choose ripe pears as they will have the maximum juice.
● Try to add as little water as possible. You need a little in the beginning to keep things moist, just until the pear juices have released.
● If you prefer, use an equal quantity of rapadura or light brown muscovado sugar instead of the maple syrup.

DIETARY INFO GLUTEN FREE | DAIRY FREE | VEGAN | EGG FREE
MAKES 125–185 ML (4–6 FL OZ/½–¾ CUP)
YOU WILL NEED TO BEGIN THIS RECIPE THE DAY BEFORE

10 dried figs (about 200 g/7 oz) or fresh figs to equal weight
2 teaspoons fig vincotto vinegar, optional
1 tablespoon rapadura sugar or raw sugar, plus 1–2 tablespoons extra
1 thin lemon sliver
1 bay leaf
½ cinnamon stick
½ vanilla bean, halved lengthways

Unless you have access to a large amount of figs for free, this is not exactly a cost-effective recipe, but it truly is sublime. This syrup is also a really wonderful alternative to maple syrup in the deep mid-winter, when only dried fruits (or bottled fruits, if you are lucky enough to have them) remain.

fig and bay syrup

The day before, combine all the ingredients (but only 1 tablespoon sugar) and 500 ml (17 fl oz/2 cups) water in a saucepan small enough that the water completely covers the figs. Cook over low heat for 1 hour, regularly topping up with a little more water to maintain the level of liquid in the pan. Remove from the heat, cover with a lid, then stand until cool. Refrigerate overnight.

The next morning, place a sieve over a bowl, ensuring the sieve does not sit too low. Line the sieve with four layers of muslin (cheesecloth). Pour the entire contents of the pan into the sieve, pull the muslin together and squeeze out as much liquid as possible. Discard the solids.

Place the liquid in a clean saucepan with 1 tablespoon sugar. Simmer for 15–20 minutes or until the liquid has reduced by half. Make sure you taste it halfway through cooking and add more sugar, fig vincotto vinegar or lemon juice, if desired. Remove the syrup from the heat and stand until cool and thickened. Pour the syrup into a clean glass jar and store in the fridge for up to 2 weeks.

KITCHEN NOTES

● The fig vincotto vinegar is not essential here, but it does add a delicious twist.

● This is absolutely divine with a little Pedro Ximénez sherry added to the pan at the beginning. This adds extra sweetness, so you may not need to add as much sugar, taste and adjust as required.

98

roasted apricots

DIETARY INFO GLUTEN FREE | DAIRY FREE
VEGAN | EGG FREE
SERVES 4–6

I use these apricots in the Roasted Apricot and Brown Rice Salad (page 144), but they would also be perfect served with any of the porridges, pancakes, panna cottas or the Vanilla Buttermilk Ice Cream (page 222).

10 ripe apricots (about 450 g/1 lb), halved and
   stones removed
2 teaspoons fat (see Roasted Fruit, page 90)
1 teaspoon rapadura sugar, or raw sugar or honey

Preheat the oven to 190°C (375°F).

Place the apricots in a shallow ovenproof dish that allows for a snug fit. Add your chosen fat and gently toss to coat, then turn the apricots so they are cut side up in the dish. Sprinkle with the sugar or drizzle with the honey and roast for 30–35 minutes, until the juices run and are bubbling and lightly caramelised. Remove from the oven and serve warm or stand until cool, then store in an airtight container in the fridge for up to 1 week.

roasted plums

DIETARY INFO GLUTEN FREE | DAIRY FREE
VEGAN | EGG FREE
SERVES 4–6

7–10 plums, halved and stones removed
2 teaspoons fat (see Roasted Fruit, page 90)
1 vanilla bean, halved lengthways, seeds scraped
1 teaspoon rapadura sugar, or raw sugar or honey

Preheat the oven to 190°C (375°F).

Place the plums in a shallow ovenproof dish or cast-iron dish that allows them to sit snugly. Add the fat, vanilla seeds and the bean and gently toss to coat. Turn the plums so that they are cut side up, then sprinkle with the sugar or drizzle with the honey. Roast for 15–25 minutes, until the juices run and are bubbling and lightly caramelised. Remove from the oven and serve warm or stand until cool, then store in an airtight container in the fridge for up to 1 week.

DIETARY INFO GLUTEN FREE | VEGAN | DAIRY FREE | EGG FREE
MAKES ABOUT 370 G (13 OZ/2 CUPS)

340 g (11¾ oz) rhubarb, leaves
   discarded and ends trimmed
250 ml (9 fl oz/1 cup) blood
   orange juice
1 vanilla bean, halved lengthways
2–3 tablespoons rapadura sugar
   or raw sugar

*In late winter, when blood oranges and rhubarb abound, this brings
a bright dash of colour and delicious flavour to the day.*

roasted rhubarb and blood orange

Preheat the oven to 190°C (375°F).

Rinse the rhubarb stalks, then cut into 3–4 cm (1¼–1½ in)
lengths. Place in a cast-iron dish with the orange juice, vanilla
bean and 2 tablespoons rapadura sugar, and gently toss through.
Roast for 30 minutes or until the rhubarb is tender and
caramelised on top. Halfway through cooking, taste a little of the
cooking liquid and add a little more sugar, if desired. Remove
from the oven and assess how much liquid is left. You're looking
for a good amount with a syrupy consistency. If there is too much
watery liquid, place the entire dish on the stovetop over medium
heat and cook, without stirring too much, for 2–5 minutes or until
the liquid has a lovely syrupy consistency. Serve warm or cool,
then store in an airtight container (vanilla bean and all) in the
fridge for up to 4–5 days.

KITCHEN NOTE
This is best made in a dish that is not so
small that all the rhubarb is submerged
in the liquid. You want the rhubarb to
caramelise in the oven rather than stew,
which will provide a good balance of
textures. I like to use an enamel-coated
cast-iron dish measuring 18 cm (7 in)
at the base, 22 cm (8½ in) at the top
and 5 cm (2 in) deep. Alternatively, you
could use a cast-iron frying pan, as in
the picture on the right.

102

two fruit smoothies

My personal preference for a smoothie is one that is not too rich, and supplies me with a shot of beneficial bacteria. I tend to favour equal amounts of yoghurt or kefir milk, coconut milk and almond milk. If I don't have coconut milk on hand, a teaspoon of coconut oil will provide those lovely anti-viral, anti-fungal, anti-microbial fatty acids to help ward less than desirable bugs away, along with quick and easy fuel.

summer smoothie

DIETARY INFO GLUTEN FREE | VEGETARIAN
EGG FREE
SERVES 2–3

125 ml (4 fl oz/½ cup) Almond Milk (page 55)
125 ml (4 fl oz/½ cup) coconut milk
125 ml (4 fl oz/½ cup) Kefir Milk (page 46) or yoghurt
fruit, to taste (try 1 large peach or 1 mango, peeled and
   stone removed, or 125 g/4½ oz fresh or frozen berries)
1 teaspoon natural vanilla extract
honey, to taste

Place all the ingredients in a blender and
process until smooth.

KITCHEN NOTE
While spirulina will alter the flavour, it will add excellent nutrient
density, as will an egg yolk. Add 1–2 teaspoons spirulina powder
and/or 1 best-quality, grass-pastured egg yolk.

winter smoothie

DIETARY INFO GLUTEN FREE | VEGETARIAN
EGG FREE
SERVES 2–3

125 ml (4 fl oz/½ cup) Almond Milk (page 55)
125 ml (4 fl oz/½ cup) coconut milk
125 ml (4 fl oz/½ cup) Kefir Milk (page 46) or yoghurt
1 banana
2–3 fresh dates, seeded and roughly chopped
½–1 teaspoon ground cinnamon
1 teaspoon natural vanilla extract
honey, to taste

Place all the ingredients in a blender and
process until smooth.

Feel free to use a combination of almond milk and coconut milk, as I have here, or make the Almond and Coconut Milk on page 55.

DIETARY INFO GLUTEN FREE | EGG FREE
MAKES 6
YOU WILL NEED TO BEGIN THIS RECIPE THE DAY BEFORE

185 ml (6 fl oz/¾ cup) thin
   (pouring) cream
1 vanilla bean, or 1 teaspoon natural
   vanilla extract
2 teaspoons powdered gelatine
310 ml (10¾ fl oz/1¼ cups) kefir
   cultured buttermilk (page 49)
90–115 g (3¼–4 oz/¼–⅓ cup)
   honey, or to taste

*Panna cotta is not just for dessert – it makes a wonderful light start
to the day in the hot summertime weather, and when the cream is
cultured you have the added benefit of good bacteria. Serve with the
Apricot Essence on page 92, or any of the stewed or roasted fruit on
pages 99–100, or the brittles on page 83.*

kefir buttermilk panna cotta

Place the cream in a small saucepan. If using a vanilla bean, halve
it lengthways, scrape out the seeds, then add the seeds to the pan
and see Kitchen Note on how to make vanilla sugar using the
bean. Whisk in the gelatine, then place over low heat and whisk
frequently until the mixture comes to just below the boil – the
cream should steam, but not boil. Remove from the heat and
continue to whisk until all the gelatine is dissolved. Set aside to
cool a little.

Whisk the kefir buttermilk and honey in a bowl to combine well.
Add the slightly cooled cream mixture and the vanilla extract, if
using, and whisk until well combined. Pour the mixture into six
90 ml (3 fl oz) capacity ramekins or jars, stand to cool a little, then
refrigerate for at least 8 hours or until set. They will keep for up
to 5 days in the fridge, but be warned, the kefir will remain active
and they can become a little more sour and fizzier (but I kind of
like them this way).

KITCHEN NOTE
Because I love to use the fragrant seeds
scraped straight from the vanilla bean
in so many recipes, I end up with quite
a few beans. The pods have exceptional
flavour and I add these to my jar of
golden caster (superfine) sugar. I often
use the vanilla sugar in baking.

DIETARY INFO GLUTEN FREE | DAIRY FREE | EGG FREE
MAKES 6
YOU WILL NEED TO BEGIN THIS RECIPE THE DAY BEFORE

500 ml (17 fl oz/2 cups) Almond
  Milk (page 55)
1–2 tablespoons golden caster
  (superfine) sugar or maple syrup
1 vanilla bean or 1 teaspoon natural
  vanilla extract
2 teaspoons powdered gelatine

This is a beautiful match with the Sweet Cherry Almond Compote (page 96), where the intense almond milk flavour brings out the best in the cherry. Because this panna cotta is dairy free, it does lack the beneficial bacteria found in the kefir buttermilk panna cotta on page 104. There are two versions of this panna cotta, one using gelatine and the other vegan version that uses agar and kudzu.

almond milk panna cotta

Place 250 ml (9 fl oz/1 cup) almond milk and 1 tablespoon sugar in a small saucepan. If using a vanilla bean, cut it lengthways down the middle, scrape out the seeds, then add the seeds to the pan (see Kitchen Note on page 104 on how to make vanilla sugar using the bean). Whisk in the gelatine, then place over low heat and whisk frequently until the milk comes to just below boiling point. Remove from the heat and continue to whisk until the gelatine is completely dissolved. Stir in the remaining almond milk and, if using, the vanilla extract. Taste and add extra sugar or maple syrup if needed.

Pour the mixture into six 90 ml (3 fl oz) capacity ramekins or jars, stand to cool a little, then refrigerate for at least 8 hours or until set.

KITCHEN NOTES
● You can replace the suggested sweeteners with rapadura or coconut palm sugar (jaggery). The flavours of rapadura sugar are best matched with almond milk, and the flavours of coconut palm sugar best with Almond and Coconut Milk (page 55) and served with tropical fruits such as mango and passion fruit.
● You can easily substitute the almond milk with Almond and Coconut Milk (page 55).
● Other than fruit, serving a little nut and seed brittle with the panna cotta will help extend the nutrient density (page 83).

500 ml (17 fl oz/2 cups) Almond
   Milk (page 55), plus 2 tablespoons
   extra, or Almond and Coconut
   Milk (page 55)
1–2 tablespoons golden caster
   (superfine) sugar or maple syrup
1 vanilla bean or 1 teaspoon natural
   vanilla extract
½ teaspoon agar powder
1 teaspoon kudzu (kuzu)

Agar and kudzu together are my favourite tools for creating beautifully textured, delicious animal-free non-dairy panna cottas and such.

my vegan almond milk panna cotta

Place 500 ml (9 fl oz/2 cups) almond milk and 1 tablespoon sugar in a small saucepan. If using a vanilla bean, cut it lengthways down the middle and scrape out the seeds, then add the seeds to the pan (see Kitchen Note on page 104 on how to make vanilla sugar using the bean). Whisk in the agar and bring the mixture to a gentle simmer over low heat, whisking frequently as the agar loves to sink to the bottom and stick. Continue to cook at a low simmer (blip, blip), whisking frequently for another 6–8 minutes. You will find that the mixture will thicken. Remove from the heat and set aside.

Place the kudzu in a small bowl with the remaining 2 tablespoons almond milk and mix into a smooth slurry. Whisking continuously, pour the kudzu mixture into the hot almond milk – it will begin to thicken immediately. Return the pan over medium heat and whisk continuously until the mixture comes to the boil. Immediately remove from the heat, taste and add extra sugar or maple syrup if needed.

Pour the mixture into six 90 ml (3 fl oz) capacity ramekins or jars, stand to cool a little, then refrigerate for at least 2 hours or until set.

sustaining fuel

A protein breakfast with a good component of fat (for example an egg or fish) provides a grounding start to the day, and long and sustaining fuel. Very little compares to the egg for ease of digestion, nutrient density and the quickness with which it cooks. We can have eggs in so many ways, but for me, it's either poached, fried or scrambled, and possibly an omelette from time to time. Eggs are perfectly matched with dark leafy green vegetables because their fat-soluble vitamins ensure all that rich mineral bounty is optimally bio-available.

to poach an egg

A really fresh egg is what makes poaching easy. A fresh egg cracked onto a plate should show a white that stands tall, holding the egg yolk high up on the white with great integrity, with a little white running at the edges. As the egg ages, that white starts to deteriorate, collapse and run. I am not a fan of adding vinegar to the water, which is a trick to tighten the egg. You can always taste the vinegar and it isn't necessary if you are using fresh eggs.

Bring a small, shallow saucepan of water to just below the boil, there should be slight bubbles on the bottom of the pan. Add a little salt and use a spoon to gently swirl the water making a small whirlpool. As the whirlpool slows a little, crack the egg and slip it gently into the centre tip of the whirlpool; success will come from having the egg very close to the water. If desired, you could crack the egg into a small bowl or cup, then slip rather than drop the egg into the water. The water should not boil again (this will create too much movement), but stay just below boiling. Continue to cook for 3–4 minutes or until the white is set and the yolk is still soft and runny. Use a slotted spoon to gently lift out, then place a tea towel (dish towel) underneath the spoon to catch excess water.

==

Adding more nutrient density to an egg- or meat-based breakfast

When having an egg breakfast, we can extend the fuel and nutrient density with added protein from meats (such as bacon or sausage) and legumes (such as baked beans, tempeh bacon, whole grains and wholegrain breads). Of course, the legumes and whole grains will also provide carbohydrate. Finally we can make use of nature's pharmacy of vegetables to provide us with an array of flavour, goodness and deliciousness – for example fried, roasted or grilled vegetables, with a fritter being a classic example. Poached eggs, sauteed mushrooms, silverbeet and kale in ghee, green drizzle sauce (see page 75), pictured right, and a handful of leftover cooked lima beans make a nourishing breakfast.

==

DIETARY INFO GLUTEN FREE | DAIRY-FREE OPTION | VEGETARIAN
SERVES 1–2

3 fresh organic eggs
2 teaspoons water, or milk, optional
2–3 teaspoons ghee or other fat
sea salt and freshly ground black
    pepper, to taste

Both of these methods for cooking eggs require a very hot pan, with a generous amount of fat – ghee is a great choice as it won't burn when set over high heat. If you want to make this dairy free, I would recommend using a meat dripping for the fat component – duck, chicken, bacon fat or lard would all be good. I find olive oil just doesn't work as well. Scrambled or as an omelette, both should also only take a few minutes to cook as too long makes the eggs tough.

scrambled eggs or omelette

Before you start, have your filling and serving plate(s) at hand. Crack the eggs into a small bowl. Add the water or, if using, milk and season to taste. Whisk until well combined.

Heat a frying pan over medium heat, then add the ghee – it should sizzle immediately.

To make scrambled eggs: Pour the egg mixture into the pan – it will start to cook instantly – and using a spatula, quickly but gently pull the edge of the egg towards the centre, tilting the pan so that the uncooked egg runs to the sides. Do this a few times for 1–2 minutes or until most of the egg is nearly set, but still soft and uncooked. The eggs will continue to cook after you turn the heat off. Transfer the eggs to a serving plate, then garnish and serve immediately.

To make an omelette: Pour the egg mixture into the pan – it will start to cook instantly – and using a spatula, quickly but gently pull the edge of the egg towards the centre, tilting the pan so that the uncooked egg runs to the sides. Do this a few times for 1–2 minutes or until most of the egg is set and will not run easily any more – you will have what looks like lovely folds. The centre will still be soft and uncooked at this point, but will continue to cook on the plate. If you are using a filling, spoon the hot mixture in a line across the centre. Gently fold the omelette over the filling into a half-moon shape. Slide the omelette onto a serving plate, then garnish and serve immediately.

KITCHEN NOTES
● Investing in a good-quality, small stainless-steel 20 cm (8 in) frying pan will make a huge difference to success. You will need a larger frying pan for cooking any more than three eggs.
● Omelettes are a fantastic way to upcycle leftovers or use up small quantities of vegetables. Seasonal fresh herbs and goat's cheese, cooked greens such as silverbeet, chard or cavolo nero, a handful of tomatoes, cooked mushrooms. Leftovers of Funked Up Roast Vegetables (page 196), Moroccan Roast Pumpkin (page 163), or ratatouille would be perfect, even small amounts go a long way in an omelette.

110

1 tablespoon extra virgin olive oil,
   plus extra for shallow-frying
1 small brown onion, finely chopped
1 garlic clove, finely chopped
250 g (9 oz) plain tempeh
2 tablespoons tamari (or wheat-free
   tamari for a gluten-free option)
1 generous teaspoon each finely
   chopped sage, oregano, marjoram
   and thyme leaves
1½ tablespoons oat flour or teff flour
¼ teaspoon paprika or sweet
   smoked paprika
½ teaspoon fennel seeds
freshly ground black pepper
maize flour, for coating

This recipe has appeared in my earlier book Wholefood for the
Family*, but I'm not sure if you have discovered that recipe, or indeed
tried it. These tempeh patties are delicious, easy to make and freeze
well. They're also perfect for adding extra nutrient density and
deliciousness to breakfast eggs in the same way sausage or bacon does.*

tempeh patties

Heat 1 tablespoon olive oil in a frying pan over low–medium heat.
Add the onion and cook gently for 3–4 minutes, then add the
garlic. Cook for another minute or until the onions are soft and
lightly caramelised, then remove from the heat.

Place the cooked onions and all the other ingredients (except the
maize flour for coating) in a food processor and process until well
combined. Shape the mixture into small walnut-size balls, then
press into patties about 5 cm (2 in) in diameter and about 5 mm
(¼ in) thick.

Place the maize flour on a plate and dust the patties. Pour enough
olive oil into a large frying pan to cover the base and place over
medium heat. When hot, but not smoking, add the patties and
cook, in batches if necessary, for 3 minutes on each side or until
golden. Drain on paper towel and serve.

DIETARY INFO   GLUTEN FREE | DAIRY FREE | VEGAN | EGG FREE
MAKES 300 G (10½ OZ) OR 16 SLICES
YOU WILL NEED TO BEGIN THIS RECIPE TWO OR THREE DAYS BEFORE

2 tablespoons maple sugar
  (or maple syrup)
1½ tablespoons sea salt
300 g (10½ oz) plain tempeh
coconut oil or olive oil, for baking
  or frying

I love bacon, but I love tempeh bacon too and it's surprisingly easy to make and delicious. You can use any tempeh here – I use a chickpea tempeh, but soy is fine. What is important is that you use uncooked tempeh. You will also need a smoker – I use my barbecue, but there are many great stovetop smokers on the market.

tempeh bacon

Choose a container that will snugly fit the tempeh, or a small resealable plastic bag. Add the maple sugar and salt to the container, roughly mix through and add the tempeh, ensuring the tempeh is well coated with the mix. Cover and place in the fridge for 2 days, turning the tempeh at least once. If you have it in a plastic bag, you can also weight the tempeh by placing a plate on the tempeh, topped with a heavy weight (such as a tin of beans).

Prepare your smoker according to the manufacturer's instructions. Remove the tempeh and smoke over medium heat for 30–40 minutes. Remove the tempeh and set aside to cool.

You can either slice the tempeh and cook all of it, or cook what you need at the time, and wrap and store the remaining tempeh in an airtight container for another time (the tempeh will keep for up to 3 weeks in the fridge). Using a sharp knife, cut the tempeh into 3–4 mm (¼ in) thick slices.

To fry, add enough oil to just cover the base of a frying pan. When the oil is hot, but not at all sizzling, add the tempeh and cook for 6–8 minutes, until golden, turn over and cook the other side. Remove and drain on paper towel before serving.

To bake, preheat the oven to 190°C (375°F). Brush 1 tablespoon oil on a baking tray, place the tempeh slices in a single layer on the tray, then brush the top with another ½–1 tablespoon oil. Bake for 10 minutes or until golden brown, then turn the tempeh and bake for another 10 minutes or until both sides are golden, brushing with a little more oil only if required. Remove and drain on paper towel before serving. Once fried, the tempeh will keep in an airtight container in the fridge for up to 1 week.

KITCHEN NOTE

This recipe essentially has three separate steps: curing the tempeh, smoking the tempeh and then crisping the tempeh. You can either fry or bake the tempeh.

whole grains for breakfast

Grains have formed the base of wholesome breakfasts for many a generation, from porridges to pancakes and everything in between. What you won't find in this section is a recipe calling for any puffed or crispy flaked cereals from a box or packet – I simply consider them far too over processed. What you will find is a range of delicious porridges, pancakes, breads, biscuits and loaves all made from whole grains, and their flours and meals. You can add nutrient density to your wholegrain breakfast with the suggestions below, but remember also that adding fat to your whole grains helps slow down how they are digested and metabolised. Bread plus butter is a good thing, porridge plus ghee is a good thing.

It is also a good idea to try and add beneficial bacteria as well as nutrient density to your wholegrain breakfasts. Do this by incorporating kefir cultured milk (page 46), kefir cultured cream (page 49), crème fraîche or cultured butter (page 50).

good bread with miso, avocado and sprouts

If you're looking for an alternative to the now, highly processed, salty Vegemite – genmai miso is it. When unpasteurised, this brown rice miso is also a rich source of beneficial bacteria and enzymes. This easy recipe is a great combination – protein from wholegrain bread and miso, fat from avocado and greens – it really is quite a substantial snack.

I like a good wholemeal sourdough but you can choose any bread you like. Spread it with as much genmai miso as desired (similar to Vegemite, a little will go a long way). Slice as much avocado on it as you like, and top with sprouts. I also like this drizzled with a little lemon or lime juice and freshly ground black pepper.

Adding nutrient density to wholegrain breakfasts

FAT: Butterfat (indeed any animal fat or fish) will provide valuable fat-soluble vitamins for mineral bio-availability.
DAIRY (IN ANY FORMAT): Egg yolk, coconut milk or cream, nuts and seeds.
PROTEIN: Dairy (in any format), nuts and seeds, egg white.

DIETARY INFO GLUTEN FREE | DAIRY-FREE OPTION | VEGETARIAN OPTION
SERVES 2
YOU WILL NEED TO BEGIN THIS RECIPE ONE DAY AHEAD

100 g (3½ oz/½ cup) quinoa
2 teaspoons whey or choice of acid
 or dairy-free option, (page 63)
sea salt
1 tablespoon ghee or butter
 1 tablespoon coconut oil (if not
 using ghee or butter, add extra)
1 teaspoon cumin seeds
1 small onion, finely chopped
2 cm (¾ in) piece fresh ginger,
 peeled and finely chopped
 or grated
2 cm (¾ in) piece fresh turmeric,
 peeled and finely chopped
 or grated
½–1 teaspoon good curry powder
1 small carrot, finely diced
230 ml (7¾ fl oz) hot fish, chicken
 or vegetable stock
60 g (2¼ oz) cauliflower, thick stem
 peeled and cut into pieces, florets
 cut into small pieces
60 g (2¼ oz) broccoli, thick stem
 peeled and cut into pieces, florets
 cut into small pieces
80 g (2¾ oz/½ cup) fresh or
 frozen peas
60 g (2¼ oz) smoked fish, flaked
2 hard-boiled eggs, peeled and cut
 into quarters
good handful of fresh herbs such
 as coriander (cilantro) or parsley
 leaves (optional)
½–1 lemon or lime
plain natural yoghurt, to serve

KITCHEN NOTE
More carbohydrate-dense root
vegetables can be diced and added
to the pan with the grain. Vegetables
that take less time to cook such as
asparagus, green beans and broccoli
can be thrown in after the grain has
been cooking for 15 minutes.

Kedgeree is a traditional English breakfast taken from colonial India. It consists of grain (basmati rice), spices and that most thrifty of nourishing standbys, salted or smoked fish. It is an astoundingly hearty and sustaining start to the day. This version of kedgeree reflects a late spring/early summer garden when the weather is not yet too hot and more fuel is required. This recipe is infinitely flexible so add whatever seasonal vegetables you like, and for a vegetarian version, swap the fish for cooked black (turtle) beans.

quinoa kedgeree

The day before, place the quinoa in a small bowl with enough water to cover by 2 cm (¾ in), then stir through the whey. Stand overnight at room temperature even when the weather is warm.

The next day, place the ghee and coconut oil in a heavy-based saucepan over low–medium heat. Add the cumin seeds and cook for 1 minute or until fragrant. Add the onion, ginger, turmeric and curry powder and cook, stirring occasionally for 5 minutes or until the onion is lightly coloured and soft. Stir in the carrot (or any other longer-cooking vegetables, if using) and season with salt.

Drain the quinoa well and add it to the pan with the hot stock. Cover with a lid and bring to a gentle boil. Immediately reduce the heat to low and cook for 20–25 minutes. After 15 minutes of cooking, add the cauliflower, broccoli and peas (or any other shorter-cooking vegetables) and gently and quickly stir through before replacing the lid. To check if the quinoa is cooked, remove the lid and tip the pan on a slight angle; if water pools you will need to replace the lid and cook it a little longer. When the quinoa is cooked, place paper towel over the top, replace the lid and leave to sit for 15 minutes before serving. The paper towel will absorb any excess moisture.

To serve, turn the cooked quinoa into a serving dish. Gently toss the flaked fish, eggs and most of the fresh herbs (if using) through the quinoa. Squeeze over the lemon or lime, then taste and adjust the seasonings as needed. Scatter with the eggs and remaining herbs, and serve with a generous dollop of yoghurt.

DIETARY INFO GLUTEN FREE | DAIRY FREE | VEGETARIAN
MAKES 1 LOAF

DRY MIX
140 g (5 oz/1 cup) teff flour
75 g (2½ oz/⅓ cup) rapadura sugar
   or raw sugar
25 g (1 oz/¼ cup) desiccated
   coconut
1½ teaspoons ground cinnamon
¼ teaspoon freshly grated nutmeg
2 teaspoons baking powder
¼ teaspoon bicarbonate of soda
   (baking soda)
85 g (3 oz/½ cup) raisins, roughly
   chopped if large
100 g (3½ oz/1 cup) pecan nuts,
   roughly chopped
310 g (11 oz/2 cups) grated carrot
1 apple, grated with skin on
125–145 g (4½–5 oz/1 cup) cooked
   and cooled hulled millet (page 67)

WET MIX
2 eggs
125 ml (4 fl oz/½ cup) coconut milk
125 ml (4 fl oz/½ cup) coconut oil
   (cool, but not at all solid) or ghee,
   plus extra, for greasing
1 teaspoon natural vanilla extract

This is a moist and delicious breakfast or snack loaf. It keeps exceptionally well, but because of the high content of moisture, is best kept in the fridge when the weather is warmer.

morning glory millet and teff loaf

Preheat the oven to 180°C (350°F). Lightly grease a 1 litre (35 fl oz/4 cup) capacity loaf (bar) tin, then line with a piece of baking paper, cutting into the corners to fit.

Place all the dry ingredients except the millet in a large bowl, sifting in the bicarbonate of soda to ensure there are no lumps. Use a whisk to combine, making sure the grated apple and carrot are well distributed and coated in the dry ingredients. Add the cooked millet and use your hands to mix through, ensuring the millet is evenly distributed.

In another medium-size bowl, mix the wet ingredients and whisk to combine well. Add the wet ingredients to the dry, and mix well. Spoon the mixture into the prepared tin and bake for 55–65 minutes, or until the centre is firm when pressed. Check the cake after about 50 minutes and if it is browning too much, reduce the temperature to 170°C (325°F). Remove from the oven and leave to cool in the tin for 15 minutes before turning out onto a wire rack to cool completely. The loaf will cut best when cool. Store in a cool dark place in an airtight container or in the fridge for up to 5 days.

KITCHEN NOTE
Make sure there is no ghee or butter in the millet, and that the grain has been cooked in water rather than a bone or vegetable stock as these things will affect the balance of fat in the recipe.

DIETARY INFO LOW GLUTEN | DAIRY-FREE OPTION | VEGETARIAN
MAKES 14–16 PANCAKES
YOU WILL NEED TO BEGIN THIS RECIPE THE DAY BEFORE

130 g (4¾ oz/1 cup) buckwheat
    flour
100 g (3½ oz/1 cup) stabilised rolled
    (porridge) oats
pinch of sea salt
500 g (1 lb 2 oz/2 cups) cultured
    buttermilk (page 50)
¾ teaspoon bicarbonate of soda
    (baking soda)
½–1 teaspoon ground cinnamon
1 tablespoon rapadura sugar or raw
    sugar, optional
2 eggs, lightly beaten
ghee and/or coconut oil, for cooking

Buckwheat and oat complement each other so well: the buckwheat provides abundant phytase to the low-phytase oats, helping to negate the phytic acid, while the oats soften the rather assertive flavour of the buckwheat. Although many fruits pair well with these pancakes, Pear 'Butter' (page 97) is perhaps the best as pear and buckwheat is a magical combination. Serve with your choice of toppings – ghee, yoghurt, cultured cream, maple syrup are all superb.

best-ever buttermilk pancakes

The night before, place the buckwheat flour, oats and salt in a bowl. Stir in the buttermilk, then cover with a tea towel (dish towel) and stand overnight at room temperature, even when hot.

The next day, sift the bicarbonate of soda over the buckwheat mixture. Add the cinnamon, sugar and eggs, then combine well.

Add enough ghee and/or coconut oil to coat the base of a medium-size frying pan by about 5 mm (¼ in) and place over medium heat. When the fat is hot, but not at all rippling or smoking – you want the batter to sizzle as it hits the fats – add 1 generous tablespoon of batter, taking care not to crowd the pan. Cook for 2–3 minutes, or until golden around the edges, then use a spatula to turn and cook the other side for 2–3 minutes, until golden. These are best served hot but are still absolutely delicious as a cold snack.

KITCHEN NOTES

● I've made this with just about every conceivable version of oat and have found that the unstabilised freshly rolled oats break down too much and give little in the way of texture to the end result. I far prefer the sturdier stabilised rolled oats, which give a toothsome and wonderful texture.

● You could add grated apple or pear, and even mashed fruit or berries (if the berries are frozen, fold them in after the batter is formed).

● For tips on cooking pancakes, see Leftover Porridge Pikelet (page 126).

● For a dairy-free version use Almond Milk, or Coconut and Almond Milk (page 55), with 1 tablespoon of water kefir or kombucha drink added.

DIETARY INFO GLUTEN-FREE OPTION | VEGETARIAN
SERVES 2

2 eggs

2 tablespoons milk, plus 2 teaspoons extra, if needed

2 teaspoons maple syrup

½ teaspoon ground cinnamon

½ teaspoon natural vanilla extract

2 slices day-old sourdough bread (or gluten-free bread), about 1–1.5 cm (½–⅝ in) thick

2 tablespoons unsalted butter or ghee

What makes French toast really good? Three things: chewy, dense sourdough; an egg mixture that has had enough time to soak into every single bit of that bread; the perfect heat that allows the egg mixture to cook and provide a golden end result. French toast will welcome any of the stewed or roasted fruits (pages 99–100), a little extra sweetness (such as the Fig and Bay Syrup on page 99, maple syrup or honey) and yoghurt to add extra deliciousness and moisture.

really good french toast

Choose a dish that will accommodate the bread snugly.

Place the eggs, 2 tablespoons milk, maple syrup, cinnamon and vanilla in a bowl and whisk until smooth. Only add extra milk if you feel the mix is too thick.

Pour into the dish, and add the bread. Leave to soak for 10 minutes, then turn the bread pieces and soak for a further 5 minutes. If the crusts are a bit dry (or perhaps they're more than a little stale), use a fork to make holes in them, which will allow the milk to soak through and soften them.

Heat the butter in a medium-size frying pan that will fit the bread pieces snugly over medium heat. The butter should be sizzling but not browning. Place the bread in the pan carefully as it will be very soft and can break; you may need to use a spatula. It should gently sizzle in the fat. Pour any leftover egg mixture onto the bread – I look for any holes or cracks to pour it into, this way none of the mixture is wasted. Cook for 2 minutes on each side until golden and the egg is cooked all the way through. Adjust your heat so it gently sizzles – if it is too hot the butter will burn the outsides and the eggy centre will be uncooked. If the bread is no longer fragile and prone to breaking apart when you lift or move it, the French toast is cooked.

DIETARY INFO GLUTEN FREE | VEGETARIAN
MAKES 12 SLICES

160 g (5½ oz/1 cup) brown rice flour
70 g (2½ oz/½ cup) teff flour
30 g (1 oz/¼ cup) chickpea flour
(besan)
1 tablespoon rapadura sugar or
raw sugar
2 teaspoons baking powder
1 teaspoon ground cinnamon
2 eggs
80 ml (2½ fl oz/⅓ cup) Cultured
Buttermilk (page 50) or plain
natural yoghurt
2 tablespoons full-cream (whole),
non-pasteurised milk
250 g (9 oz/1 cup) mashed sweet
potato, cooled
100 g (3½ oz) cold unsalted butter,
cut into small pieces
pinch of sea salt

120

An exceptionally easy and delicious bread, this will keep for some time and it toasts brilliantly even if a couple of days old. The bread is wonderful enjoyed as is, or paired with the date butter (page 79), or tempeh bacon (page 112) or patties (page 111), or smoky pinto beans (page 172). It also freezes well.

sweet potato, cinnamon bread

Preheat the oven to 180°C (350°F) and generously butter a loaf (bar) tin (see Kitchen Note).

Place the flours, sugar, baking powder and cinnamon in a bowl. Mix through with a whisk to combine the ingredients and break up any lumps of flour.

Place the eggs, buttermilk and milk in a small bowl and whisk to combine well, then add the mashed sweet potato and mix until well combined.

Using your fingers or a pastry cutter, cut the butter into the flour until the mixture resembles coarse breadcrumbs – some bits should be the size of a pea. Add the wet mixture and stir through until just combined. Spoon into the prepared tin and bake for 40–45 minutes, until a skewer inserted into the middle comes out clean. Leave to cool for 15 minutes before turning out onto a wire rack to cool completely.

To store, wrap in a piece of foil lined with baking paper and store in a cool dark place for up to 5 days. To freeze, slice and store in a sealed container.

KITCHEN NOTE

This is best made in a loaf tin that is narrower rather than wider; providing less surface area for the bread to hold together once cut. You can happily make this in a 1 litre (35 fl oz/4 cup) capacity loaf tin, but I prefer a smaller 750 ml (26 fl oz/3 cup) capacity cast-iron terrine dish measuring around 27 × 8 × 4 cm (10¾ × 3¼ × 1½ in) that will make a lovely narrow loaf.

DIETARY INFO DAIRY-FREE OPTION | VEGETARIAN OPTION | WHEAT FREE | EGG FREE
MAKES 12

100 g (3½ oz/⅔ cup) very cold
    duck fat or butter
260 g (9¼ oz/2 cups) white
    unbleached spelt flour, plus
    extra to dust
2 teaspoons baking powder
good pinch of sea salt and freshly
    ground black pepper
2 tablespoons chopped fresh herbs,
    such as sage, rosemary, basil
    and oregano
200 ml (7 fl oz) Cultured
    Buttermilk (page 50)

I adore biscuits, that wonderful American term that refers to a denser scone, a savoury number that could be put together on the spot and eaten not long after. They're far easier than making bread. These can be made with butter, but when made with duck fat they are just insanely delicious, especially if that duck fat has come from a dish you have rendered yourself, with the extra bounty of flavour. They're a treat with egg and bacon of any sorts for breakfast.

herb biscuits

Before you begin, ensure that the duck fat is very cold. Measure it out and place the fat in the fridge to chill further.

Preheat the oven to 200°C (400°F). Lightly flour a baking tray, or line with baking paper. (If making a dairy-free version – see Kitchen Notes – add the vinegar to the almond milk and set aside.)

Place the flour, baking powder, salt, pepper and herbs in a food processor and pulse to distribute the ingredients. Using a butter knife, cut the cold fat into chunks and add to the processor. Pulse a few times or until the fat has become very small pieces, taking care not to overwork the mixture. Turn into a bowl, add the buttermilk and stir just until it comes together.

Turn the dough out onto a lightly floured work surface and, with a little flour on your hands, pat the dough out to a rectangle about 2–2.5 cm (¾–1 in) thick. Cut into 12 squares, place on the prepared baking tray leaving a small gap between each one and bake for 10–15 minutes, until golden.

KITCHEN NOTES

● To make these biscuits dairy free, replace the buttermilk with 200 ml (7 fl oz) almond milk, 2 teaspoons apple cider vinegar and increase the duck fat to 120 g (4¼oz).

● It may be that your white spelt has a percentage of bran and germ, and thus may absorb more liquid. In this case, you may need to add a little more milk to the dough. Aim for a dough that is not at all dry, but not at all wet, easy to pat out without being sticky and requires just a little flour on your hands to do so.

DIETARY INFO DAIRY-FREE OPTION | VEGETARIAN | EGG FREE | WHEAT FREE
SERVES 3-4
YOU WILL NEED TO BEGIN THIS RECIPE THE DAY BEFORE

100 g (3½ oz/½ cup) spelt berries
100 g (3½ oz/½ cup) oat kernels
1 tablespoon whey or choice of acid
  or dairy-free option (page 59)
stewed or roasted fruit or your
  choice of toppings (page 99–100),
  optional

Toothsome and slightly chewy, spelt berries are a perfect match for the oat kernel, providing extra phytase to the oats to break down phtyic acid. Oats in turn lend a delicious creaminess to the porridge. This is a delicious example of a wholegrain porridge.

oat kernel and spelt berry porridge

The night before, place the spelt berries in a food processor and process until very roughly ground. Add the oat kernels and continue to process until you have a rough meal. Transfer to a bowl and add enough water to cover by about 3 cm (1¼ in). Stir in the whey and stand overnight at room temperature, even when it is warm.

The next day, pour off the excess water – avoid putting it through a sieve as you will lose too much of the finely ground grain – and place in a saucepan. Add 625–750 ml (21½–26 fl oz/2½–3 cups) water and cook over low heat, stirring frequently for 45 minutes to 1 hour. The porridge will take this amount of time to ensure the grain is fully cooked, which should be creamy rather than al dente for best digestion. If you feel it is too thick and needs more water, add it as you go. You will have to stir it almost continuously towards the end of cooking when the porridge thickens. It may also benefit from a heat diffuser at this point because the porridge needs a very gentle heat to stop it from catching. If it is still too moist after this time, increase the heat slightly and stir continuously until thickened. Serve immediately with toppings of your choice.

KITCHEN NOTE
If you would prefer a lower gluten option, replace the spelt berries with rye berries.

124

DIETARY INFO LOW GLUTEN | DAIRY-FREE OPTION | EGG FREE | WHEAT FREE
SERVES 2-3
YOU WILL NEED TO BEGIN THIS RECIPE THE DAY BEFORE

100 g (3½ oz/1 cup) stabilised or freshly rolled (porridge) oats

100 g (3½ oz/½ cup) buckwheat kernels

1 tablespoon whey or choice of acid or dairy-free option (page 63)

stewed or roasted fruit or your choice of toppings (pages 99–100), if desired

Buckwheat is another high-phytase option for soaking with low-phytase oats, and will ensure all deliciousness from the grain is bio-available. If you are using unstabilised rolled oats, especially those you have rolled yourself, the end result will be smoother and less textured in consistency, but likely more nourishing.

rolled oat and buckwheat kernel porridge

The night before, place the oats and buckwheat in a bowl and cover with 250 ml (9 fl oz/1 cup) water. Stir in the whey, then stand overnight at room temperature.

The next morning, place the grains in a sieve; the goal is to remove most of, rather than all the liquid, especially with freshly rolled oats. Transfer to a medium-size saucepan and add 500 ml (17 fl oz/2 cups) water. Cook over low–medium heat, stirring frequently for 25–30 minutes. Ensure you stir it almost continuously towards the end of cooking when the porridge thickens; it may also need a heat diffuser at this point. The porridge will take this amount of time to ensure the buckwheat is fully cooked, which should be creamy rather than al dente for best digestion. Serve immediately with toppings of your choice.

KITCHEN NOTE
Depending on the condition of your stabilised oats (quite dry), you may need to add 60 ml (2 fl oz/¼ cup) more water to the porridge.

DIETARY INFO LOW GLUTEN | DAIRY-FREE OPTION | VEGETARIAN | WHEAT FREE
MAKES 7–8 SMALL BUT SUBSTANTIAL PIKELETS

1 egg
200 g (7 oz/1 cup) leftover cold porridge (see Rolled Oat and Buckwheat Kernel Porridge (page 125) or Oat Kernel and Spelt Berry Porridge (page 124)
½–1 teaspoon ground cinnamon
½ apple, grated (if it is very juicy, squeeze a little of the juice out)
45 g (1½ oz/¼ cup) currants, sultanas (golden raisins) or raisins, coarsely chopped if large
ghee and/or coconut oil, for frying
stewed or roasted fruit or your choice of toppings (pages 99–100), if desired

Leftover porridge should never be wasted, and it can be transformed into pikelets, which make for a tasty (and when cool, transportable) end result. When hot, the pikelets will need a spoon and toppings as desired.

leftover porridge pikelets

Crack the egg into a mixing bowl and lightly beat. Add the porridge and stir until well combined. Add the cinnamon, apple and dried fruit and combine well.

Add enough ghee and/or coconut oil to coat the base of a 24 cm (9½ in) frying pan by 5 mm (¼ in). Place over medium heat and when hot, but not at all smoking, add tablespoons of batter, making sure you don't crowd the pan – the batter should sizzle as it hits the fat. Cook for 5 minutes or until very golden on the base and well cooked. You may need to reduce your heat to low–medium as you want to keep an even gentle sizzle throughout the cooking process. When the pikelets are well cooked, use a stainless-steel spatula to turn, then cook the other side for 3–4 minutes, until golden. Serve with your favourite toppings, if desired.

KITCHEN NOTES

● Other than the egg (which will bind the mix), the porridge welcomes a range of additions in the form of spices, other fresh fruit or dried fruit. You might also like to try adding vegetables.

● I like to use a combination of both ghee and coconut oil when frying. The coconut oil provides a delicious crispiness to the edges while the ghee cuts through the overwhelming coconut flavour. The key to successful pikelets here is to make sure they are well cooked and very golden on one side before turning. They are tricky to turn, but will be easier if well cooked and if you use a nice, sharp stainless-steel spatula to ease them off the pan.

50 g (1¾ oz/¼ cup) amaranth

2 teaspoons whey or choice of acid or dairy-free option (page 59)

50 g (1¾ oz/¼ cup) sulphur-free tapioca or sago

375 ml (13 fl oz/1½ cups) Almond and Coconut Milk (page 55), plus extra for serving

zest of 1 small lime

Blueberry and Lime Sauce (page 92)

Coconut Palm Sugar Syrup (page 80), optional, to serve

As a high-protein, low-carbohydrate grain, amaranth is a perfect choice (along with rice) for a warmer weather 'porridge'. However, just amaranth can be a little confronting so it's a good idea to add tapioca. Once cooked, this firms up like all porridges; simply stir through some extra nut milk, warmed up, to loosen before serving. It also makes a great snack, with fruit and extra milk (or yoghurt).

amaranth and tapioca coconut porridge

The night before, place the amaranth into a bowl and add enough water to cover by 2 cm (¾ in). Stir through the whey, then stand overnight at room temperature, even when the weather is warm. In a separate bowl, soak the tapioca in 125 ml (4 fl oz/½ cup) of the almond and coconut milk in the fridge.

The next day, drain the amaranth through a fine sieve, then place into a medium-size saucepan with the soaked tapioca, including any of the tapioca soaking liquid. Stir in the remaining 250 ml (9 fl oz/1 cup) almond and coconut milk, 250 ml (9 fl oz/1 cup) water and the lime zest. Cook over low heat, stirring often and adding extra water if needed, for 40 minutes or until tender. During cooking you want to see a very gentle simmer – a blip, blip. Serve drizzled with extra almond and coconut milk, topped with blueberry and lime sauce and a drizzle of coconut palm sugar syrup, if using.

KITCHEN NOTE

If making this with 100 per cent amaranth, increase the amount to 100 g (3½ oz/½ cup).

FRESH RECIPES THAT WORK WITH YOUR LIFE

light
VEGETARIAN

DIETARY INFO GLUTEN FREE | DAIRY FREE | VEGETARIAN OPTION | EGG FREE
SERVES 6–8

265 g (9¼ oz/1¼ cups) cooked
   French green lentils (page 60)
2 tablespoons extra virgin olive oil
1 small brown onion, finely chopped
2 garlic cloves, finely chopped
1 good-size thyme sprig, leaves
   picked
1 teaspoon smoked paprika
280 g (10 oz/2 cups) grated
   beetroot
2–3 teaspoons sweet white miso
   (shiro)
crackers, crudité and Cristel's
   Lemony Labne (page 54) or feta,
   to serve

130

KITCHEN NOTES

● This is best made with lentils cooked
in chicken stock – it will give greater
depth to the dish, and make the lentils
easier to digest. It's not essential
though, and you will still get a fabulous
vegetarian dip, using vegetable stock.

● Smoked paprika varies enormously
and I have used from ¾ teaspoon of one
brand and 1½ teaspoons of another for
the same effect. I would advise adding
a smaller amount first, tasting halfway
through cooking the beetroot and
adjusting the amount as required. The
smoky flavour should come through
but shouldn't be overwhelming.

*While this dip doesn't set into an easy-to-slice terrine, it will firm
up somewhat if put into a terrine dish, and refrigerated overnight.
It really is the most delicious dip, and comes to life when served with
a goat's cheese, salty feta, or Cristel's Lemony Labne on page 54.*

smoky lentil and beetroot dip

Drain the lentils, reserving 2–3 tablespoons of the cooking liquid.
Remove and discard the bay leaf. If you used kombu to cook the
lentils, leave a little in with the lentils.

Place 1 tablespoon olive oil in a medium-size frying pan over low
heat. Add the onion, garlic and thyme leaves and cook, stirring
frequently, for 10–15 minutes or until cooked through. The onion
should be ever so lightly golden and caramelised, but in no way
fried or crispy. Stir in the paprika and beetroot and cook, stirring
frequently, for a further 10 minutes or until the beetroot is cooked
through, then remove from the heat.

Place the lentils and 2 tablespoons of the reserved lentil cooking
liquid in a food processer. Add the warm beetroot, remaining olive
oil and 2 teaspoons miso. Process until smooth, scraping down the
sides every now and then. Taste, and add more miso if required.
Serve with crackers, crudité and lemony labne or feta.

PHOTO ON PAGE 132

arame tapenade

DIETARY INFO GLUTEN FREE | DAIRY FREE
VEGAN | EGG FREE
MAKES ABOUT 350 G (12 OZ/1½ CUPS)

Lorna Sass is a fabulous American wholefood writer, and this recipe is inspired by her. Arame is a sea vegetable and a great way to include mineral-rich sea vegetables in your diet. Because it has quite a strong flavour, the robust flavour of olives helps to balance this out. While arame is rich in iron, it's wise to bear in mind that it carries non-heme iron, which is not absorbed in the same way as the heme iron that is found in red meat. Adding a food rich in vitamin C (such as lemon juice) helps you to absorb that non-heme iron. This tapenade is also lovely sprinkled with some finely chopped fresh rosemary or thyme, or drizzled with rosemary olive oil (page 72).

28 g (1 oz) arame
1–2 garlic cloves, finely chopped
125 g (4½ oz/1 cup) good-quality pitted black olives
50 g (1¾ oz/¼ cup) good-quality capers, drained, or rinsed
  if packed in salt
2 tablespoons extra virgin olive oil
1–2 teaspoons finely grated lemon zest
sea salt, to taste

Place the arame in a large bowl and pour over enough boiling water to cover by at least 5 cm (2 in). Stand for 10–15 minutes or until soft, then drain well.

Place all the ingredients, including the drained arame, in a food processor and process until a rough paste forms. Taste and adjust the seasoning with lemon juice and sea salt (bearing in mind the saltiness of the olives and capers), as needed. Store in a clean glass jar in the fridge for up to 2 weeks.

PHOTO ON PAGE 133

pine nut 'cheese'

DIETARY INFO GLUTEN FREE | VEGAN OPTION
DAIRY-FREE OPTION | EGG FREE
MAKES 60 G (2¼ OZ/GENEROUS ¼ CUP)
YOU WILL NEED TO BEGIN THIS RECIPE
8 HOURS BEFORE

In a world of heavy nut 'cheeses', this pine nut 'cheese' shines with delicious flavour and a light but gorgeous creaminess.

145 g (5 oz/1 cup) pine nuts
1 tablespoon cultured acid such as yoghurt, whey
  or buttermilk (for a dairy-free option use kombucha
  or water kefir drink - see page 59)
2 teaspoons sweet white miso (shiro)
1–2 teaspoons olive oil
2 teaspoons lemon juice, or to taste
1–2 tablespoons finely chopped chives
1 tablespoon thyme leaves
1 tablespoon finely chopped parsley
1 garlic clove, crushed
freshly ground black pepper, to taste

Place the pine nuts, 250 ml (9 fl oz/1 cup) warm water, whey and 1 teaspoon miso in a food processor or blender and process until very smooth. Place a sieve over a bowl, ensuring the base of the sieve is not sitting too low in the bowl. Line with four layers of muslin (cheesecloth), then tip the pine nut mixture into the sieve, fold over the muslin corners and leave to sit in a warm (but not hot) place for 8 hours.

After this time, turn out what is sitting in the muslin (the cheese) into a bowl. Transfer the liquid (whey) into a small jar. Stir all the remaining ingredients into the cheese, tasting and adjusting the flavours as needed – it should be quite salty from the miso. Store in an airtight container in the fridge for up to 1 week.

PHOTO ON PAGE 133

131

FROM LEFT: SMOKY LENTIL AND
BEETROOT DIP, ARAME TAPENADE
AND PINE NUT 'CHEESE'

DIETARY INFO GLUTEN FREE | DAIRY FREE | VEGAN | EGG FREE
SERVES 4 AS A LIGHT MEAL

2 pears (I like the sturdy Beurré
    Bosc variety)
2 tablespoons extra virgin olive oil
60 ml (2 fl oz/¼ cup) Pedro
    Ximénez 12 month-old
    sherry vinegar
2 tablespoons Pedro Ximénez sherry
50 g (1¾ oz) rocket (arugula) leaves
    or mustard greens (or both, as I've
    used here)
1 quantity cooked French Green
    Lentils (page 60), drained
40–75 g (1½–2½ oz/¼–½ cup)
    hazelnuts, roasted, skins rubbed
    off, roughly chopped
hazelnut oil for drizzling, optional

134

KITCHEN NOTES

● A good goat's cheese would be a
nice addition to offset any sweetness.
Crumble a little over the top of the
salad once assembled.
● If you have access to fresh and
artisanal hazelnut oil, this would be
the perfect finish for this salad.
● You could use chicken stock to give
greater depth to the dish, and make
the lentils easier to digest.
● Use the best-quality Pedro Ximénez
sherry for this salad – ideally one that
is fruity and sweet. If yours is slightly
acidic, add a teaspoon of rapadura sugar
to balance the flavour.

A blog post from one of my favourites, The Yellow House, *by Sarah Searle, discussed the phenomenon of what she calls 'The Wedding Salad': basically greens, sweet fruit (usually dried cherries or cranberries), nuts, a dressing and perhaps some goat's cheese or feta, which you would usually find a version of at a wedding. You don't need a million recipes, it's a basic format. Here is my version, and honestly it is delicious.*

green lentils, caramelised pear and pedro ximénez salad

Cut the pears into eighths, and remove and discard the cores.

Place the olive oil, 2 tablespoons sherry vinegar and the sherry in a small frying pan no larger than 20 cm (8 in). This size pan will give more depth of liquid (and thus more flavour) to the pears, and contribute to less evaporation. Toss the pears through the liquid, place over medium heat and bring to a gentle boil. Cook for 15–20 minutes, turning the pears every now and then. At the end of this time, there should be about 2 tablespoons of liquid left in the pan. If it looks like there is more, increase the heat slightly and continue to cook until it has reduced. Remove the pears and set aside on a plate. Add the remaining tablespoon of sherry vinegar to the pan and stir – this is now your dressing. Remove from the heat and set aside to cool.

To put the salad together, arrange the rocket leaves on a serving platter and spoon the cooked lentils over the top. Using your fingers, gently toss together. Place the cooked pears over the lentils and scatter over the hazelnuts. Gently pour the cooled dressing over the salad and drizzle with a little hazelnut oil, if using.

DIETARY INFO GLUTEN-FREE OPTION | DAIRY FREE | VEGAN OPTION | EGG FREE
SERVES 6-8 AS A SIDE

2 carrots (about 215 g/7½ oz),
   well scrubbed and unpeeled
2 medium beetroot (beets)
   (about 165 g/5¾ oz), peeled
1 large apple, unpeeled
35 g (1¼ oz/½ cup) shredded
   coconut
30 g (1 oz/1 cup) coriander
   (cilantro) leaves
20–35 g (¾–1¼ oz/½–1 cup)
   mint leaves
80 g (2¾ oz/½ cup) Tamari
   Almonds (page 81), halved lengthways or chopped into quarters
good pinch of salt

CURRY DRESSING
1 tablespoon lemon juice
60 ml (2 fl oz/¼ cup) extra virgin
   olive oil
1 tablespoon apple cider vinegar
2 teaspoons honey or maple syrup
1 teaspoon sweet fragrant curry
   powder

I have a very soft spot for a curry dressing, and it's a wonderful match with carrot and beetroot. Apple gives this salad a moist and fresh bite while the coconut and tamari almonds give it a little more heft. It keeps very well, tasting better the next day, though the almonds might have softened a little.

carrot and beetroot salad with a curry dressing

To make the dressing, place all the ingredients in a clean glass jar, seal with the lid and shake well. Taste and adjust – depending on the acidity of the lemon, you may need to add a little more honey, or lemon juice, to get the balance right.

Grate the carrots, beetroot and apple into a bowl. Add the coconut, herbs and dressing and toss through. Add the chopped tamari almonds, then taste and add salt as needed – the salt will temper any sweetness in the salad.

KITCHEN NOTES
● Mint does work here, but as I'm not a fan of mint I've left the decision of how much to use up to you.
● If making the gluten-free option, use wheat-free tamari when making the almonds on page 81.

1 fennel bulb
½ sugarloaf cabbage or other
  cabbage variety
6 tender inner celery stalks (about
  220 g/7¾ oz), very thinly sliced
  on the diagonal
2 handfuls fresh herbs, such as
  flat-leaf (Italian) parsley,
  coriander (cilantro) leaves,
  chervil, tarragon and basil
1 quantity Celery Leaf Pesto (page
  141), optional

BRIGHT LEMON DRESSING
2 tablespoons extra virgin olive oil
1 tablespoon lemon juice
1 garlic clove, finely grated
¼ teaspoon honey, vincotto
  or maple syrup
pinch of sea salt

KITCHEN NOTES
● Younger fennel is best here as older
fennel has thick, tough outer layers
that, while great for cooking, are not
ideal in salad.
● Thinly sliced radish and double
peeled, blanched broad (fava) beans
are both delicious additions.
● If you would like to make, or have
Celery Leaf Pesto (page 141) on hand
and would like to use it as the dressing,
add more lemon juice to the pesto to
thin it out and omit the bright lemon
dressing, or happily use both.

I consider this to be my default salad – it makes a fabulous lunch on its own and partners well with any number of foods. Consider this a template of sorts, the fundamentals being sweet cabbage, fennel and the bright lemon dressing. Try it served with fried haloumi, shaved parmesan or pecorino, or alongside the cauliflower fritters on page 166. Pear is a welcome addition, but should you have only cabbage on hand, it is still delicious. In its own right, pear, fennel and celery is a fabulous combination, and with the lemon dressing and/or Celery Leaf Pesto on page 141 served with a lovely chunk of Taleggio cheese, it's exquisite.

cabbage and fennel salad with a bright lemon dressing

To make the dressing, whisk all the ingredients in a large mixing bowl. Taste and adjust – this should have a sharp, but balanced lemon flavour.

Cut off and discard the tough stems of the fennel and set aside the softer central stem with new growth and young fronds. Cut in half and discard any of the outside layers if they appear too thick. Using a mandoline or large sharp knife, slice the fennel as thinly as possible, then immediately add to the bowl with the lemon dressing. Finely shave down the sides of the cabbage, leaving the core. Add to the bowl with the fennel, then add the celery. Take the reserved central stem of the fennel, rich with fronds, and cut it into very thin slices. Add to the bowl with your chosen herbs. Toss through and serve with a good dollop of celery leaf pesto, if desired.

137

DIETARY INFO DAIRY FREE | VEGAN OPTION | EGG FREE
SERVES 4-6

1 quantity cooked Borlotti Beans
    (page 62), drained
1 quantity Rosemary, Preserved
    Lemon and Tomato Dressing
    (page 74)
2 tablespoons very coarsely chopped
    rosemary leaves
extra virgin olive oil or Rosemary-
    infused Olive Oil (page 72),
    for frying
1 red capsicum (pepper), seeds and
    membrane removed, cut into 1 cm
    (½ in) dice
1 zucchini (courgette) (about
    200g/7 oz), cut into 1 cm
    (½ in) dice
sea salt, to taste
1 eggplant (aubergine), cut into
    1.5 cm (⅝ in) dice
freshly ground black pepper, to taste
handful of basil leaves, roughly torn
large handful of flat-leaf (Italian)
    parsley leaves, well rinsed and
    roughly chopped
1 quantity cooked spelt berries,
    drained (page 65)

138

KITCHEN NOTES
● If you have time, marinate the
borlotti beans in the dressing and
rosemary overnight. The flavour will
be better for it.
● Additions: cooked cavolo nero (see
page 140) adds lovely colour. Olives can
be added as desired, but go carefully as
they have the ability to overpower the
delicious flavours already there.
● Don't dice the eggplant until you are
ready to start cooking or it will oxidise.

*Spelt berries are a good match for borlotti beans. They have history
together that goes back hundreds of years, having grown up in the
same area. This is a hearty and robust salad that is even more
sublime when fresh borlotti beans are available.*

spelt berry, ratatouille and borlotti bean salad

Combine the cooked borlotti beans, dressing and rosemary in
a bowl. Stand for at least 1 hour. Meanwhile, pour enough olive
oil into a 24 cm (9½ in) frying pan to just cover the base (about
¾ tablespoon should be plenty). Place the pan over medium heat
and when hot, add the capsicum and cook, stirring regularly, for
10–15 minutes, until soft but not brown. Using a slotted spoon,
remove the capsicum from the pan and set aside, leaving the
flavoured oil in the pan.

If needed, add another 1 teaspoon olive oil. Add the zucchini and
a pinch of salt and cook over medium heat for 10 minutes, or until
just tender and the juices have evaporated. Using a slotted spoon,
remove the zucchini from the pan, leaving as much oil behind as
possible, and add them to the capsicum.

Return the pan to medium heat. Toss the eggplant with
1 tablespoon olive oil and add to the pan. Cook the eggplant for
25–30 minutes, turning every now and then and more frequently
towards the end of cooking, until golden all over. Remove and add
to the capsicum and zucchini. Season the vegetables to taste with
freshly ground black pepper. Set aside to cool, then toss through
the basil and parsley. To put the salad together, place the cooked
spelt berries, vegetables, beans and dressing in a bowl and
gently toss together.

DIETARY INFO GLUTEN-FREE OPTION | DAIRY FREE | VEGAN OPTION | EGG FREE
SERVES 4–6

1 quantity cooked borlotti beans (page 62)

1 quantity Rosemary, Preserved Lemon and Tomato Dressing (page 74)

30 g (1 oz/½ cup) roughly chopped basil

2 tablespoons extra virgin olive oil

2 garlic cloves, crushed

150 g (5½ oz) good-quality day-old sourdough bread (or gluten-free bread), crusts removed, torn into rough 2 cm (¾ in) pieces

sea salt

5 cavolo nero leaves, thick stems removed (about 50 g/1¾ oz after trimming)

500 g (1 lb 2 oz) juicy very ripe tomatoes, quartered

2–4 teaspoons balsamic vinegar

handful of fresh flat-leaf (Italian) parsley leaves, well rinsed and roughly chopped

freshly ground black pepper, to taste

140

A robust and hearty salad to serve when tomatoes are at their peak and will be well complemented with a small dollop of Arame Tapenade (page 131). If you are tempted to add some parmesan or pecorino cheese, it wouldn't go astray here.

borlotti bean panzanella

Place the borlotti beans, dressing and basil in a bowl and stir to combine well. Cover and stand for 1 hour or overnight.

Meanwhile, to make the croutons, preheat the oven to 180°C (350°F). Place the olive oil and garlic in a medium-size bowl. Add the torn bread and use your hands to massage through, ensuring the oil and garlic are evenly distributed. Sprinkle generously with sea salt. Place on a baking tray and bake for 10–15 minutes, until lightly coloured and crisp on the outside but not yet dried out. Set aside to cool.

To prepare the cavolo nero, bring a medium-size saucepan of water to the boil. Add a pinch of sea salt and the cavolo nero leaves and cook for about 5 minutes (smaller, younger leaves will need less time). Drain in a colander, then run under cold water. When cool, squeeze out any excess water and cut into 2–3 cm (¾–1¼ in) thick ribbons.

To put the salad together, place the croutons and tomatoes in a large bowl with the marinated beans and dressing. Toss through, giving the tomato an encouraging bit of pressure to help their juices ooze into the croutons. Add 2 teaspoons balsamic vinegar to start with, toss through and taste, adding more if desired. Add the blanched cavolo nero, parsley and a grind of black pepper, then toss through to combine. Arrange on a platter to serve.

KITCHEN NOTES

● You need a sharp balsamic vinegar with good acidity here. Some of the very good-quality balsamic vinegars can be a little sweet.

● If you have time, marinate the borlotti beans in the dressing and chopped basil overnight as the whole dish will be better for it.

400 g (14 oz) new-season potatoes,
  cut into even sizes
good pinch of sea salt
100 g (3½ oz) young tender inner
  celery stems, sliced very thinly
  on the diagonal

CELERY LEAF PESTO

15 g (½ oz/¾) flat-leaf (Italian)
  parsley leaves
15 g (½ oz) tender inner celery
  leaves (these are usually more
  yellow in colour than the green
  outer stalks)
1 teaspoon capers in salt, rinsed
2 garlic cloves
40 g (1½ oz/¼ cup) toasted
  pine nuts
25 g (1 oz/¼ cup) finely grated
  pecorino cheese
¼–½ teaspoon freshly ground
  black pepper
1 tablespoon lemon juice
2 teaspoons finely grated lemon zest
60 ml (2 fl oz/¼ cup) best fruity
  extra virgin olive oil, plus extra
  to cover

New-season potatoes, at their best straight out of the garden, are the star of this salad. Simply cooked, and tossed with tender, inner celery stems and celery leaf pesto, they are sublime. The inner leaves of celery are remarkably sweet and delicious – perfect for pesto.

potato and celery salad with celery leaf pesto

First, make the pesto. Place the parsley, celery leaves and capers in a good-size mortar and pestle and gently pound until you have a rough mash. Gently pound in the garlic and pine nuts, then stir in the remaining ingredients. Taste and adjust the flavours as needed.

Place the potatoes in a saucepan of cold water with the sea salt. Bring to the boil, then simmer until the potatoes are just tender when pierced with a small knife. Drain and place in a serving bowl. Add the celery and pesto and toss through with your fingers (carefully – it might be a little hot). Taste and adjust the seasoning, adding a little extra salt if needed.

KITCHEN NOTE
I prefer using a mortar and pestle for this pesto as it gives you more control over the texture and taste. The inner ribs of celery are wonderful added to salads, the middle ribs good for stews and braising, while the tougher outer stems are ideal for using in stock.

DIETARY INFO GLUTEN FREE | DAIRY FREE | VEGAN | EGG FREE
SERVES 3-4 AS A MEAL, OR MORE AS A SIDE

350 g (12 oz) pumpkin (winter
  squash) (such as jap or kent)
extra virgin olive oil, to drizzle
sea salt and freshly ground
  black pepper
2-3 small jalapeño chillies
  (about 65 g/2¼ oz total)
4 small zucchini (courgettes)
  (about 200 g/7 oz), halved
  lengthways
1 corncob, papery husks discarded
1 quantity cooked Christmas
  lima beans (page 62), drained

DRESSING
60 ml (2 fl oz/¼ cup) extra virgin
  olive oil
1 tablespoon lemon juice
1 tablespoon Sweet Sultana and
  Chilli Sauce (page 77)
¼ teaspoon smoked sweet paprika,
  or to taste
1 garlic clove, crushed
pinch of sea salt

KITCHEN NOTES
● When blackened or grilled (broiled),
peppers become sweeter, more subtle
and hotter. Because jalapeño peppers
are small and only have a thin layer of
flesh, when blackening them you need
to keep an eye on them. Also take care
not to breathe in the fumes or smoke.
● Smaller zucchini (courgettes) are
more flavourful. If yours are larger,
cut them lengthways into 2 cm (¾ in)
thick slices.

*Beans, squash and corn are known as the 'three sisters', and are
considered sacred to the Native Americans. Corn provides the pole
for the beans to climb on, squash covers and mulches the ground,
and at the same time they nutritionally complement each other.*

three sisters Christmas lima bean salad

Preheat the oven to 190°C (375°F). Cut the pumpkin into wedges
no more than 4 cm (1½ in) thick, leaving the seeds in if possible.
Place on a baking tray, drizzle with a little olive oil and toss to
coat. Stand each piece of pumpkin up on its skin, and ensure that
any pumpkin seeds are on top of the pumpkin (to prevent the
seeds from burning). Sprinkle generously with sea salt and pepper.
Bake for 20-30 minutes, until the pumpkin is caramelised and
tender. Smaller pieces will cook more quickly.

Meanwhile, place a wire rack over a gas flame and arrange the
chillies on top. Allow to score well, turning frequently until
the peppers are lightly blackened and blistered – a fair bit of
blackened skin is okay, but don't overdo it. (You can also do this
on a barbecue.) Place in a small bowl, cover and allow to cool.
Slip the skins off, discard the seeds and slice into thin strips.

Preheat a barbecue or chargrill pan over high heat. Brush the
zucchini with a little olive oil, then cook for 3-5 minutes or
until well scored. Turn over and cook the other side. Next, brush
the corn with a little olive oil and cook for 10 minutes, turning
frequently, or until the corn is cooked and scored. Set aside to
cool. Lay the corn upright on a chopping board and carefully cut
the corn into chunks.

To make the dressing, place all the ingredients in a small jar, seal
and shake to combine well. Taste and adjust the flavour as needed.
To put the salad together, place all the ingredients on a platter,
drizzle with the dressing, then toss gently and serve.

DIETARY INFO EGG FREE | DAIRY FREE | VEGAN OPTION
SERVES 4–6
YOU WILL NEED TO BEGIN THIS RECIPE THE DAY BEFORE

220 g (7¾ oz/1 cup) medium-grain brown rice

1 tablespoon whey or choice of acid or dairy-free option (page 59)

1 cinnamon stick

sea salt, to taste

1 quantity Roasted Apricots (page 99)

200 g (7 oz/1 cup) cooked chickpeas (or 65 g/2½ oz/⅓ cup uncooked chickpeas, cooked following method for a pot of beans on page 62)

75 g (2½ oz/½ cup) pumpkin seeds (pepitas), lightly toasted

140 g (5 oz/1 cup) pistachios, lightly toasted and roughly chopped

75 g (2½ oz/½ cup) currants

1 quantity Lime, Cumin and Honey Dressing (page 75)

small handful of mint leaves, optional

Many years ago, back in my Earth Market days, I used to make a dried apricot, sultana and couscous salad. I've long since forgotten the recipe, but this is a more wholesome version of that baby. If you can, I urge you to make the dressing ahead of time and soak the currants in it – they will swell and become extra delicious.

roasted apricot and brown rice salad

The night before, put the rice and whey in a large bowl with enough water to cover by 10 cm (4 in) and leave to soak overnight. Soak the chickpeas as per the instructions on page 62.

The next day, strain the soaked rice through a sieve and pat dry with a tea towel (dish towel) as described on page 66. Place in a medium-size saucepan with the cinnamon, a pinch of sea salt and 435 ml (15¼ fl oz/1¾ cups) water. Cover with a lid and cook over the lowest heat possible for 35–40 minutes or until the liquid is absorbed and the rice is cooked. Turn off the heat, remove the lid, place a clean tea towel on top of the rice and replace the lid, then stand until cool.

To put the salad together, place all the ingredients in a mixing bowl and gently toss to combine. Taste and adjust the flavours as needed – it might just need a little drizzle of extra honey. Spoon into a serving bowl.

144

500 g (1 lb 2 oz/4 cups) cauliflower
   florets (about 1 small cauliflower)

1 teaspoon garam masala

1 teaspoon ground cumin

1 teaspoon ground coriander

good pinch each of sea salt and
   freshly ground black pepper

60 ml (2 fl oz/¼ cup) extra
   virgin olive oil

1 small brown onion, halved and
   thinly sliced lengthways

200 g (7 oz/1 cup) cooked chickpeas
   (or 65 g/2½ oz/⅓ cup uncooked
   chickpeas, cooked following
   method for a pot of beans on
   page 62)

3 fresh dates, seeds removed and
   cut into small pieces

15 g (½ oz/½ cup) coriander
   (cilantro) leaves

ORANGE TAHINI SAUCE

65 g (2¼ oz/¼ cup) hulled tahini

125 ml (4 fl oz/½ cup) orange juice

1 teaspoon finely grated orange zest

1–2 tablespoons lemon juice

1 garlic clove, crushed

1 teaspoon honey or maple syrup

I find cauliflower very easy to grow in the cooler months and am always looking for ways to use it. It is a good friend of both chickpeas and tahini, both of whom love a bit of spice in their lives, resulting in a simple, but delicious combination.

baked spicy cauliflower, chickpeas and fresh dates

Preheat the oven to 190°C (375°F).

Place the cauliflower florets in a bowl with the spices, salt and pepper, and toss to coat well. Drizzle with 2 tablespoons olive oil and toss to combine well. Spread over a baking tray, making sure all the spicy oil from the bowl ends up on the cauliflower. Bake for 20–25 minutes, until the cauliflower is cooked and caramelised.

Meanwhile, heat the remaining tablespoon of olive oil in a frying pan over medium heat. Add the onion and cook for 5–8 minutes or until translucent and slightly caramelised. Add the chickpeas and toss until warmed through, then remove from the heat.

To make the sauce, place the tahini in a bowl and whisk in a little orange juice – it will clag up initially, but will relax as you add more. Whisk in the remaining ingredients and adjust the acidity and sweetness as desired.

When the cauliflower is ready, arrange on a serving dish, top with the warm chickpeas, onion, dates and coriander leaves and gently toss through. Drizzle half the sauce over the top, then serve with the remaining sauce in a small bowl to be added as needed.

145

DIETARY INFO GLUTEN FREE | VEGETARIAN | EGG FREE
SERVES 4

200 g (7 oz) haloumi cheese, cut
   into thick slices
butter, ghee or extra virgin olive oil,
   for frying

BAKED PEACH SALSA
2 small–medium jalapeño chillies
4 peaches, stones removed and cut
   into wedges
250 g (9 oz) mixed ripe tomatoes,
   quartered or left whole if small
   cherry tomatoes
2–3 small red onions (about
   80 g/2¾ oz each), peeled and cut
   into thick slices
1 tablespoon extra virgin olive oil
sea salt
1–2 teaspoons raspberry vincotto
   vinegar
small handful of basil leaves

KITCHEN NOTE
Blackened tomatoes are also a nice
touch in the salsa. To blacken the
tomatoes, place them, whole, onto a
wire rack sitting over a medium flame
and cook, turning occasionally for
5 minutes or until the skins are
blackened and blistered. Set aside to
cool, then remove the skin, cut the
flesh into coarse pieces and crush them
lightly with your hands as you add them
to the salsa with any tomato juices.

*Served with a bowl of lemony greens, this is a tasty and substantial
meal. The baked peach salsa by itself would be delicious served with
greens and goat's cheese. The salsa also pairs wonderfully with
baked whole fish such as red mullet.*

baked peach salsa and haloumi

To make the salsa, place the jalapeño chillies on a wire rack over a
gas flame and cook, turning frequently until lightly blackened and
blistered – be a little careful as chillies have only a thin layer of
flesh and you don't want to overdo it. You can also do this on the
barbecue. Place the chillies in a small bowl, cover and stand until
cool. Remove and discard the skins (they should slip off easily)
and the seeds, then cut the flesh into thin strips.

Preheat the oven to 200°C (400°F). Place the peaches and the
tomatoes on a baking tray along with the onions. Drizzle with the
olive oil and sprinkle with salt. Bake for 20 minutes, or until the
onion is lightly caramelised and cooked. There may be a touch of
caramelisation on the peaches also, and some juice will have run.
Remove from the oven and allow to cool enough to handle. Peel
off and discard the skins of any larger tomatoes, then give them
a little squeeze to release some of their juices. Add the sliced
jalapeño chillies to the tray. Drizzle with the vinegar, then transfer
to a bowl.

For the haloumi, brush a chargrill pan (or frying pan) with a little
butter. Cook the haloumi slices over medium heat for 1–2 minutes
on each side, or until golden and well marked. Remove and drain
on paper towel. Serve the haloumi with the peach salsa warm or
at room temperature, and scatter with the basil leaves.

146

DIETARY INFO GLUTEN-FREE OPTION | DAIRY FREE | VEGETARIAN OPTION
SERVES 4-6
YOU WILL NEED TO BEGIN THIS RECIPE THE DAY BEFORE

90 g (3¼ oz/½ cup) Christmas lima beans
2 x 2 cm (¾ in) pieces kombu
1 bay leaf
3 juniper berries
3 black peppercorns
5 teaspoons extra virgin olive oil
1 large brown onion, finely chopped
80 g (2¾ oz) carrot, finely chopped
80 g (2¾ oz) celery, finely chopped
pinch of sea salt
1 teaspoon finely chopped rosemary
1 bay leaf, roughly torn
3 thyme sprigs
250 ml (9 fl oz/1 cup) chicken stock
1 tablespoon Rosemary-infused Olive Oil (page 72), plus a little extra for brushing
100 g (3½ oz/1 cup) pecans, toasted and roughly chopped
1 tablespoon tamari (or wheat-free tamari for a gluten-free option)
115 g (4 oz/⅓ cup) Fig, Balsamic and Onion Jam (page 76)
1 tablespoon arrowroot
freshly ground black pepper

148

KITCHEN NOTES
• I use an enamel-coated cast-iron terrine dish, which measures 25 × 8.5 × 7 cm (10 × 3¼ ×2¾ in). Alternatively, a glass or china dish covered with baking paper and foil will do, but your cooking time may vary.
• For a vegetarian option, replace the chicken stock with 185 ml (6 fl oz/ ¾ cup) vegetable stock and 60 ml (2 fl oz/½ cup) bean cooking liquid. Whisk ⅛ teaspoon agar powder into the cold stock in the saucepan and simmer over low heat, stirring occasionally, until reduced by half.

One deeply flavoured and hearty terrine. It's best made with a well-jellied chicken stock because the gelatine in the stock helps the terrine hold together. It also makes the beans easier to digest.

Christmas lima bean terrine

The day before, place the beans, 1 piece kombu, bay leaf, juniper berries and peppercorns in a large bowl with water to cover by 10 cm (4 in).

The next day, follow the instructions on page 62 for cooking the beans. Place the olive oil, onion, carrot, celery, salt, rosemary, bay leaf and thyme in a large frying pan and cook over low heat for 10–15 minutes, until the vegetables are just softened. Add 125 ml (4 fl oz./½ cup) chicken stock and cook for another 10–15 minutes, until the vegetables are tender. Increase the heat to medium to reduce any remaining liquid and gently fry the vegetables – you should hear a faint sizzle. Remove from the heat and leave to cool.

Place the remaining stock in a small saucepan and simmer over medium–high heat for 5 minutes, until reduced by half.

Preheat the oven to 180°C (350°F) and brush a terrine dish (see Kitchen Notes) with the extra rosemary-infused olive oil. Drain the beans, keeping a little of the kombu, and discard the rest of the flavourings. Add the beans and kombu to the food processor and blitz until just combined. Tip into a bowl and stir in the pecans, cooked vegetables (remove any thyme stems), reduced stock, tamari, fig balsamic jam and rosemary oil. Season with pepper, then stir in the arrowroot. Spoon into the greased dish and smooth the top. Cover with a lid or baking paper and foil, and bake for 30 minutes. Remove the lid and bake for another 25 minutes – the sides should pull away from the edges and the centre slightly puffed. Remove from oven and set aside for 15–25 minutes.

Place a plate over the terrine dish and invert the terrine onto a plate. Using a sharp knife, gently cut into slices. Any leftovers will store in an airtight container for 2–3 days in the fridge.

2 eggplants (aubergines)
  (about 500 g/1 lb 2 oz), cut into
  1–1½ cm (½–⅝ in) thick slices
sea salt, for sprinkling
2–3 tablespoons extra virgin olive
  oil, plus extra for brushing
¼ teaspoon smoked paprika
2–3 garlic cloves, finely chopped
15 g (½ oz/½ cup) coriander
  (cilantro) leaves,
  coarsely chopped
generous grind of black pepper

CHICKPEA AND TOMATO JAM

1 tablespoon extra virgin olive oil
1 red onion, halved and
  thinly sliced lengthways
pinch of sea salt
1 cinnamon stick
¾–1 teaspoon ground cumin
¾–1 teaspoon ground coriander
2–3 teaspoons apple cider vinegar
2–3 teaspoons honey
200 g (7 oz/1 cup) cooked chickpeas
  (or 65 g/2½ oz/⅓ cup uncooked
  chickpeas, cooked following
  method for a pot of beans on
  page 62)
440 g (15½ oz) tinned tomatoes
  or fresh to equal

KITCHEN NOTE

Salting eggplant isn't altogether
necessary because most of their
bitterness is bred out of them these
days. I prefer using young eggplants,
which do not require salting and have
yet to develop seeds. Here, the salting
process draws out the bitter juices from
the eggplants. I also find that once
salted, they don't absorb as much oil.

This makes a tasty and fragrant meal, and would partner beautifully with a bowl of hulled millet. The fragrant eggplants, just as they are, make a fabulous stand-alone nibble.

paprika eggplant with chickpea and tomato jam

Place the eggplant on a tray and sprinkle with a little sea salt. Stand for 15–20 minutes or until you see juices weeping from the eggplant. Rinse the eggplant and pat dry with paper towel.

Pour enough oil into a large-size frying pan to cover the base by about 2 mm (1/12 in) and place over medium heat. Lay as many eggplant slices as will fit into the pan in a single layer and brush the tops with the extra oil. Cook for 10 minutes or until golden, then turn and cook the other side. As the eggplant slices cook, they will start to release some of the oil. If necessary, brush them with a little extra oil – this is much easier than adding extra oil to the whole pan. Repeat with the remaining eggplant. Drain on paper towel, cut into rough chunks and place in a bowl. Add the remaining ingredients and stir gently.

To make the tomato and chickpea jam, heat the olive oil in a frying pan over low heat. Add the onion and pinch of salt and cook for 10 minutes, or until soft and lightly caramelised. Add the spices, starting with ¾ teaspoon each of cumin and coriander and let them cook for 1–2 minutes. Stir in 2 teaspoons each of vinegar and honey, the chickpeas and tomatoes, then simmer gently for 10 minutes. Taste and add extra spice, vinegar and honey, if needed. Cook for another 10–20 minutes or until thick and jam-like in consistency. Stir in the eggplant and serve warm or at room temperature. The jam will keep in an airtight container in the fridge for up to 3 days.

FROM TOP LEFT: SIMPLE TRAY BAKED TART SHELL; RUSTIC TART OF SEASONAL GREENS; MUSHROOM, LEEK AND GRUYÈRE TART

DIETARY INFO LOW GLUTEN | DAIRY-FREE OPTION | VEGETARIAN | WHEAT FREE
SERVES 2

1 quantity Barley and Spelt
   Shortcrust Pastry (page 84)
spelt flour, for dusting
1 egg, lightly beaten

A tart is a wonderful lunch or dinner served with a salad of greens, with the added bonus that leftovers are just as good the next day, and they freeze brilliantly. I know that pastry can be overwhelming for many, but read through the recipe for Barley and Spelt Savoury Shortcrust Pastry on page 84, then have a good read through here for how to roll it. Because of the low gluten, this can be a little tricky to roll and bake. But it is easy and this is how you do it.

simple tray bake tart shell

Preheat the oven to 190°C (375°F) and grease your tin.

Following the instructions on page 84, roll out the pastry into a rectangle about 2 mm (1/12 in) thick (see Kitchen Note). Lift into the prepared tin and gently ease the pastry into the base, corners and up the sides. Using kitchen scissors or a knife, trim any overhanging pieces on the edges. Reserve any scraps and lay them on top of each other (don't roll them up into a ball), then cover and refrigerate. Place the pastry-lined tin in the freezer to chill for 5 minutes.

Remove the lined tin from the freezer and place a large sheet of baking paper over the pastry. Fill with baking weights, dried beans or rice ensuring they fill the tin. Bake for 10–15 minutes, until the edges are beginning to colour. Remove from the oven, reduce the temperature to 170°C (325°F), then remove the baking weights and paper. If there are any cracks, flatten a small piece of the chilled scraps and patch up the cracks, letting the heat of the pastry soften it and become 'one' with the pastry. Just take care to be super gentle, as too much pressure can break this pastry at this point. Brush all over with the beaten egg and bake for 5–10 minutes or until the pastry is just about cooked. If at any point the bottom of the pastry puffs up, reduce the oven temperature to 160°C (315°F).

Remove the tart shell from the oven. The tart is now ready to fill with the recipes on pages 153–154.

KITCHEN NOTE

I shape my tarts into a rectangle as they are easier to slice that way. I use a 3 cm (1¼ in) deep, 30 × 20 cm (12 × 8 in) slab tin or you can use a 3 cm (1½ in) deep, 24–26 cm (9½–10½ in) round tart tin with a loose base.

PHOTO ON PAGE 150

DIETARY INFO LOW GLUTEN | WHEAT-FREE OPTION | VEGETARIAN
SERVES 6–8 WITH A SIDE SALAD

1 Simple Tray Bake Tart Shell
  (opposite)
100 g (3½ oz/1 cup) gruyère cheese,
  grated

MUSHROOMS
10 dried shiitake mushrooms
30 g (1 oz/1 tablespoon) ghee or
  1½ tablespoons butter
3–4 garlic cloves, finely chopped
1 teaspoon tamari (or wheat-free
  tamari)
1 teaspoon mirin (rice wine)
pinch of freshly ground black
  pepper

LEEKS
1½ tablespoons ghee or
  2 tablespoons butter
1 medium leek, whites sliced
  and rinsed (green tops reserved
  for stock)
5 thyme sprigs, leaves picked
1 bay leaf, roughly torn
sea salt

CUSTARD
500 ml (17 fl oz/2 cups) full-cream
  (whole), non-homogenised milk
1 egg
2 egg yolks

KITCHEN NOTE
The amount of ghee or butter in the
recipe is deliberate, making up some
of the fat in the custard.

While fairly rich, this is a deeply flavoured and delicious tart.

mushroom, leek and gruyère tart

Place the mushrooms in a small saucepan with 250 ml (9 fl oz/ 1 cup) water. Cover and bring to the boil, then remove from the heat and stand for 1 hour.

Preheat the oven to 190°C (375°F) and place a baking tray inside. For the leeks, melt the ghee in a medium-size frying pan over low heat. Add the leek, thyme, bay leaf and a pinch of salt and cook for 10 minutes or until the leek is soft and tender. Season to taste with pepper, then transfer the leek to a plate and reserve the pan.

Drain the mushrooms (reserving the soaking water), remove and discard the stalks, and slice thinly. Melt the ghee in the reserved frying pan over low–medium heat. Add the sliced mushrooms along with their soaking water, leaving any gritty bits behind. Simmer gently for 10–15 minutes, until only a little liquid remains. Add the garlic, tamari, mirin and pepper and cook over low heat for about 10 minutes, until all of the liquid has evaporated and the mushrooms are glossy. Remove from the heat.

Whisk the milk, egg and egg yolks in a bowl. Spread half the gruyère over the base of the prepared tart shell, then the leeks, followed by the mushrooms. Carefully pour two-thirds of the custard into the tart shell and place on the baking tray in the oven. Bake for 10 minutes, then reduce the oven temperature to 180°C (350°F). Pour in the remaining custard and sprinkle over the remaining gruyère. Bake for 15 minutes, reduce the temperature to 160°C (315°F), then cook for another 5–10 minutes or until the filling is just cooked. If the custard puffs up during cooking, reduce the temperature immediately to 160°C (315°F). Remove from the oven and stand for 10–15 minutes before serving.

PHOTO ON PAGE 151

DIETARY INFO LOW GLUTEN | VEGETARIAN | WHEAT FREE
SERVES 6–8 WITH A SIDE SALAD

1 Simple Tray Bake Tart Shell
(page 152)
2 tablespoons ghee or 60 g
(2¼ oz) unsalted butter
1 medium leek, whites thinly sliced
and rinsed (green tops reserved
for stock)
sea salt and freshly ground black
pepper, to taste
2 carrots, scrubbed and grated
150 g (5½ oz) jap (winter squash) or
butternut (squash) pumpkin,
peeled, seeded and grated
1 parsnip, peeled, cored and grated
2 medium potatoes, scrubbed and
grated
5 large sage leaves, finely chopped
2 teaspoons finely chopped
rosemary
2 teaspoons thyme leaves
2 tablespoons finely chopped chives
2 garlic cloves, finely chopped
100 g (3½ oz/1 cup) tasty cheddar
cheese, grated

CUSTARD
500 ml (17 fl oz/2 cups) full-cream
whole, non-homogenised milk
1 egg
2 egg yolks

KITCHEN NOTE
Grate the vegetables on the
medium-size holes of a grater, not too
finely. Try to grate the potato at the
last moment, as it will oxidise quickly.

*Carrots, leeks and herbs are easy to grow and to find at farmers'
markets. This is a tart of good, elemental flavours and it is perfect
for the cooler weather.*

a tart of wintery root vegetables

Melt 1 tablespoon ghee in a large frying pan over low heat. Add
the leek and a pinch of salt and cook, stirring often for 5 minutes
or until soft and tender. Remove from the pan and set aside, then
return the pan to the heat. Add the carrots, pumpkin, parsnip,
potatoes and a good pinch of salt and pepper, and cook over
low–medium heat for 15–20 minutes, until the vegetables are just
about cooked. You may find they stick to the base of the frying pan
– which is fine and will only add to the flavour – just use an egg
flip to move them off the bottom. When cooked, remove from the
heat and stir in the herbs, garlic, leek and two-thirds of the grated
cheese, then season to taste.

Preheat the oven to 190°C (375°F) and put a baking tray inside.

To make the custard, place all the ingredients in a bowl and whisk
to combine well. There should be adequate salt and pepper from
the vegetables so you shouldn't need to add extra to the custard.

Spread the vegetable mixture evenly over the base of the prepared
tart shell. Gently pour two-thirds of the custard into the tart shell
and place on the baking tray in the oven. Bake for 10 minutes to set
the custard, then reduce the oven temperature to 170°C (325°F).
Gently pour in the remaining custard and scatter the remaining
cheese on top. Cook for another 15 minutes, then reduce the oven
temperature to 160°C (315°F) and bake for another 5–10 minutes,
or until cooked. If the custard puffs around the edge the first stage
of baking, reduce the heat immediately to 160°C (315°F). Remove
from the oven and stand for 10–15 minutes before serving.

154

DIETARY INFO LOW GLUTEN | VEGETARIAN | WHEAT FREE
SERVES 6

1 quantity Barley and Spelt
   Shortcrust Pastry (page 84)

FILLING

1–2 tablespoons extra virgin olive oil

2–3 small–medium leeks, whites
   thinly sliced and rinsed (green tops
   reserved for stock)

15–20 silverbeet (Swiss chard) or
   rainbow chard leaves with
   stems intact

7–10 small cavolo nero leaves

2 garlic cloves, finely chopped

sea salt, to taste

good handful of basil, roughly
   chopped

85 g (3 oz/⅓ cup) sour cream or
   cultured cream (page 48)

good grating of parmesan or
   pecorino cheese

200 g (7 oz) goat's cheese or feta
   cheese, crumbled

sea salt and freshly ground black
   pepper

KITCHEN NOTE

A good dollop of celery leaf pesto (page
141) or a basil pesto is a lovely addition
stirred into the filling at the very end.

*Extremely flexible, this tart will welcome the abundance of
silverbeet and cavolo nero that are both so easy to grow. I really love
the cream and cheese in the tart; both helping to buffer the oxalic
acid in the silverbeet.*

rustic tart of seasonal greens

To make the filling, heat the olive oil in a medium-size frying pan
over low heat. Add the leeks and cook, stirring often, for 5 minutes
or until tender.

Meanwhile, prepare the silverbeet and cavolo nero. If the
silverbeet leaves are very fresh, you can happily cut some of the
stem into 5 mm (¼ in) slices. Otherwise, cut off the tough stems
from the cavolo nero and silverbeet leaves and discard, then cut
the leaves into 1 cm (½ in) slices.

Add the silverbeet stems, garlic and a pinch of salt to the pan with
the leeks. Toss over medium heat, until they begin to look soft
and 'melting'. Add the silverbeet and cavolo nero leaves and the
basil, 1 small handful at a time, tossing them through and cooking
for a few minutes before adding the next. Cook for 5–10 minutes,
turning frequently, until soft. Remove and set aside to cool. Add
the sour cream and cheeses, stir through and season to taste.

Preheat the oven to 190°C (375°F) and line a baking tray with
baking paper. Following the instructions on page 84, roll out the
cold pastry into a circle about 30–35 cm (12–14 in) diameter and
3 mm (⅛ in) thick and transfer to the tray. Place the filling on top of
the pastry, leaving an 8 cm (3¼ in) border. Fold any overhanging
edges over and place in the freezer for 5–8 minutes, or in the
fridge until very cold. Bake for 40–50 minutes, until golden,
checking the tart after 25 minutes – if it is browning too quickly,
reduce the oven temperature. Serve hot, or at room temperature.

PHOTO ON PAGE 150

155

DIETARY INFO LOW GLUTEN | VEGETARIAN | WHEAT FREE
SERVES 4–6 WITH SIDE SALAD

½ quantity Barley and Spelt
  Shortcrust Pastry (page 84)
1 egg, lightly beaten
7–8 plums (I use the black amber
  variety), halved and stones
  removed
extra virgin olive oil, for drizzling
200 g (7 oz/1 cup) goat's curd
2 tablespoons Fig, Balsamic and
  Onion Jam (page 76)
5–6 small basil leaves

This tart would also be delicious topped with roasted beetroot and sprinkled with finely chopped rosemary instead of the plums and basil.

roast plum, goat's curd and basil tart

Preheat the oven to 190°C (375°F) and line a baking tray with baking paper. To prepare the pastry base, following the instructions on page 84, roll out the pastry into a 26 cm (10½ in) round, then lift onto the lined baking tray. While the pastry is still quite cool, roll the edges inward, creating a wall about 1 cm (½ in) high. The diameter should be around 23 cm (9 in). Prick the base of the pastry with a fork and place in the freezer for 5 minutes. Meanwhile, cut a 23–24 cm (9–9½ in) round piece of baking paper to fit the new diameter of the tart shell.

Remove the pastry from the freezer and place the baking paper on the pastry. Fill the base with baking weights, dried beans or uncooked rice. Bake for 10–15 minutes, until the edges are beginning to colour. Remove from the oven, then remove the baking weights and paper. Brush the base and sides all over with the beaten egg. Reduce the oven temperature to 180°C (350°F) and continue to bake for a further 8–10 minutes or until golden. Remove from the oven and set aside. Increase the oven temperature to 190°C (375°F) in preparation for the plums.

Place the plums, cut side up, in an ovenproof dish that allows for a snug fit and drizzle with a little olive oil. Roast for 15–20 minutes, until just cooked but no juices have released. Remove and allow to cool enough to handle.

To assemble the tart, carefully spread the goat's curd over the tart base. Scatter the onion, fig, balsamic and onion jam on top of the curd, followed by the plums. Sprinkle the basil leaves over the plums and serve immediately.

KITCHEN NOTE
Assemble the tart just before serving to prevent the pastry becoming soggy. All the components can be prepared ahead of time.

158

pocket pies

Pocket pies are one of my favourite things to make as they are so easy. Make them for eating at home or to pack in a picnic; they are good any time of the day, and delicious either hot or cold.

tips for pocket pie success

ROLLING The key is to keep the pastry cool, so try to work with just half the amount of pastry at a time, rolling and filling half the pocket pies before proceeding to use the other half. Note that the dairy-free pastry (pages 86–87) will be less flexible because coconut oil has no give.

FILLING Make sure the filling is absolutely cold before putting together the pies. Solid ingredients such as uncooked vegetables or fruit are more of a challenge to work with because they are less malleable than cooked ingredients when you fold the pastry over. This is especially true when working with dairy-free pastries.

STORAGE Any leftover pocket pies can be stored in an airtight container in the fridge for up to 1 day, or frozen. These reheat brilliantly. To heat from frozen, place the pies on a tray in an oven preheated to 170°C (325°F) and cook for 20–30 minutes, until hot throughout.

apple and cheddar

DIETARY INFO LOW GLUTEN | WHEAT FREE | VEGETARIAN
MAKES 8 POCKET PIES

These are best made with apples that will hold their shape when cooked. I like to use golden delicious.

1 quantity Barley and Spelt Shortcrust
  Pastry (page 84)
2 apples, peeled, quartered,
  cored and cut into 3 mm (½ in)
  thick slices
5–6 small–medium sage leaves,
  roughly sliced

100 g (3½ oz) best-quality tasty
  cheddar, thinly sliced
1 egg, lightly beaten, for brushing
1 tablespoon rapadura sugar or
  raw sugar

Preheat the oven to 190°C (375°F).

Divide the pastry into two and place one half in the fridge. Roll out one quantity of pastry into a 23–24 cm (9–9½ in) square, 2–3 mm (1/12–1/8 in) thick. Cut into four and leave it exactly where it is (that is, don't separate it once you have cut it).

To fill, divide half the quantity of apple slices between the bottom half of each piece of pastry, laying the straight edge of the apple facing the fold line, overlapping them as you go and leaving no more than a 1 cm (½ in) border. Scatter with half the sage, then top with half the cheese. Use a large palette knife to carefully fold the pastry over the filling, gradually moving the pie away from the remaining pastry squares as you do so. Next, use a fork to press the edges of the pastry to seal, and transfer to a baking tray lined with baking paper. Repeat with the remaining pastry, apples, sage and cheese.

Brush the beaten egg generously over the pastry tops. Using a small sharp knife, make a small cross on top of the pies, then sprinkle over the sugar. Bake for 30–35 minutes, until golden and the juices are sizzling at the sides of the pie. Remove from the oven, allow to cool enough to handle, then eat.

moroccan-spiced pumpkin, silverbeet and goat's cheese

DIETARY INFO LOW GLUTEN | WHEAT FREE | VEGETARIAN
MAKES 8 POCKET PIES

*It may be that you just have a bit of pumpkin left over after a meal and a bit of pastry
in the freezer. Basically, you will need about 40 g (1½ oz) cooked pumpkin per pie.*

1 quantity Barley and Spelt Shortcrust Pastry (page 84)
1 egg, lightly beaten

FILLING

8 small silverbeet (Swiss chard) or rainbow chard leaves
   (about 100 g/3½ oz in total)
2 teaspoons extra virgin olive oil
sea salt and freshly ground black pepper
1 quantity cold Moroccan-spiced Roast Pumpkin
   (page 163), skins discarded and cut into small chunks
190 g (6½ oz/½ cup) Fig, Balsamic and Onion jam
   (page 76)
40 g (1½ oz) soft goat's cheese (chevre) or feta

For the filling, cut the silverbeet leaves into
1 cm (½ in) wide slices. If your silverbeet is
young and fresh, use about 4 cm (1½ in) of
stem, discarding the rest, and cut into 5 mm
(¼ in) slices. If the stems are tough and
fibrous, discard them.

Place the olive oil in a small frying pan over
medium heat. If using the silverbeet stems, add
them to the pan and cook for 2 minutes, stirring
occasionally. Add the leaves and cook for
5 minutes, until well wilted and any juices have
evaporated. Transfer to a small bowl and set
aside until completely cooled. Just before using,
strain off any remaining juices and liberally
season with salt and pepper.

Preheat the oven to 190°C (375°F).

Divide the pastry into two and place one half
in the fridge. Roll out the remaining half of the
pastry into a 23–24 cm (9–9½ in) square,
2–3 mm (1/12–⅛ in) thick. Cut into four and
leave it exactly where it is (that is, don't
separate it once you have cut it). Divide half the
amount of pumpkin between the bottom half
of each pastry piece, along the fold line, leaving
no more than a 1 cm (½ in) border. Top with
one-eighth of the cooked and cooled silverbeet,
1 tablespoon fig, balsamic and onion jam and
1 teaspoon goat's cheese. Use a large palette
knife to carefully fold the pastry over the filling,
gradually moving the pie away from the other
pastry squares as you do so. Next, use a fork to
press the edges of the pastry to seal, and transfer
to a baking tray lined with baking paper. Repeat
with the remaining pastry and filling.

Brush the beaten egg generously over the pies.
Using a small sharp knife make a small cross on
top of the pies. Bake for 30–35 minutes, until
golden. Remove from the oven, allow to cool
enough to handle, then eat.

160

fragrant coconut chicken and sweet potato

DIETARY INFO DAIRY FREE | WHEAT FREE
MAKES 8 POCKET PIES

1 quantity Dairy-free Coconut Oil and Sesame Pastry
  (page 86)
1 egg, lightly beaten

FILLING
2 teaspoons coconut oil
50 g (1¾ oz) shallots (about 1–2), finely chopped
15 g (½ oz) peeled fresh ginger, finely chopped or grated
1 tablespoon finely chopped coriander (cilantro) stems
100 g (3½ oz) orange sweet potato, peeled and
  cut into 5 mm (¼ in) dice
100 g (3½ oz/½ cup) corn kernels
170 ml (5½ fl oz/⅔ cup) coconut milk
2 boneless skinless chicken thighs (about 200 g/
  7 oz), cut into rough 5 mm (¼ in) dice
1–2 teaspoons fish sauce
handful of coriander (cilantro) leaves, finely chopped
freshly ground black pepper, to taste

For the filling, heat the coconut oil in a medium-size frying pan (about 24 cm/9½ in) over medium heat. Add the shallots, ginger, coriander stems and sweet potato, and cook, stirring occasionally for 5–8 minutes, or until the vegetables are beginning to soften. Add the corn and coconut milk, then cover with the lid and cook for about 3 minutes, or until the sweet potato is just cooked. Remove the lid, add the chicken and cook, stirring occasionally for another 2 minutes, or until the chicken is just cooked. Transfer to a bowl, allow to cool briefly, then place in the fridge to cool completely.

Preheat the oven to 190°C (375°F). When ready to assemble the pies, stir the fish sauce and coriander leaves through the mixture and season to taste with black pepper.

Divide the pastry into two and place one half in the fridge. Roll out the remaining half of the pastry into a 23–24 cm (9–9½ in) square, 2–3 mm (¹⁄₁₂–⅛ in) thick. Cut into four and leave it exactly where it is (that is, don't separate it once you have cut it). Divide half the filling between the bottom half of each piece of pastry, leaving no more than a 1 cm (½ in) border. Use a large palette knife to carefully fold the pastry over the filling, gradually moving the pie away from the other pastry squares as you do so. Next, use a fork to press the edges of the pastry to seal, and transfer to a baking tray lined with baking paper. Repeat with the remaining pastry and filling. Brush the beaten egg generously over the pies. Bake for 30–35 minutes, until golden. Remove from the oven, allow to cool enough to handle, then eat.

Variation: Black beluga lentil and sweet potato and coconut
If you have leftover Black Beluga Lentil, Sweet Potato and Coconut Stew (page 176), this makes a fantastic pocket pie filling. Or, if you like, make the full recipe for the stew and one quantity of the pastry above and fill the pies as per above.

1 teaspoon ground coriander
1 teaspoon ground cumin
½ teaspoon ground fennel
½ teaspoon sea salt
½ teaspoon freshly ground
  black pepper
700 g (1 lb 9 oz) jap (kent) pumpkin
  (winter squash)
1 tablespoon extra virgin olive oil

*I love serving this with yoghurt and Green Drizzle Sauce (page 75).
It's a good companion for the Baked Spicy Cauliflower, Chickpeas
and Fresh Dates (page 145).*

moroccan-spiced roast pumpkin

163

Preheat the oven to 190°C (375°F).

First, combine all the spices in a small bowl.

Cut the pumpkin into wedges, leaving the seeds in. You are looking
for the centre to be about 4–4.5 cm (1½–1¾ in) thick, tapering to
about 1–2 cm (½–¾ in) thick at the ends. Depending on the size
of the pumpkin, you may need to cut the wedge into 2–3 sections
giving you two ends that taper, and one fairly even middle piece.
Place the pumpkin in a bowl and drizzle with enough olive oil to
coat well, massaging it in to the pumpkin. Rub the spice mix over
the pumpkin, then place on a baking tray and sit each piece of
pumpkin up on its skin, ensuring that any pumpkin seeds are on
top otherwise they will burn on the tray. Scrape out any spice mix
left in the bowl and sprinkle it on the pumpkin.

Bake for 30–40 minutes, until caramelised and tender. Smaller
pieces will cook more quickly and may need to be removed as they
become ready.

DIETARY INFO DAIRY-FREE OPTION | VEGETARIAN OPTION | GLUTEN-FREE OPTION | EGG FREE
SERVES 4–6
YOU WILL NEED TO BEGIN THIS RECIPE THE DAY BEFORE

250 g (9 oz) green split peas, rinsed

1 generous tablespoon ghee or butter

1 large leek, whites thinly sliced and rinsed (reserve the green tops for stock)

1–2 tablespoons chopped fennel fronds (see Kitchen Notes)

2–3 thyme sprigs

good pinch of sea salt

2 celery stalks, cut into 1 cm (½ in) dice

1 fennel bulb, cut into 1 cm (½ in) dice

1 parsnip, peeled, cored and cut into 1 cm (½ in) dice

1 medium sweet potato, peeled and cut into 1 cm (½ in) dice

2–3 carrots, peeled (if organic, unpeeled), cut into 1 cm (½ in) dice

100–250 g (3½–9 oz) pumpkin (butternut squash or jap/kent are both good), peeled and cut into approximately 1.5 cm (⅝ in) dice

approximately 2 litres (70 fl oz/ 8 cups) chicken stock (page 42)

tamari (or wheat-free tamari for a gluten-free option) and mirin, to balance if needed

1–2 tablespoons finely chopped coriander (cilantro) or flat-leaf (Italian) parsley leaves

KITCHEN NOTES

● For a dairy-free option, simply use olive oil. And if you have some rendered chicken fat, all the better.

● I prefer to buy my fennel with their fronds – the softer inner fronds will add welcome flavour.

● For a vegetarian option, choose a deeply flavoured vegetable stock (page 41) instead of the chicken stock.

Quick-cook green split peas make a delicious and hearty soup with very little effort. Soaking them first will make them a little more digestible and even quicker to cook.

split pea, fennel and winter vegetable soup

The night before, soak the split peas overnight following the instructions on page 59.

The next day, melt the ghee in a medium–large saucepan over low–medium heat. Add the leek, fennel fronds, thyme sprigs and sea salt and cook, stirring occasionally for about 5 minutes. Add the celery, fennel, parsnip, sweet potato, carrot and pumpkin as you cut them, letting the vegetables in the pan cook while you cut the remaining ones. Drain the soaked split peas and add them to the pan with the stock. Simmer, stirring occasionally, for 50 minutes or until the peas are tender, or leave them to totally break down (this will also thicken the soup). Taste to check the seasoning and add a little tamari or mirin, if needed. Stir in the coriander or parsley just before serving.

DIETARY INFO GLUTEN FREE | DAIRY-FREE OPTION | VEGETARIAN | EGG FREE
SERVES 4–6

1½ tablespoons ghee or
2 tablespoons butter
(or 2 tablespoons olive oil for
a dairy-free option)
2 leeks (about 155 g/5½ oz), whites
thinly sliced and rinsed (reserve
the green tops for stock)
1 teaspoon fennel seeds, toasted and
ground (or 1¼ teaspoon ground)
½ teaspoon coriander seeds, toasted
and ground (or ½ generous
teaspoon ground)
¼–½ teaspoon ground cinnamon
20 g (¾ oz) piece of fresh ginger,
peeled and finely chopped
4 sage leaves, sliced
sea salt and freshly ground black
pepper, to taste
1 kg (2 lb 4 oz) jap (kent)
pumpkin (winter squash), seeds
removed and discarded, peeled and
cut into rough chunks
1 pear, peeled, cored and roughly
chopped
1 medium fennel bulb, roughly
chopped, 1–2 tablespoons chopped
fronds reserved
1 litre (35 fl oz/4 cups) vegetable
stock (page 41)
tamari (or wheat-free tamari for a
gluten-free option), for seasoning

As well as being a lovely twist on a classic pumpkin soup, this dish is another use for the abundant fennel that it seems I am able to grow quite successfully.

pear, fennel and pumpkin soup

Melt the ghee in a 24 cm (9½ in) saucepan over low heat. Add the leeks, ground spices, ginger, sage and a good pinch each of salt and pepper, and cook, stirring occasionally for 5 minutes or until the leeks are wilted and the flavours begin to mingle. Add the pumpkin, pear, fennel and stock and bring to a gentle simmer. Cover and simmer gently for 30 minutes or until the pumpkin and fennel are tender when pierced with a knife. Leave to cool for 10 minutes, then transfer to a blender and, holding the lid, start the motor slowly to prevent the hot soup from popping the lid off and landing everywhere. Blend until smooth, then taste the soup and adjust if necessary. If your pumpkin is very sweet, it may need a little tamari to ground it. If adding tamari, start with just a couple of drops. Ladle into bowls, sprinkle with the reserved chopped fennel fronds and serve.

KITCHEN NOTE
You will achieve a better flavour in this soup if you can toast the spices just before using.

DIETARY INFO GLUTEN FREE | DAIRY FREE | VEGETARIAN
MAKES 12

375 g (13 oz/3 cups) cauliflower
  florets with little stems
2 teaspoons extra virgin olive oil,
  plus extra for frying
1 small brown onion, finely chopped
1–2 tablespoons finely chopped
  garlic chives
25–35 g (1–1¼ oz/½–¾ cup)
  chopped coriander (cilantro) leaves
100 g (3½ oz/½ cup) cooked
  amaranth (page 64)
sea salt and freshly ground black
  pepper, to taste
1 large or 2 small eggs, lightly beaten

Infinitely flexible, fritters are one of my favourite snack or lunch tactics. Not only does the egg bind the ingredients (mostly vegetable, with an option of a little grain) but it provides exceptional nutrient density. In turn, the vegetables, herbs and grain extend the expensive egg – it's a win-win any way you look at it.

cauliflower and amaranth fritters

In a metal steamer, add the cauliflower. Cover with a tight-fitting lid and steam over a saucepan of simmering water for 3 minutes, until just cooked and still a little toothsome. Place in a food processor and pulse until coarsely chopped, taking care not to over-blend it into a smooth paste. Transfer to a mixing bowl.

Heat 2 teaspoons olive oil in a small frying pan over low heat. Add the onion and cook, stirring often for 5–6 minutes, until soft and lightly coloured, but not at all fried or crispy.

Add the cooked onion to the cauliflower along with the garlic chives, coriander and amaranth, then season with salt and pepper to taste. Using your hands, mix through to evenly distribute the amaranth – it can be quite sticky. Add the beaten egg and stir through. Leave to sit for a couple of minutes to firm up, then form into 12 small flat patties.

Add enough oil to coat the base of a frying pan by 1.5 mm (¹⁄₁₆ in) and place over medium–high heat. When the oil is hot, but not at all smoking, add the patties (in batches if necessary) – they should sizzle as they hit the oil. Cook for about 7 minutes, or until golden brown. After about 2–3 minutes of cooking, use your spatula to flatten the patties just a little. Turn and cook for the same amount of time on the other side, adding a little extra oil if needed and leaving the fritters to cook until nice and golden. Remove and drain on paper towel before serving. The fritters keep well in an airtight container in the fridge for up to 1 week.

KITCHEN NOTE
These patties take longer than you'd think to cook. They must be well cooked and golden with a definite crust before flipping; this will help hold them together. The fritters will also firm up as they cool and are great in lunch boxes.

2 medium parsnips
1 tablespoon extra virgin olive oil
1 small onion, finely chopped
½ teaspoon ground fennel
¼ teaspoon ground coriander
¼ cup cooked grain (such as
   quinoa, page 63)
1 tablespoon coarsely chopped
   chives
5 medium–large sage leaves,
   coarsely chopped
generous grind of black pepper
sea salt, to taste
2 eggs, lightly beaten
1 medium apple
ghee, for frying (or olive oil
   if dairy free)

If your parsnips are very fresh, you can simply scrub their skin well before cooking. However, if they're old they will need to be peeled. Choose apples that are tart rather than sweet, and don't hold back on the sage – it works so well with parsnip. With regards to the onion – anything will work. If all you have is spring onions, thinly slice and use those. Leek, shallot or brown and red onions will just require a little longer cooking time.

parsnip, apple and sage fritters

Bring a saucepan of lightly salted water to the boil over high heat. Meanwhile, cut the parsnips into thirds – the top third cut into quarters, the middle third cut in half and leave the thin bottom third as is. *Carefully* cut the woody core from the quarters and discard. Add the parsnips to the boiling water and cook for 5 minutes, or until just tender but not at all floppy. Drain and set aside to cool briefly.

Heat the olive oil in a small frying pan and cook the onion over medium heat for 1–2 minutes. Stir in the ground fennel and coriander and cook for another 5 minutes or until lightly caramelised, then remove from the heat.

Place the cooked parsnip in a food processor and pulse until it appears roughly grated – don't overdo it. Transfer to a bowl, add the onion mixture, cooked grain, chives, sage leaves, pepper, salt and eggs. Core, then grate the apple, skin and all, and add to the bowl along with the parsnip. Mix together until well combined.

Add enough ghee and olive oil to the frying pan to come about 3 mm (¹⁄₁₂ in) up the side of the pan (I use about two parts ghee and one part oil) and place over low–medium heat. When hot, but not at all smoking, add spoonfuls of the mixture, and use a spatula to gently pat the fritters down as they cook. Fry for about 5 minutes on both sides, or until very golden brown. Avoid turning the fritters too much during cooking – you want to achieve a nice crust. Drain on paper towel before serving.

HEARTY DISHES THAT NOURISH ON EVERY LEVEL

heartier
VEGETARIAN,
meat & fish

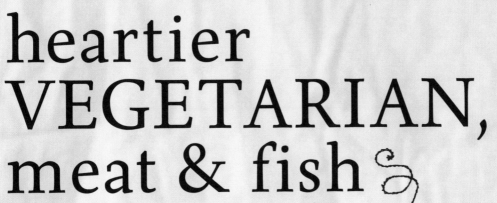

DIETARY INFO LOW GLUTEN | VEGETARIAN | VEGAN OPTION | EGG FREE
SERVES 4–6
YOU WILL NEED TO BEGIN THIS RECIPE THE DAY BEFORE

100 g (3½ oz/½ cup) pearl barley

2 tablespoons green lentils

3 teaspoons whey or choice of acid or dairy-free options (page 59)

2 tablespoons extra virgin olive oil, plus extra for drizzling

1 medium leek, whites thinly sliced and rinsed (reserve the green tops for stock) (or 1 onion, finely chopped)

3–4 garlic cloves, finely chopped

2 teaspoons finely chopped rosemary

2 cm (¾ in) piece kombu

2 bay leaves

500 ml (17 fl oz/2 cups) chicken or vegetable stock

1 teaspoon ghee (or extra virgin olive oil, if vegan)

12 small–medium rainbow chard or silverbeet (Swiss chard) leaves (about 160 g/5¾ oz), well rinsed, leaves and tender stems cut into wide strips

sea salt and freshly ground black pepper, to taste

1–2 tablespoons lemon juice

25–50 g (1–1¾ oz/¼–½ cup) grated parmesan or pecorino cheese

40 g (1½ oz/¼ cup) toasted pine nuts

KITCHEN NOTE

Sausage would be a delicious addition to this dish. Add the sausage to the pan with the onions. It will add more fat to the dish so you may want to reduce the amount of extra virgin olive oil, or serve it on the side.

You can make this with vegetable stock, however a bone stock, such as chicken, will make the dish far more nourishing and delicious.

barley, rainbow chard and lemon risotto

The night before, place the barley and lentils in separate bowls and add enough water to cover by 2 cm (¾ in). Stir 2 teaspoons whey into the barley and 1 teaspoon into the lentils. Set aside at room temperature for at least 8 hours or overnight.

The next day, make the risotto. Place the olive oil, leek, garlic and rosemary in a heavy-based 20 cm (8 in) cast-iron pan. Cook over low heat, stirring occasionally for 10 minutes, until translucent.

Drain the barley and lentils, then add to the pan with the kombu and bay leaves, and stir through. Add the stock and bring to a simmer, then cover and cook over low heat for 40–50 minutes, until the barley and lentils are cooked and tender to the bite; there should still be plenty of liquid left.

Next, heat the ghee in a medium-size frying pan over low heat. Add the chard stems and cook gently, stirring occasionally for 10 minutes. Toss in the leaves and cook for another 10 minutes, until they are well wilted. Increase the heat to reduce the liquid.

When the barley and lentils are ready, stir in the chard and simmer, uncovered, for 5 minutes or until most of the liquid has evaporated. The barley will continue to absorb liquid as it sits. If it looks a little dry, add a little more stock or water to loosen. Season generously with sea salt and pepper (this is a dish that loves pepper), then stir in the lemon juice and parmesan cheese to taste. Scatter with the pine nuts, then drizzle with a little extra virgin olive oil and serve.

DIETARY INFO GLUTEN-FREE OPTION | DAIRY-FREE OPTION | VEGETARIAN OPTION | EGG FREE
SERVES 4–6
YOU WILL NEED TO BEGIN THIS RECIPE THE DAY BEFORE

200 g (7 oz/1 cup) dried pinto beans

5 cm (2 in) piece kombu

1 tablespoon extra virgin olive oil

1 tablespoon ghee (or chicken fat
for a dairy-free option)

1 brown onion, finely chopped

2 garlic cloves, finely chopped

1 teaspoon each dried basil and
oregano, or about 1–2 tablespoons
roughly chopped fresh oregano or
basil leaves

¼ teaspoon dried thyme or
1 teaspoon fresh thyme leaves

¼ teaspoon dried sage

2 bay leaves

1 medium carrot, halved lengthways
and cut into 1 cm (½ in) slices

2 celery stalks, cut into 1 cm (½ in)
slices or parsley stems

250 g (9 oz) sweet potato, peeled
and cut into 2 cm (¾ in) dice

1–2 teaspoons smoked sweet paprika
(see Kitchen Note)

freshly ground black pepper, to taste

1.5 litres (52 fl oz/6 cups) vegetable
or chicken stock (page 41)

1–2 tablespoons tomato paste
(concentrated puree)

1–2 teaspoons tamari (or wheat-free
tamari for a gluten-free option)

1–2 tablespoons coarsely chopped
flat-leaf (Italian) parsley

I love this twist on traditional baked beans. Chicken stock will give this recipe a slightly sweeter, silkier and more nutrient-dense end result, but vegetable stock will do just fine.

smoky sweet potato and pinto beans

The night before, place the beans and kombu in a large bowl and add enough water to cover by 10 cm (4 in). Set aside at room temperature for 12–24 hours.

The next day, heat the olive oil and ghee in a heavy-based flameproof casserole dish (a 24 cm/9½ in) enamel-coated cast-iron pan is ideal) over very low heat. Add the onion, garlic, herbs and vegetables and cook, stirring occasionally for 10 minutes or until the onion is translucent and lightly caramelised. Stir in the paprika and pepper, to taste, and cook for 1 minute.

Drain the beans, rinse well and reserve the kombu. Add the beans and kombu to the dish with the stock. Partly cover with a lid, increase the heat to low–medium and bring to a gentle simmer. Cook for 2–3 hours or until the beans are soft. Add the tomato paste and tamari and simmer, uncovered, for another 1–2 hours or until the beans are very soft and creamy. If the beans yield a soft creamy centre to gentle pressure, increase the heat to medium and simmer, uncovered for 10–15 minutes, stirring often until the beans are reduced to a thick, saucy consistency. If not yet soft and creamy in the centre, continue to simmer with the lid on until ready. When the beans are ready, you might like to mash some of them to help thicken the sauce. Check the seasoning and adjust if necessary, then serve scattered with the parsley.

KITCHEN NOTE
Smoked paprika can vary in flavour
from brand to brand, so add a little,
then taste before adding the remainder.

172

500 g (1 lb 2 oz) floury potatoes, well scrubbed and cut into chunks

4 spring onions (scallions), whites and some greens finely chopped

2 teaspoons finely grated lemon or lime zest

1 tablespoon very finely chopped celery (inner stalks are best)

2–3 tablespoons finely chopped herbs (I like fennel fronds, flat-leaf/Italian parsley and inner celery leaf, basil or coriander/cilantro)

sea salt and freshly ground black pepper, to taste

200 g (7 oz) mixed cooked fish (see Kitchen Note)

1 large or 2 smaller eggs

120 g (4¼ oz/2 cups) sourdough breadcrumbs, made from day-old sourdough bread (or gluten-free bread)

ghee, for frying (or olive oil if dairy free)

Tartare Sauce (page 71), to serve

KITCHEN NOTE

The general ratio for the fish in this recipe is: 50 g (1¾ oz) high omega-3 strongly flavoured and oily fish such as mackerel, 50 g (1¾ oz) smoked high omega-3 oily fish milder in flavour (such as mullet), and 100 g (3½ oz) lighter flavoured fish. If you have cold-smoked fish or uncooked lighter flavoured fish, this will need to be cooked before adding to the recipe. To do this, place the fish in a small saucepan, cover with milk or fish stock (if dairy free), add a pinch of salt and pepper and a bay leaf and simmer for 5–10 minutes, just until opaque. Set aside to cool in the milk or stock.

What makes these the best fish cakes ever? Smoked fish and real potatoes (as in fresh and grown in great soil) are a good start, followed by a crispy golden outside and a soft, but not too squishy, middle. Plan these for when you have some cooked mackerel left over, and add whichever herbs take your fancy.

the best fish cakes ever

Place the potatoes in a saucepan of lightly salted water and bring to the boil. Simmer until tender, then drain well. Place the potatoes in a bowl and coarsely mash. Add the spring onions, lemon zest, celery, herbs, salt and pepper and combine well. Add the fish in generous-size pieces and gently mix through, trying not to break them up too much. Taste and adjust with salt and pepper as needed. Shape the mixture into 8 balls, then flatten to make cakes about 3 cm (1¼ in) thick. Place on a tray, cover and refrigerate for 30 minutes.

When ready to cook, lightly beat the egg with a little salt and pepper in a shallow bowl. Place the breadcrumbs on a plate and season if desired. Working one at a time, dip the fish cakes in the egg mixture, then coat in breadcrumbs.

Add enough ghee and olive oil to a small frying pan to come a quarter of the way up the side of a fish cake (it is better to use a smaller pan where less fat will achieve this more easily). Place over medium–high heat and when the fat is very hot, but not at all smoking, cook the fish cakes, in batches, for 8–10 minutes on each side, until gloriously golden. Adjust the heat as the fish cakes cook, being careful that it is not too hot otherwise they will burn. Drain on paper towel, then serve with tartare sauce and a simple salad. These fish cakes will keep for up to 2 days in an airtight container in the fridge and will reheat readily in a warm oven.

173

DIETARY INFO GLUTEN FREE | VEGETARIAN
SERVES 4–6

3 medium eggplants (aubergines)
(about 750 g/1 lb 10 oz), cut into
1–1.5 cm (½–⅝ in) thick slices
sea salt, for sprinkling
extra virgin olive oil, for frying

MUSHROOM BASE
3 tablespoons ghee
or 80 g (2¾ oz) butter
1 brown onion, halved and thinly
sliced lengthways
400 g (14 oz) mushrooms
(Swiss browns work well), cut into
5 mm (¼ in) slices
2 teaspoons chopped oregano leaves
2 teaspoons thyme leaves
2 bay leaves
4 garlic cloves, finely chopped
freshly ground black pepper, to taste
60 ml (2 fl oz/¼ cup) good, well-
bodied red wine (such as Shiraz)
170 g (6 oz) tomato paste
(concentrated puree)

YOGHURT CUSTARD
500 g (1 lb 2 oz/2 cups) Labne
(page 52)
250 ml (9 fl oz/1 cup) full-cream
(whole), non-homogenised milk
4 eggs
2 egg yolks
100 g (3½ oz/1 cup) finely grated
parmesan cheese

174

Here is a deeply flavoured, rich dish for late summer, when eggplants (aubergines) are at their peak and the cooler weather is asking us for a little more. Yes, it does have rather a lot of ghee in it, and the eggplants are fried, but this will help buffer the nightshade eggplant and, indeed, the abundance of nightshades at this time of the year.

mushroom and eggplant moussaka

Place the eggplant slices on a tray and sprinkle with a little sea salt – a couple of pinches is ample. Stand for 15–20 minutes, until you see juices weeping from the eggplant. Rinse and pat dry with paper towel.

Pour enough olive oil into a medium-size frying pan to cover the base by about 2 mm ($\frac{1}{12}$ in) and place over medium heat. Lay as many eggplant slices as will fit into the pan and brush the tops with the extra oil. Cook for 10 minutes or until golden, then turn and cook the other side. As the eggplants cook, they will start to release some of the oil. If necessary, brush them with a little extra oil – this is much easier than adding extra oil to the whole pan. Drain on paper towel.

For the mushroom base, heat 1 tablespoon ghee in a medium-size frying pan over medium heat. Add the onion and a pinch of salt and cook, stirring occasionally, for 10–15 minutes, until the onion is translucent and lightly caramelised. Remove from the pan and set aside. Add the remaining ghee, mushrooms and a pinch of salt to the pan and cook, stirring frequently, for 15–20 minutes. As the mushrooms begin to cook, they will absorb the ghee and appear dry, then as their liquid is released, they will look moist. Reduce the heat as they begin to release their liquid to prevent them from frying. The final stage is when the mushrooms appear shiny and no liquid remains. When the mushrooms reach the shiny stage, cook for a couple more minutes, then stir in the herbs, garlic and black pepper. Cook for a further minute, then stir in the cooked onion.

If you prefer, both the eggplant and
the mushroom base can be made a day
ahead ready to assemble the next day.

Pour in the red wine, then stir in the tomato paste. Simmer gently,
stirring occasionally, for 5–10 minutes, or until slightly thickened
and well combined. Remove from the heat and set aside.

To make the yoghurt custard, place all the ingredients in a bowl
and whisk together until smooth and well combined.

To assemble the moussaka, preheat the oven to 180°C (350°F).
Spread half the mushroom mixture over the base of a 25 × 20 ×
5.5 cm deep (10 × 8 × 2¼ in) baking dish. Arrange half the eggplant
on top, then repeat the layers. Pour over the yoghurt custard and
bake for 45 minutes to 1 hour, until the custard is gently firm to
the touch in the centre. After 30 minutes in the oven, check to see
if the yoghurt custard is puffing up, or beginning to crack – if so,
reduce the temperature immediately to 160°C (315°F). Remove
from the oven and stand for 10–15 minutes before serving.

DIETARY INFO GLUTEN FREE | DAIRY FREE | VEGAN | EGG FREE
SERVES 4–6

3 teaspoons coconut oil

1 small brown onion, thinly sliced

1 garlic clove, thinly sliced

25 g (1 oz) piece of fresh ginger, peeled and finely chopped

15 g (½ oz) piece of fresh turmeric, peeled and finely chopped (or 1 teaspoon ground turmeric)

1 teaspoon ground coriander

1 teaspoon cumin seeds

½ teaspoon curry powder

250 ml (9 fl oz/1 cup) coconut milk

250 g (9 oz) sweet potato, peeled and cut into 1.5–2 cm (⅝–¾ in) dice

200 g (7 oz/1 cup) cooked and drained Black Beluga Lentils (page 61)

1–2 tablespoons lime juice

½–1 teaspoon coconut sugar, or to taste

coriander (cilantro) leaves, to serve

A simple weeknight stew, this is quick to make and delicious served with a cooked grain such as brown rice or quinoa. You could happily use cooked black beans instead of lentils here, if that is what you have on hand. Any leftovers can be easily used up in the dairy-free pocket pies on page 162.

black beluga lentil, sweet potato and coconut stew

Place the coconut oil and onion in a 20 cm (8 in) cast-iron saucepan (the size of the pan is quite important here, see Kitchen Note) and cook over medium heat, stirring occasionally, for 5 minutes or until the onion is nearly translucent, soft and lovely. Stir in the garlic, ginger, turmeric, ground coriander, cumin seeds and curry powder and cook for another 2–3 minutes until aromatic. Add the coconut milk, sweet potato and, if necessary, a little water to come just underneath the vegetables (the water should not cover the vegetables). Place the lid on top of the pan and cook over low heat for 30 minutes or until the sweet potato is tender when pierced with a knife. Gently stir in the cooked black lentils and stir until warmed through. Add the lime juice and coconut sugar to taste, then scatter with chopped coriander just before serving. This stew will keep refrigerated for up to 2 days in an airtight container.

KITCHEN NOTE

It's important to use a saucepan no bigger than 20 cm (8 in) in diameter. This will ensure there's enough liquid to come just below the vegetables without having to add water.

176

DIETARY INFO GLUTEN FREE | VEGETARIAN | EGG FREE
SERVES 6

150 g (5½ oz/¾ cup) millet
50 g (1¾ oz/¼ cup) amaranth
750 ml (26 fl oz/ 3 cups)
   hot stock or water
pinch of sea salt, to taste
extra virgin olive oil for frying,
   plus extra to grease
grated parmesan, pecorino or
   romano cheese, to serve

PUMPKIN TOPPING

1½ generous tablespoons ghee
750 g (1 lb 10 oz) butternut
   pumpkin (squash), peeled, seeded
   and cut into 2 cm (¾ inch) dice
40 g (1½ oz) butter
5 garlic cloves, halved lengthways,
   then thinly sliced
20 sage leaves, or more if very small

This is one of those dishes that will take a little bit more work and time, but it's a great occasion dish. I usually make extra pumpkin topping (in another frying pan) and have that sitting in the fridge to use over the next couple of days. Using stock to cook the grain will increase the flavour, and if you use a bone stock it will increase the nutrient density as well.

polenta of millet and amaranth with pumpkin, sage and garlic

Lightly oil a 20 cm (8 in) square dish – about 1–1.5 cm (½–⅝ in) in height is ideal. Don't worry if you don't have exactly the right size, just choose one that will give you the depth of polenta you desire.

Place the millet and amaranth in a medium-size saucepan. You are better off with a wider (but shallower) pan here. Cook over medium–high heat for 3–5 minutes, until you can smell a delicious nuttiness, taking care not to burn the grains. As they begin to heat, the amaranth will pop – you will need to take the pan off the heat and shake it regularly to not only cool it down a little and stop any burning, but also to redistribute the grains. Reduce the heat to low again, add the hot stock or water, taking care as it will bubble a bit as it hits the hot pan. Stir in a good pinch of salt, then cover, increase the heat to high and bring to the boil. Reduce the heat to low so no steam escapes the lid. Simmer for 40–50 minutes, until the liquid is all absorbed. Remove from the heat, take off the lid and cover with a piece of paper towel to absorb any excess moisture. Allow to stand for 5 minutes. Transfer the polenta to the prepared dish, smooth over the top, cover with a tea towel (dish towel) and set aside until cool enough to handle.

When the polenta is cool, turn it out onto a chopping board and cut into 4 rows, then cut each row into 3 pieces. Cut each piece in half on the diagonal, giving you a total of 24 pieces.

When ready to put the dish together, preheat the oven to 100°C (200°F). Line a baking tray with paper towel.

Pat the bottom of the polenta triangles dry with paper towel – this helps prevent the polenta from sticking during cooking. Add enough olive oil to a large frying pan to cover the base well and place over high heat. When the oil is hot but not at all smoking, cook the polenta in batches so you don't overcrowd the pan, for 5–6 minutes on each side or until golden. This takes longer than you think, and requires a high heat. Place the fried polenta triangles on the lined baking tray, then put in the oven to keep warm.

For the pumpkin topping, heat the ghee in a 30 cm (12 in) frying pan over medium–high heat. (If you don't have a pan as large as this, you are best cooking the pumpkin in 2 batches.) Add the pumpkin and cook, shaking the pan occasionally to prevent sticking, for 15 minutes or until cooked and well caramelised. When ready, remove from the pan and set aside.

Add the butter to the pan and shake over medium heat for 1–2 minutes, until the butter melts and turns a light, nutty brown – don't let it burn. Immediately add the garlic and sage, and shake the pan over the heat for 10–15 seconds or until the sage is crisp and the garlic is light golden. Remove from the heat, add the pumpkin and shake the pan to mix through (avoid stirring). Remove the polenta from the oven and transfer to a large plate. Spoon over the pumpkin, pour the sage and garlic butter over the top, then scatter with cheese and serve immediately.

PHOTO ON PAGE 180

KITCHEN NOTES

- The recipe calls for butter and ghee. When frying and caramelising the pumpkin, use ghee as it will withstand the high heat needed and will enable you to shake and turn the pumpkin easily. Butter will give you the best result when making the brown butter.
- Both the polenta triangles and pumpkin topping can be made in advance. Just warm them before making the sage and garlic butter.

POLENTA OF MILLET AND
AMARANTH WITH PUMPKIN,
SAGE AND GARLIC

heartier vegetarian, meat and fish

DIETARY INFO GLUTEN-FREE OPTION | DAIRY FREE | VEGETARIAN
MAKES 12-14

6 g (⅛ oz) wakame
500 g (1 lb 2 oz) sweet potato
1½ tablespoons extra virgin olive oil,
    plus extra for frying
1¼ teaspoons roasted sesame oil
225 g (8 oz/1½ cups) sesame seeds,
    lightly toasted
1 brown onion, finely chopped
1 garlic clove, finely chopped
freshly ground black pepper,
    to taste
2 small eggs, lightly beaten
2 teaspoons tamari (use wheat-free
    tamari for a gluten-free option)
large handful of coriander (cilantro)
    leaves, roughly chopped

These patties are my updated version of the classic Margaret River sesame and carrot patties for burgers, of which I've cooked thousands in my life. I was well and truly ready for a change, so sweet potato it is. One thing: don't be tempted to fry these in coconut oil because this can make the patties far too sweet. Serve these in a burger or as they are with Sweet Sultana and Chilli Sauce (page 77) and Tempeh Bacon (page 112).

sweet potato, wakame and sesame patties

Preheat the oven to 170°C (325°F).

Place the wakame on a baking tray and toast in the oven for 10 minutes, or until crisp and completely dried out. Take care not to burn the wakame, it may take less time. Remove from the oven and increase the temperature to 200°C (400°F).

Peel the sweet potato and cut lengthways into pieces about 2–3 cm (¾–1¼ in) thick, then place on a baking tray. Combine 3 teaspoons olive oil and ¼ teaspoon sesame oil, then rub the oils all over the sweet potato to coat well. Bake for 30–40 minutes, or until just lightly coloured and soft to the touch. Be careful not to overcook and dry out the sweet potato. Remove from the oven and set aside to cool a little.

Meanwhile, prepare the wakame sesame seeds. Pound the wakame using a mortar and pestle, discarding any stems, until roughly ground. Add the toasted sesame seeds and gently grind until the seeds begin to smell fragrant and glisten – you will hear a popping sound as they begin to break a little. Do not grind to a meal or paste. Set aside.

Place the remaining sesame oil and olive oil, the onion and garlic in a medium-size saucepan and cook over low–medium heat, stirring frequently, for 5 minutes or until the onion is translucent

182

One thing: don't be tempted to fry these in coconut oil because this can make the patties far too sweet.

and beginning to caramelise. Add a little pepper, then transfer to a mixing bowl. Roughly break up the sweet potato and add to the onions with the wakame sesame seeds. Stir until roughly combined and use a butter knife to cut the sesame seeds and onion into the sweet potato – you want to keep the sweet potato in chunks. Add the beaten eggs, tamari and chopped coriander, and stir gently until just combined.

Shape the mixture into 12–14 patties about 6 cm (2½ in) in diameter and no more than 2 cm (¾ in) thick. Place on a tray and stand for 30 minutes to allow the patties to firm up a little. When the weather is warm, put them in the fridge.

Pour enough oil into a medium-size frying pan to coat the base by 5 mm (¼ in) and place over medium heat. When the oil is hot but not at all smoking, use a metal spatula to lift the patties into the oil; they will gently sizzle as they hit the oil. Fry for about 6 minutes, until golden, before turning to cook the other side. If the heat is too high they will brown too quickly before they have a good chance to set. Parts of the sweet potato may brown – these highly caramelised sweet potato bits are one of my favourite things about these patties. Drain on paper towel and serve.

PHOTO ON PAGE 181

DIETARY INFO GLUTEN FREE | DAIRY FREE | EGG FREE
SERVES 4–6
YOU WILL NEED TO BEGIN THIS RECIPE THE DAY BEFORE

95 g (3¼ oz/½ cup) dried Christmas
    lima beans or borlotti beans
2 x 2 cm (¾ in) pieces kombu
1 tablespoon Rosemary-infused
    Olive Oil (page 72), or extra virgin
    olive oil with 1 good rosemary sprig
1 small brown onion, finely chopped
1 medium leek, whites and as much
    green as is in good shape, cut into
    5 mm (¼ in) thick slices
3 bay leaves
3–4 thyme sprigs
4–5 medium–large sage leaves,
    coarsely sliced
3 carrots (about 210 g/7½ oz),
    scrubbed and cut into 1 cm
    (½ in) dice
2 celery stalks (about 150 g/5½ oz),
    cut into 5 mm (¼ in) thick slices
4 garlic cloves, coarsely chopped
generous grind of black pepper
265 g (9¼ oz) jap (kent) or
    butternut pumpkin (squash),
    peeled and cut into 1 cm
    (½ in) dice
2 litres (68 fl oz/8 cups) bone stock
    (lamb stock is particularly good)
410 g (14½ oz) tinned tomatoes
sea salt and freshly ground black
    pepper

KITCHEN NOTES
● The quality of the stock here is
paramount and will influence the
end result.
● At the end of cooking, if you find
the flavour a little acidic, add a couple
of drops of apple juice concentrate or
rapadura sugar. If it is too sweet, add
a touch of wheat-free tamari.
● Add either cooked or pre-soaked
uncooked whole grains. If using cooked
whole grains add with the tomatoes,
and for uncooked, add with the beans.

Mum would make this type of frugal brew to keep the wolf from the door in winter. I humbly offer you carrots, celery, herbs, dried beans and bone stock. This can be made with any bean, but I am particularly fond of Christmas lima beans, which become big, fat and juicy in this soup. Make it, freeze it, and I'm betting that you will return to it again and again. Infinitely flexible, this will welcome any winter vegetable – both swede (rutabaga) and turnip work well.

a humble bean and vegetable soup

The day before, place the beans and 1 piece kombu in a bowl and add enough cold water to cover by at least 10 cm (4 in). Stand overnight at room temperature.

The next day, heat the olive oil in a heavy-based 24–26 cm (9½–10½ in) saucepan over low heat. Add the onion, leek and herbs and cook, stirring occasionally, for 10 minutes or until soft. You are aiming to soften, not fry, the vegetables, so they should be gently sizzling in the pan. Stir in the carrots, celery, garlic and pepper, then increase the heat to medium–high and cook, stirring frequently for 10–15 minutes, until the vegetables are very lightly coloured. Drain and rinse the beans, discard the kombu, then add to the pan along with the remaining kombu, the pumpkin and stock. Reduce the heat to low, cover and simmer gently for 2–3 hours or until the beans are soft. Add the tomatoes and cook for another hour or until the beans are soft and creamy. If the soup is too thin at the end of cooking, increase the heat to medium–high and simmer for a further 5 minutes until slightly thickened, but if you have added grain, this won't be necessary. Taste, season with salt and pepper and adjust the flavour as required (see Kitchen Notes).

DIETARY INFO DAIRY-FREE OPTION | GLUTEN FREE
SERVES 4–6

1 tablespoon ghee or extra virgin olive oil

1 medium brown onion, finely chopped, or 1 leek, thinly sliced and rinsed (reserve the green tops for stock)

1–2 carrots (about 150 g/5½ oz), cut into 1 cm (½ in) dice

2 celery stalks (about 150 g/5½ oz), cut into 1 cm (½ in) dice

2 bay leaves

3 thyme sprigs

sea salt and freshly ground black pepper, to taste

1 teaspoon curry powder

2 potatoes (about 250 g/9 oz), scrubbed and cut into 1 cm (½ in) dice

1 litre (35 fl oz/4 cups) good-quality fish stock (page 40), plus 2 tablespoons extra

600 g (1 lb 5 oz) mixed fish (such as 200 g/7 oz each of mullet, lighter-tasting fish and artisan smoked fish – avoid soft-smoked fish such as smoked salmon)

1 tablespoon kudzu (kuzu) or cornstarch (cornflour)

1–2 tablespoons chopped flat-leaf (Italian) parsley

Kefir Cream (page 49), or crème fraîche, to serve

Inspired by the chowder that chef Hamish McLeay from Bunkers Beach Café makes, this delicious chowder is quick to put together, uses very simple vegetables, is incredibly nutrient dense and easy to digest. There's not much more we could ask for in a recipe. It's also a great place to use a little (or a lot) of stronger-tasting fish such as mullet.

fish chowder

Place the ghee, onion, carrot, celery, bay leaves and thyme in a medium-size heavy-based saucepan (I use a 24 cm/9½ in) cast-iron pan). Add a good pinch of salt and pepper and cook over medium heat, stirring occasionally for about 5 minutes or until the vegetables are just starting to caramelise. Stir in the curry powder, then add the potatoes and 1 litre (35 fl oz/4 cups) stock and simmer for 15 minutes or until the vegetables are just cooked. Remove the thyme sprigs and bay leaves and discard.

Meanwhile, check the fish to ensure that there are no scales or bones, then cut into good bite-size pieces that are not too small. If your smoked fish is already cooked and the edges are quite dry, cut it into smaller pieces so it can soften in the broth.

Place the kudzu and extra 2 tablespoons stock in a small bowl and mix to a smooth slurry. Whisk the mixture into the chowder – it will begin to thicken immediately – and continue whisking until it comes to the boil. Gently stir in the fish, being careful not to break up the pieces too much, and simmer for 5 minutes (it will continue to cook after this). Taste and add salt and pepper as required, then gently stir in the parsley. Ladle the chowder into bowls and serve with a dollop of kefir cream or crème fraîche.

KITCHEN NOTES

● The success of the chowder rests on a robust and well-flavoured fish stock.

● If making a dairy-free alternative, use a fish stock made without ghee, replacing it with extra virgin olive oil, and replace the kefir cream with a squeeze of lemon.

DIETARY INFO GLUTEN FREE | DAIRY-FREE OPTION | VEGETARIAN | VEGAN OPTION
SERVES 3–4 AS A SIDE

1 litre (35 fl oz/4 cups) water, bone
   or vegetable stock (or if making
   soft polenta, use 1.25 litres/
   44 fl oz/5 cups)
sea salt, to taste
190 g (6¾ oz/1 cup) polenta

*The key to a good polenta is to cook it until it is deliciously creamy.
This takes time, and often longer than you'd think – at the very least,
25 minutes from the time it comes to a simmer.*

polenta

Place the stock and a pinch of salt in a deep heavy-based saucepan
and bring to the boil. Whisking continuously, gradually rain the
polenta into the water, then reduce the heat to as low as possible.
Simmer, stirring frequently, for 20–35 minutes, until the polenta
becomes thick and creamy. Stir in your chosen flavourings (see
below Variations), season to taste and serve immediately, or see
Kitchen Notes.

Variations on flavour: Cooking polenta in a fatty chicken stock
will make the flavour shine, but adding butter, or ghee, and cheese
will also make it incredibly mouthwatering. It is possible however
to make polenta quite successfully without dairy products, using
fresh herbs and olive oil instead. You can add whatever you like,
these are just some additions to choose from: finely chopped
rosemary, basil, drizzle of your best extra virgin olive oil, finely
grated parmesan or pecorino cheese.

KITCHEN NOTES
● Firm polenta: If made with 1 litre
(35 fl oz/4 cups) liquid, polenta has
the great advantage of drying into an
almost solid state, and can take on any
desired shape. You can leave it to set
until firm in a greased tray, cut it into
pieces, then fry it in olive oil or grill it.
Alternatively, try it spread very thinly
on a large tray, cooled, then cut into
sections to be used as lasagne sheets;
this is especially excellent if you are
gluten intolerant as it is a far tastier
alternative to the commercial gluten-
free lasagne sheets out there.
● Soft polenta: If made with
1.25 litres (44 fl oz/5 cups) liquid,
the polenta can be spooned directly
into the bowl, a perfect match for a
simple stew such as the Spelt Berry
Ratatouille (page 138), then drizzled
with extra virgin olive oil and sprinkled
with shavings of parmesan cheese and
perhaps a little Green Drizzle Sauce
(page 75). Served with a side of roasted
red capsicums (peppers) and oven-
baked tomatoes, a little salad, say,
of rocket (arugula) and fresh greens,
this is a superb lunch or light dinner.

1.25 litres (44 fl oz/5 cups) water,
  chicken or vegetable stock
  (page 42 or 41)
sea salt, to taste
190 g (6¾ oz/1 cup) coarse polenta
40 g (1½ oz) unsalted butter
2 corncobs, kernels cut off and cob
  discarded (or reserve the cobs for
  using in stock)
freshly ground black pepper, to taste
2 × quantities Refried Black Beans
  (page 62), warmed
1 quantity Lime, Cumin and Honey
  Dressing (page 75)

This is a simple, robust peasant meal. It's delicious with a little tomato and avocado tossed together with the Lime, Cumin and Honey Dressing on page 75.

creamy fresh corn polenta with refried black beans

Make the polenta according to the method opposite.

About 10 minutes before the polenta is ready, melt the butter in a frying pan over medium heat. Add the corn kernels and stir for 2–3 minutes, or until just tender. Season to taste with salt and pepper, then stir into the cooked polenta.

Spoon the warm polenta into a bowl, top with the warm refried black beans and drizzle with the dressing.

187

DIETARY INFO GLUTEN FREE | VEGETARIAN | WHEAT FREE
SERVES 4–6 AS A SIDE

800 g (1 lb 12 oz/4 cups) corn
    kernels (about 4–5 cobs)
1 tablespoon masa flour
good pinch of sea salt and freshly
    ground black pepper
4 eggs
250 g (9 oz/1 cup) crème fraîche or
    Kefir Sour Cream (page 49)
125 ml (4 fl oz/½ cup) full-fat
    (whole), non-pasteurised milk
60 g (2¼ oz) unsalted butter

You absolutely must make this once, when corn is at its sweetest and best. Butter, cream and corn are made for each other, indeed summer time and the living is easy. This is perfect served with Three Sisters Christmas Lima Bean Salad (page 142), omitting the corn.

corn pudding

Preheat the oven to 180°C (350°F).

Place half the corn in a blender or food processor and process until creamy. Transfer to a large mixing bowl, then add the remaining corn, masa flour, salt and pepper and mix through.

Whisk the eggs, crème fraîche and milk together in a separate bowl and set aside.

Melt the butter in a 24 cm (9½ in) ovenproof frying pan. Pour most of the butter, leaving a little in the pan, into the egg mixture and whisk through. Add the egg mixture to the corn and combine. Pour the mixture back into the pan and bake for 30–35 minutes, or until the pudding is a little puffed, lightly golden around the edge and still just a bit wobbly in the centre. If at any time you see cracks appearing (especially around the edges where it has puffed) the oven is too hot and the egg can split, so reduce the temperature to 160°C/315°F.

1 quantity uncooked Masa Tortillas
(page 190)
200 g (7 oz/1 cup) cooked and
cooled Refried Black Beans (page
62), lightly mashed with a fork
1½ tablespoons goat's cheese,
optional
lard (or extra virgin olive oil for a
vegetarian option), for frying
cos (romaine) lettuce, shredded,
to serve
Sweet Sultana and Chilli Sauce
(page 77), cultured cream (page
48) and the Lime, Cumin and
Honey Dressing (page 75),
to serve

These lovely little pies also work beautifully when stuffed with goat's cheese, mozzarella and zucchini (courgette) or pumpkin (winter squash) blossoms.

refried black bean stuffed empanadas

Make the tortilla dough following the method on page 190, but divide the dough into 6 portions not 8. Roll out according to the recipe instructions, but do not cook.

Working with one rolled piece of dough at a time, place 1 tablespoon of refried beans on one side, then top with 1 teaspoon goat's cheese, if using. Fold the other side over and seal gently around the edge; you should have a half-moon shape. Holding it gently in your hand, go along and fold the edges over, forming a rope-like pattern as you go. Place on a tray or chopping board and cover with a slightly damp tea towel (dish towel) while you assemble the others.

Place enough lard in a medium-size frying pan to cover the base of the pan well – the more fat there is, the quicker the empanadas will cook. Place the pan over high heat and when the fat is hot, but not at all rippling or smoking, add the empanadas in batches if necessary – they should sizzle robustly. Cook for 2–3 minutes on each side, or until golden. As they cook, you may need to adjust the heat to ensure that the oil is not too hot or smoking at all. Drain on paper towel and serve warm with shredded lettuce, Sweet Sultana and Chilli Sauce and any of the other condiments in the ingredients list.

189

DIETARY INFO GLUTEN FREE | DAIRY FREE | VEGETARIAN | VEGAN OPTION
MAKES EIGHT 10 CM (4 IN) TORTILLAS

140 g (5 oz/1 cup) masa flour
1 tablespoon lard or ghee (optional)
185 ml (6 fl oz/¾ cup) warm water

Fresh corn tortillas are one of the most delicious foods, and one of the easiest to make – you can read more about Masa on page 20. While you can easily roll these with a rolling pin, or a heavy cast-iron frying pan to press them out, a tortilla press makes it a quicker and easier job. Any leftover tortillas will keep wrapped tightly in baking paper and foil to store in the fridge. Then simply remove the baking paper to heat in the foil.

masa tortillas

Place the masa flour and the fat (if using) in a mixing bowl, add the warm water and mix together well, adding extra water as needed. Form into a ball, and press a finger into the dough to check it is the right consistency (see Kitchen Notes). Cover and leave to cool a little, before dividing into 8 balls. The dough will keep well in the fridge for a couple of days, but it must be very well wrapped in plastic wrap to prevent it from drying out.

Working with a ball at a time, place it between two sheets of baking paper, then flatten using a tortilla press or by gently applying pressure with a cast-iron frying pan.

To cook, preheat a flat cast-iron pan over very high heat – you are looking for as much heat as possible. No fat is required. Once very hot, peel off one piece of baking paper from the tortilla and lay the tortilla flat on the pan, then peel off the remaining piece of baking paper – it should be hot enough that when the tortilla hits the pan it puffs up a little from the heat. Cook for 1–2 minutes, until lightly speckled and coloured before turning and cooking the other side. Stack the cooked tortillas on a plate and keep them covered with a clean tea towel (dish towel) until ready to use.

KITCHEN NOTES

● As a very general rule you need 185 ml (6 fl oz/¾ cup) of water for every cup of masa, possibly more, depending on the masa. You need to add enough water to allow you to press your finger into a ball of dough without leaving any cracks around the edge of the finger indentation.

● You want your tortilla to be about 2 mm (⅟₁₆ in) thick.

Beautiful served with fresh coriander, lime, honey and cumin dressing, cultured cream, sweet sultana chilli sauce and some refried black beans.

DIETARY INFO GLUTEN FREE | DAIRY-FREE OPTION | EGG FREE
SERVES 1–2 GENEROUSLY

1 × 420 g (15 oz) mackerel, scaled and gutted
1–2 teaspoons ghee, extra virgin olive oil or lard
sea salt

Baking a whole fish has many benefits: it's incredibly simple, it's quick, it's cheap and it produces a fish with very moist flesh. Yes there will be bones, but really, with just a little time and care they can be removed as you eat. Ask your fishmonger to scale and gut the fish. When finished with, you will still have the head, backbone, tail and some side bones, which can then be used to make stock. I prefer lighter tasting fish bones for making stock (read more about making a fish stock on page 40) and wouldn't fancy using strong tasting fish bones, such as mackerel, so I tend to discard them. The cabbage salad on page 137 would be the perfect accompaniment for the fish. If you have leftovers, use them in the salad overleaf, or as the oily fish component for the fish cakes on page 173.

baked whole mackerel

Preheat the oven to 200°C (400°F).

Rinse the fish and pat dry with paper towel. Starting about 2–3 cm (¾–1¼ in) down from the gills and following the same direction, score the flesh 3 times on each side, taking care not to cut down to the bone. Rub the fish all over with the ghee, then generously salt inside and out.

Place a wire rack over a baking tray. Fold a sheet of baking paper in half to suit the size of the fish, place on top of the wire rack and then put the fish on top. Bake for 10–15 minutes or until the flesh is opaque right down to the bone. There can be a fine line between undercooked and overcooked, so I prefer to take the fish out of the oven at 10 minutes, and check the thickest part of the fish, then give it more time in the oven if needed.

Serve warm or at room temperature. If baking the mackerel to make the salad, stand until cooled, then flake the meat off the bones, discarding the skin and bones as you go.

KITCHEN NOTE
Using ghee will help to soften the strong flavour of an oily fish. Herring, tailor and skipjack are all good alternatives to mackerel. Bake the smaller herring for 10 minutes only.

BAKED WHOLE MACKEREL WITH
BAKED MACKEREL SALAD
(RECIPE PAGE 194)

DIETARY INFO GLUTEN FREE | DAIRY-FREE OPTION | EGG FREE
SERVES 2-4

1 quantity Rosemary and
    Preserved Lemon Mayonnaise
    (made with 1 egg yolk, page 70)
extra preserved lemon, finely
    chopped, optional
2 tablespoons very finely chopped
    fennel
2 tablespoon very finely chopped
    celery heart and leaves
2 teaspoons very finely diced shallot
2 teaspoons finely chopped inner
    fennel fronds
1 teaspoon finely chopped flat-leaf
    (Italian) parsley
generous grind of black pepper
190 g (6¾ oz/1 cup) flaked baked
    mackerel flesh (see page 192)

*Most often, tuna or salmon are chosen as fish options for a salad,
but because I don't live in the Northern Hemisphere I don't have the
option of using salmon, and I don't use tuna. For this recipe, I prefer
to choose other, often overlooked, oily, sustainable fish that are high
in omega-3, such as mackerel, tailor or herring.*

baked mackerel salad

Place all the ingredients, except the mackerel, in a bowl and
stir to combine. Taste and add extra preserved lemon if needed.
Be bold with the lemon as it will balance out the rich mackerel.
You shouldn't need to add salt because it will be salty from the
preserved lemon. Gently stir through the flaked fish, then taste
and adjust the flavours as required. Store in an airtight, clean
glass jar in the refrigerator for up to 2 days.

PHOTO ON PAGE 193

KITCHEN NOTE
Any fresh herb will do here – dill
especially – but since I'm not a fan
of dill, I prefer not to use it. Capers
would work brilliantly also, just be
careful with seasoning if using salted
capers and salty preserved lemons.

DIETARY INFO GLUTEN FREE | DAIRY-FREE OPTION | EGG FREE
SERVES 3-4

4 small potatoes, scrubbed

1 tablespoon extra virgin olive oil

60 ml (2 fl oz/¼ cup) Green Drizzle Sauce (page 75), plus extra as desired

sea salt and freshly ground black pepper, to taste

1 mackerel (about 420 g/15 oz), scaled and gutted

1–2 teaspoons ghee, extra virgin olive oil or lard, for greasing the fish

Cabbage and Fennel Salad with a Bright Lemon Dressing (page 137), to serve

An easy and good-for-you dish, any leftover fish can be used in the Baked Mackerel Salad opposite or the fish cakes on page 173. Black bream and herring would also be great substitutes here for the mackerel, if available.

mackerel with green herb drizzle and crisp potatoes

Place the potatoes in a saucepan of lightly salted water and bring to the boil. Simmer for 7 minutes, or until *just* tender, then drain. When cool enough to handle, cut into 5 mm (¼ in) thick slices.

Preheat the oven to 200°C (400°F).

Put the potatoes into a roasting tin (I like to use a heavy shallow tin that will transfer heat well, such as cast-iron or enamel pans), add the olive oil, 1 tablespoon green drizzle sauce, salt and pepper, and toss to combine well. Bake for 15 minutes or until the potatoes look delicious and crisp, but are happy to cope with another 10–15 minutes of cooking.

Meanwhile, prepare and score the fish following the instructions on page 192. Rub the fish all over with the ghee, then rub and press the remaining green drizzle sauce into the cuts in the fish. Season generously, inside and outside, with salt.

When the potatoes look crisp, place the fish on top and bake for a further 10–15 minutes or until the fish is opaque right down to the bone. (It is a good idea to take it out at 10 minutes to check the fish at the thickest part and give it more time if needed.) Serve with the remaining green drizzle sauce.

195

DIETARY INFO GLUTEN-FREE OPTION | DAIRY-FREE OPTION | VEGAN | EGG FREE
SERVES 4 AS A SIDE DISH

200 g (7 oz) parsnips (about 4–5), rinsed and cut in half lengthways
good pinch of sea salt and freshly ground black pepper
350 g (12 oz) jap (kent) or butternut pumpkin (squash), seeds reserved and prepared according to Moroccan-spiced Roast Pumpkin (page 163)
300 g (10½ oz) orange or purple sweet potato, scrubbed and cut into wedges about 6 cm (2½ in) long and 3 cm (1¼ in) wide
150 g (5½ oz) baby carrots
2 teaspoons roasted sesame oil
2 teaspoons extra virgin olive oil
40 g (1½ oz/¼ cup) sunflower seeds
40 g (1½ oz/¼ cup) pumpkin seeds (pepitas) (over and above what the pumpkin yields)

DRESSING

1 tablespoon molasses
1 teaspoon tamari (or wheat-free tamari for a gluten-free option)
1 tablespoon maple syrup
1 tablespoon genmai miso (brown rice miso)
60 ml (2 fl oz/¼ cup) orange juice
1 tablespoon lemon juice
¼–½ teaspoon ground cinnamon

KITCHEN NOTES

● You basically need a total of 1 kg (2 lb 4 oz) vegetables.
● Once you've added the dressing to the vegetables, keep an eye on it; the vegetables and seeds need to be crisp, caramelised and toasted but the dressing should still remain a little liquid but quite sticky.

This recipe is inspired by Bryant Terry, a whole, natural foods and vegan chef and activist from the US. It's very dependent on knowing your oven. Once the dressing goes on the vegetables and they go into the hot oven, there needs to be enough heat to reduce the dressing and help it caramelise on the vegetables, but not burn.

funked up roast vegetables

Preheat the oven to 200°C (400°F).

For the dressing, place all the ingredients in a small bowl and stir to combine well.

To prepare the parsnip, bring a medium-size saucepan of water to the boil with a pinch of sea salt. Add the parsnip and blanch for 3–4 minutes, until just barely tender. Drain and place in a bowl of cold water to stop the cooking process.

In a large ovenproof dish (I use a 30 × 23 cm/12 × 9 in) dish that isn't too deep but still has a bit of height to hold the liquid when added), toss together the vegetables, any seeds collected from the pumpkin, both the oils and some salt and pepper. Arrange the vegetables so they are not crowded and so they have maximum exposure to the heat; for example, the pumpkin will be best sitting on its thickest part rather than lying on it. Roast for 30–45 minutes or until the vegetables are nearly cooked through and lightly caramelised at the edges.

Remove from the oven, then pour the dressing over and toss through. Sprinkle over the seeds, return to the oven and roast for another 10–15 minutes or until the vegetables and seeds are crisp and the cooking juices are only just caramelised and sticky. During cooking, occasionally spoon any pooling dressing over the vegetables. If there are obvious hot spots in the oven, turn the tray to ensure the heat is evenly distributed.

DIETARY INFO GLUTEN-FREE OPTION | DAIRY-FREE OPTION | EGG FREE
SERVES 4, OR 6 WITH SIDES

1 × 1.4 kg (3 lb 2 oz) whole chicken
generous pinch of sea salt and
  freshly ground black pepper
3–4 thyme sprigs, leaves picked
  (lemon thyme is a lovely option)
1 tablespoon ghee, duck fat or extra
  virgin olive oil
6–8 young, very small bulb spring
  onions (scallions), or shallots
4–6 green garlic cloves
2–3 baby fennel bulbs
375 ml (13 fl oz/1½ cups) apple cider
375 ml (13 fl oz/1½ cups)
  chicken stock (page 42)
tamari (or wheat-free tamari for a
  gluten-free option) and apple juice
  concentrate, if necessary
1 teaspoon kudzu (kuzu) or
  cornstarch (cornflour)

If you're looking for a gorgeous meal for family and friends to sit down to, look no further. When served with sides such as freshly dug potatoes and peas or asparagus, it proves that you don't need a lot of expensive chicken to make a meal. If you prefer, serve it with a salad; the Cabbage and Fennel Salad on page 137 would be perfect.

braised spring chicken with cider, fennel and young garlic

Using a pair of kitchen shears, cut the chicken into 8 portions (thighs, legs, breast and wings). (If you'd prefer, leave the breasts still on the bone.) Set the carcass and neck aside for stock.

Combine the salt, pepper and thyme leaves on a plate or small baking tray. Press the skin side of the chicken pieces into the salt and herb mix, ensuring all of the mix is used.

Heat the ghee or oil in a large heavy-based flameproof casserole dish (an enamel-coated cast-iron pan is ideal) over medium heat. For the best results, the fat in the dish should be hot but not at any time smoking. When the fat is hot, add the chicken pieces, skin-side down – they should gently sizzle when they hit the fat. Leave the chicken to brown for 10 minutes (resisting the urge to check it and thus releasing moisture), turning the legs once, if required, to brown the chicken evenly.

Meanwhile, top and tail the bulb spring onions – they should not need peeling, but if using shallots, they will. Remove any tough stem or outer skin from the garlic and discard, then coarsely chop any soft stem. Trim away the base and tops of the fennel bulbs so the stems are even to the top of the bulb, reserving any green fronds. Cut the bulbs in half lengthways, then cut into 2 cm (¾ in) thick slices, from the top right through the core at the base.

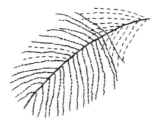

Coarsely chop some of the green fennel fronds (about a small handful's worth) and set aside.

Preheat the oven to 160°C (315°F).

As the chicken pieces become golden, remove them from the dish and set aside on a plate. Add the onions to the pan, and cook, turning occasionally for 10 minutes or until caramelised. Add the fennel and green garlic. Reduce the heat to low–medium and cook for a further 10 minutes or until the onions are lightly caramelised. Add the cider and stock, mixing well to lift all the juicy brown bits from the base of the dish. Add the fennel fronds and chicken pieces along with any juices from the plate. Gently stir through, cover with a lid or foil and bake for 30–40 minutes, or until the chicken is cooked through.

When ready, remove the chicken from the dish and set aside on a clean plate. Place the dish on the stovetop over medium–high heat and simmer until reduced by one-third. Reduce the heat to very low, then taste and assess the flavour. If it is too sweet, add a drop or 2 of tamari. If it is not sweet enough, add a drop or 2 of apple juice concentrate. When you are happy with the flavour, combine the kudzu and 1 tablespoon extra stock, or water, in a small bowl to form a smooth paste. Add this to the dish, stirring continuously, and bring to the boil. Immediately turn off the heat, and return the chicken to the dish, tossing it through the delicious gravy.

KITCHEN NOTES

● It is the sweetness of the young white onions that contributes to the success of this dish. If you can't find them, use large shallots instead.

● When balancing this dish with apple juice concentrate, how much you need will depend on the sweetness of the apple cider used.

● This is a dish that truly benefits from browning the chicken well. It will take time, so don't be tempted to rush.

DIETARY INFO GLUTEN FREE | EGG FREE
SERVES 3–4 GENEROUSLY
YOU WILL NEED TO BEGIN THIS RECIPE THE DAY BEFORE

375 ml (13 fl oz/1½ cups) cultured
  buttermilk (page 50)
2 good-size rosemary sprigs,
  leaves picked
5–6 lemon thyme sprigs, leaves
  picked
3–4 garlic cloves, peeled
zest of 1 lemon, peeled in wide strips
1 teaspoon salt
generous grind of black pepper
1 × 1.6–2 kg (3 lb 8 oz–4 lb 8 oz)
  whole chicken
extra virgin olive oil or ghee,
  for drizzling

*This is one of the most delicious and easiest ways to eat chicken –
especially an heirloom breed that may be a little tougher. The
buttermilk marinade tenderises the meat and infuses it with flavour.
I dare say, it's also very easy to make.*

roast buttermilk chicken

The day before, place the buttermilk, rosemary and thyme leaves
in a bowl, reserving the herb stems. Smash the garlic with the back
of a knife and add them to the bowl. Remove any white pith from
the lemon zest and slice into 5 mm (¼ in) lengths. Add these to
the buttermilk with the salt and pepper, and stir to combine.

Pat the chicken dry using paper towel. Use kitchen shears to
cut off the chicken neck, then down both sides of the backbone.
Reserve the neck and backbone for stock. Choose a container
with a lid that will fit the chicken lying flat and pour in the
buttermilk mixture. Lay the chicken, breast-side down, in the
container and add the herb stems. Cover with a lid and refrigerate
for 8–12 hours. Turn the chicken over so it is now sitting on its
back and marinate for another 8–12 hours. This can be marinated
up to 2 days in advance.

The next day, or when ready to cook, preheat the oven to 180°C
(350°F). Put the chicken, breast side up, into a large ovenproof
dish that will fit it lying flat, allowing a little room around it. Press
down on the chicken a little to flatten it. Pour over the buttermilk
mixture, arrange most of the herb stems underneath and the herbs
and lemon zest on top. Drizzle with olive oil or ghee, then roast
for 1–1¼ hours or until the chicken is golden and cooked through,
basting with the juices every 15 minutes. It is natural for the
buttermilk to curdle a little into a fairly solid milky bit, so don't
stress if that is what you see. You can serve this as is, or if desired,
place the dish over a flame and reduce the liquid a little.

KITCHEN NOTE
I prefer smaller chickens as they have
a stunning flavour, and encourage
making two at the same time, giving
you leftovers.

DIETARY INFO DAIRY-FREE OPTION | EGG FREE
SERVES 6-8

1 × 1.5–1.6 kg (3 lb 5 oz–3 lb 8 oz) whole chicken

35 g (1¼ oz/¼ cup) white unbleached spelt flour

sea salt and freshly ground black pepper, to taste

1 teaspoon thyme leaves

2 tablespoons ghee or chicken fat drippings

2 tablespoons extra virgin olive oil

1 leek, cut into 5 mm (¼ in) slices, rinsed (reserve the green tops for the stock)

2 carrots (about 180 g/6½ oz), scrubbed and cut into 1 cm (½ in) pieces

2 celery stalks (about 150 g/5½ oz), cut into 1 cm (½ in) slices

2 garlic cloves, finely chopped

5 good-size sage leaves, or more to equal

½ teaspoon dried thyme

2 bay leaves

1 litre (35 fl oz/4 cups) chicken or duck stock (page 42)

handful of parsley, roughly chopped, to serve

DUMPLINGS

260 g (9¼ oz/1¾ cups) white unbleached spelt flour

2 teaspoons baking powder

sea salt and freshly ground black pepper, to taste

2 tablespoons chopped fresh herbs such as sage, chives, rosemary, basil and oregano

100 g (3½ oz) cold unsalted butter, diced

250 ml (9 fl oz/1 cup) Cultured Buttermilk (page 50)

202

My take on the Southern classic, chicken and dumplings, this is a dish that is not difficult to make, and also provides a hearty, comforting and fabulous meal in the cooler weather. This is best served with greens such as peas, brussels sprouts, beans or broccoli. In late summer, corn makes a delicious addition, but can also sweeten the end result, so it may need a little balancing with tamari.

chicken with buttermilk herb dumplings

Using a pair of kitchen shears, cut the chicken into 8 portions (thighs, legs, breasts and wings). If preferred, cut the breasts still on the bone. Set the carcass and neck aside for stock.

Combine the flour, salt, pepper and thyme leaves on a plate or small baking tray.

Heat the ghee and olive oil in a large, cast-iron dish or ovenproof stainless steel frying pan over medium–high heat. Press the skin side of the chicken pieces into the salt and herb mix, ensuring all the mix is used. When the fat in the dish is hot but not smoking, add the chicken pieces, skin side down; they should gently sizzle when they hit the fat. Leave the chicken to brown for 10 minutes (resisting the urge to disturb or check it), turning the legs once if required so all the skin has as much opportunity to brown as possible. As the process continues, fat from the skin should render and mingle with the oil. When the chicken is golden, remove to a plate and set aside.

Add the leek, carrots, celery, garlic, herbs and salt and pepper to the dish, and cook over medium heat, stirring occasionally for 10 minutes or until the vegetables are lightly caramelised. Return the chicken to the dish and add the stock. Cover and cook over very low heat for 40–45 minutes, until the chicken is tender. Take care that it simmers very gently to avoid overcooking the chicken.

Skim off 1 tablespoon of fat at this point and store for another use.

Transfer the chicken to a plate or bowl. When cool enough to handle, shred the meat (and the lovely golden skin) from the bone, and discard the bones (keeping them for stock if desired). If I'm making this for adults, I simply add the whole wings back – they're lovely to chew on – but for children I would shred the wing. Add the shredded meat and skin to the vegetables, stir through, then taste and add more herbs and salt and pepper if desired. Set aside while you make the dumplings.

Preheat the oven to 190°C (375°F).

If making dairy-free dumplings, add the vinegar to the almond milk (see Kitchen Notes) and set aside.

For the dumplings, place the flour, baking powder, salt, pepper and herbs into a food processor and pulse to distribute the ingredients. Add the chilled butter (or duck fat for dairy free) and pulse 1–4 times, or just until the fat is broken up into very small pieces, taking care not to overwork it to fine crumbs. Turn into a bowl and add the buttermilk (or vinegared milk, if using), then use a spoon to bring the dough together.

Alternatively, make the dumplings by hand. Using your fingers or a pastry cutter, cut the fat into the flour until the mixture resembles coarse breadcrumbs – some bits should be the size of a pea. Add the buttermilk (or vinegared milk, if using) and use a spoon to bring the dough together.

Drop tablespoonsful of the dough on top of the chicken and vegetables in the dish. You should get about 16 dumplings. Bake in the oven for 12–15 minutes, or until the dumplings are just cooked. If you have the option of a grill (broiler) in your oven, just spoon some of the juices over the dumplings and grill for 5 minutes or until lightly golden. Sprinkle with a little chopped parsley to serve.

PHOTO ON PAGE 204

KITCHEN NOTES

● Chicken thrift: If you'd prefer to make a smaller dish, you could happily use a smaller chicken or omit using the breasts. Reduce the vegetables, seasonings and stock by a quarter, choose a smaller dish and halve the dumpling recipe.

● This is best cooked in a heavy enamel-coated cast-iron dish. Choose one that is wide enough to fit the chicken snugly and just deep enough to hold the chicken and juices with enough room for the dumplings. If you don't have a cast-iron dish, a good-size ovenproof frying pan will be fine.

● For dairy-free buttermilk dumplings, replace the butter with 110 g (3¾ oz) chilled duck fat and replace the buttermilk with 250 ml (9 fl oz/1 cup) almond milk and 2 teaspoons apple cider vinegar.

CHICKEN WITH BUTTERMILK
HERB DUMPLINGS

heartier vegetarian, meat and fish

DIETARY INFO GLUTEN-FREE OPTION | DAIRY FREE | EGG FREE
SERVES 4–6
YOU WILL NEED TO BEGIN THIS RECIPE THE DAY BEFORE

8 very small red onions, halved
(or if larger, cut into rough
1.5–2 cm (⅝–¾ in) chunks

2 star anise

8 plums (see Kitchen Note), halved
and stones removed

80 ml (2½ fl oz/⅓ cup) tamari
(or wheat-free tamari for a
gluten-free option)

25 g (1 oz) piece of fresh ginger,
peeled and finely chopped
or grated

5 teaspoons maple syrup, or
rapadura sugar or raw sugar

3 bay leaves

1 × 1.8–2 kg (4 lb–4 lb 8 oz)
whole duck

sea salt

STUFFING

200 g (7 oz/1 cup) red quinoa

1 teaspoon whey or choice of acid or
dairy-free option (page 59)

85 g (3 oz /½ cup) raisins (I like
muscat raisins)

125 ml (4 fl oz/½ cup) duck or
chicken stock (page 42)

It was Whole and Natural Foods pioneer Holly Davis who introduced to me the idea of cooking a whole duck stuffed with a grain such as quinoa, and held my hand through my journey of discovery in cooking this bird. I adore duck – especially any sweet and sour or plum version – but sadly, it doesn't seem to be made with real ingredients anywhere I can find. This is my rendition, where two favourites are rolled into one.

sweet and sour duck

The night before, prepare the stuffing. Place the quinoa and whey in a bowl with enough water to cover the grain well, and set aside. Place the raisins and the stock in a separate bowl and allow to soak overnight in the fridge.

The next day, preheat the oven to 190°C (375°F). Strain the quinoa, then place in a bowl with the raisins and stock. Stir in a pinch of sea salt.

Place the onions, star anise, plums, tamari, ginger, maple syrup and bay leaves in a bowl and combine well.

Rinse the duck and pat dry with paper towel. Sprinkle a little salt into the cavity and onto the bird. Stuff the quinoa into the cavity, ensuring as much liquid as possible gets in there too. Use a skewer or toothpick to seal the main cavity. Seal the neck opening if the neck has been removed. (This will ensure that the heat is contained inside the bird to cook the quinoa.) Brush away any quinoa on the surface of the duck and transfer the duck to a roasting tin. Arrange the onions and plums around the duck and pour the liquid over the top.

Roast in the oven for 30 minutes, then reduce the temperature to 180°C (350°F). Baste the bird with the juices and cook for a further 1–1½ hours, or until the onions and plums are nicely caramelised and the duck and quinoa are cooked, basting from time to time. Remove the duck to carve, and place a folded tea towel (dish towel) under the reserved roasting tin with the sauce so it is on an angle, sending all the sauce to one corner; this will enable you to skim away most of the fat (to store for another use) quite easily with a spoon. There will most likely be around ½ cup of fat. Roughly mash the plums into the juices if desired.

If the onions and plums are well cooked and caramelised, before the duck is cooked, remove the roasting tin from the oven and transfer the duck from the tin into a heavy-based ovenproof frying pan. Set aside the roasting tin with the sauce in it and place the duck in the pan back into the oven to finish cooking. During this time, more fat will render from the duck and the skin should be golden. Remove from the oven and check that the quinoa is cooked. If not, pop it back in the oven for a few more minutes.

To serve, remove the stuffing from the duck cavity and place in a small bowl. Cut the duck into portions and return to the roasting tin, or lay on a serving platter and pour the sweet and sour sauce over the duck. Serve the quinoa stuffing separately for guests to help themselves.

Variation using duck leg quarters (without stuffing)
*Substitute the whole duck for 4 duck leg quarters

Preheat the oven to 190°C (375°F). Choose a shallow cast-iron or stainless steel frying pan that will fit the duck pieces snugly, but without crowding. Preheat the frying pan over medium heat until very hot (there is no need to add any fat to the pan), then add the duck pieces, skin side down –they should sizzle immediately. Using a spatula, press down on the duck for a few seconds so that as much fat touches the hot surface as possible. Leave to cook for 10 minutes, until the edges of the skin are very golden. A lot of fat will render at this stage and you may prefer to pour it off from time to time to stop it spitting. If a piece of duck needs turning, avoid doing so until it releases easily from the pan (it can take some time, about 10 minutes, for the skin to become golden and release). Put the duck pieces in a roasting tin, or if you are using the frying pan, pour off all of the fat and return the pieces back into the pan.

Combine the onions, star anise, plums, tamari, ginger, maple syrup and bay leaves in a bowl and combine well. Scatter the onions and plums, cut side up, around the duck, then pour the liquid over the top. Bake for 10 minutes, then check to ensure the sauce is not burning. Reduce the oven temperature to 180°C (350°F) and cook for another 10–15 minutes or until the duck is just cooked. Remove from the oven. Roughly mash the plum into the juices, then pour over the duck and serve.

PHOTO ON PAGE 205

KITCHEN NOTES
- Choose fragrant tasting, dark coloured plums such as Black Amber, Satsuma or Santa Rosa.
- To cook the quinoa stuffing through, it needs at least 1½ hours to cook as a minimum. If your bird is around the 1.4–1.6 kg (3 lb 2 oz–3 lb 8 oz) weight range, it can be overcooked by the time the stuffing is cooked. For best results, stick to the weight guideline for the duck in this recipe.
- You could bypass the stuffing completely and cut your bird into pieces or buy duck leg quarters to save time (see left).
- The duck should come with the glands on the back of the parsons nose removed – if not, ensure you cut these out and remove any giblets left in the cavity of the duck. If the neck is still attached, use kitchen shears to cut this off and reserve for stock or Duck Neck and Lentils (page 208).

DIETARY INFO GLUTEN FREE | DAIRY FREE | EGG FREE
SERVES 4–6 GENEROUSLY
YOU WILL NEED TO BEGIN THIS RECIPE THE DAY BEFORE

100 g (3½ oz/½ cup) green lentils
2 teaspoons whey or choice of acid
　or dairy-free option (page 59)
2 duck necks (about 420 g/15 oz)
1 medium brown onion, finely diced
1 medium carrot, finely diced
1–2 celery stalks, finely diced
2 bay leaves
6 sage leaves, roughly sliced
3 thyme sprigs
1 small apple, peeled, cored and cut
　into 5 mm (¼ in) dice, optional
sea salt and freshly ground black
　pepper

A wonderful example of thrift, duck necks provide just enough meat and are the most perfect of partners for lentils. This is a rich dish for the cold weather. Serve with cabbage or brussels sprouts.

duck neck and green lentils

The day before, place the lentils in a bowl with enough water to cover by at least 2 cm (¾ in). Stir in the whey, then stand overnight at room temperature.

The next day, heat a heavy-based frying pan (I use a shallow 30 cm/12 in cast-iron pan with a lid) over medium–high heat. Add the duck necks and cook for 15–20 minutes, turning occasionally, until golden all over. It will take longer than you think to render a good amount of fat (as the fat releases, you may want to reduce the heat a little so it doesn't spit too much). When golden, stir in the vegetables, herbs and apple, a pinch of salt and generous grind of pepper. Cook, stirring occasionally, for 15–20 minutes.

Drain the lentils and add them to the pan with 750 ml (26 fl oz/ 3 cups) water. Bring to a simmer, cover and cook at a gentle simmer for 2–2½ hours or until the meat is falling from the bone. Ensure that no steam is escaping from under the lid during this time.

When ready, remove the meat from the bone, discarding the skin, bone and any sinew. If the stew is too liquid, remove the lid and boil over high heat for 2–3 minutes, until it has reached a sauce consistency. Return the meat to the stew. Taste and season as required, and serve.

KITCHEN NOTE
This is one recipe where you will get an excellent, nourishing dish by using water instead of stock as the dish makes its own stock while it cooks. But if you prefer, you can always use duck, chicken or vegetable stock instead.

800 g–1 kg (1 lb 12 oz/2 lb 4 oz)
  lamb riblets
60 ml (2 fl oz/¼ cup) dry white wine
3 bay leaves

LAMB RUB
½ teaspoon ground coriander
½ teaspoon ground cumin
½ teaspoon sea salt
½ teaspoon freshly ground black
  pepper
½ teaspoon ground cinnamon
3 garlic cloves, crushed

**SWEET SULTANA AND CHILLI
BARBECUE SAUCE**
60 ml (2 fl oz/¼ cup) Sweet Sultana
  and Chilli Sauce (page 77)
60 g (2¼ fl oz/¼ cup) tomato paste
  (concentrated puree)
1 tablespoon balsamic vinegar
½ teaspoon ground cumin
½ teaspoon ground cinnamon
2 teaspoons wholegrain mustard

I love ribs. I'm not a pork girl, but lamb I love. The breast is an incredibly cheap cut of meat, and in most cases it will come already cut into riblets. If you have access to a whole rib, then all the better as this will give a moister end result. The whole rib of lamb may well have a flap of skin attached so you will need to remove this.

lamb ribs with sweet sultana and chilli barbecue sauce

Preheat the oven to 150°C (300°F).

To make the lamb rub, combine all the ingredients in a small bowl, then rub all over the ribs.

Place the ribs in a roasting tin that will fit them snugly. Add enough water to come three-quarters of the way up the side of the tin. Pour the wine into the tin and add the bay leaves. Cover with a lid, or with baking paper and foil and bake for 2 hours or until very tender, then remove from the oven.

Meanwhile, to make the sauce, combine all the ingredients in a small bowl and set aside.

When ready to serve, increase the oven temperature to 200°C (400°F). Place a wire rack over a baking tray, and when the ribs are ready, use a pair of tongs to remove them from the cooking liquid. Coat them with the barbecue sauce, then sit them bone side down on the rack. (If you have cooked a whole breast, cut into riblets before coating with the sauce.) Cook for 15–20 minutes, until they are sticky and gorgeous – it's a fine line between the fat becoming deliciously crispy and the meat becoming dry and overcooked so keep an eye on them.

209

DIETARY INFO GLUTEN FREE | DAIRY FREE | EGG FREE
SERVES 6-8
YOU WILL NEED TO BEGIN THIS RECIPE THE DAY BEFORE

100 g (3½ oz/½ cup) dried borlotti
beans, or fresh borlotti beans to
equal (don't soak fresh beans)
2 cm (¾ in) piece kombu
1.5 kg (3 lb 5 oz) lamb shoulder,
hogget or mutton shoulder,
on the bone
3–4 small–medium fennel bulbs,
stems trimmed and bulbs cut
into wedges, fronds chopped
and reserved
5 small red onions, quartered, or
halved if very small
3 bay leaves
3–5 small rosemary sprigs
250 ml (9 fl oz/1 cup) chicken or
lamb stock
2 teaspoons worcestershire sauce

MARINADE
1 teaspoon coriander seeds, toasted
1 teaspoon fennel seeds, toasted
4 garlic cloves, coarsely chopped
2 teaspoons coarsely chopped
rosemary leaves
½ teaspoon sea salt
generous grind of black pepper
2 tablespoons extra virgin olive oil

This is my default Sunday family lunch dish (served late-ish) and it covers many principles that I hold dear: firstly, meat cooked on the bone; secondly, extending the value of expensive and precious meat; thirdly, requiring little work on my part; and finally, embodying a loaves and fishes theme.

lamb shoulder, fennel and borlotti beans

The night before, soak the dried borlotti beans and kombu in enough water to cover by 10cm (4 in). Stand overnight. For the marinade, use a mortar and pestle to coarsely crush the seeds with the garlic, rosemary, salt and pepper. Stir in the olive oil. Make 2–3 deep incisions into the lamb and massage the marinade all over and into the cuts. Cover and refrigerate overnight.

The next day, take the meat out of the fridge to come to room temperature 1 hour before cooking. Preheat the oven to 200°C (400°F). Place the lamb in a roasting tin or cast-iron pan and roast for 30 minutes.

Meanwhile, drain the borlotti beans and discard the kombu. When the meat is ready, add the fennel to the tin along with the onions, drained beans, bay leaves, rosemary sprigs and stock (if using fresh borlotti beans, simply add). Reduce the oven temperature to 160°C (315°F), cover with foil and bake for 3–5 hours, until the lamb is exceptionally tender and can be pulled apart with a fork.

Transfer the meat to a plate, cover and set aside while you make the gravy. Place the roasting tin or pan directly on the stovetop, over medium heat, and simmer for 2–5 minutes, until you have a sauce consistency, being careful to not mash the beans or vegetables too much. Taste and add the worcestershire sauce and season as needed. Carve the meat from the bone and return to the tin along with any juices. Gently stir through, sprinkle with the chopped reserved fennel fronds and serve.

KITCHEN NOTES
● I prefer making this with hogget or mutton, however both will take longer to cook. Mutton can take up to 1–1½ hours extra.
● If making this dish without the borlotti beans, omit the stock.

DIETARY INFO GLUTEN-FREE OPTION | DAIRY FREE
MAKES 6

30 g (1 oz) two-day-old sourdough
    bread (or gluten-free bread),
    crusts removed
1 teaspoon finely chopped rosemary
generous grind of black pepper
generous pinch of sea salt
1 egg
6 lamb or hogget cutlets, fat
    trimmed (about 120 g/4¼ oz
    trimmed weight)
extra virgin olive oil, for frying, or
    rendered lamb fat if available
Rosemary and Raspberry Jelly
    (page 78), to serve

*Yes, lamb cutlets are an expensive cut of meat, but as 'an every
now and then' treat, they make for a very quick and easy meal.
The rosemary and raspberry jelly not only makes them easier to
digest, but also super delicious. Once crumbed, these will freeze
easily for another day.*

crumbed cutlets with rosemary and raspberry jelly

Place the bread, rosemary, pepper and salt in a food processor
and process until fine breadcrumbs form, then transfer to a plate.
Place the egg in a shallow bowl and lightly beat with a fork.

To flatten out the meat on the cutlets, place the cutlets on a
chopping board and use a potato masher to firmly press down
on them, until the meat is about 1 cm (½ in) thick. Working
with one at a time, hold a cutlet by the bone, dip in the beaten
egg, then coat in the crumb mix, ensuring both sides are covered.
Place the crumbed cutlet on a clean plate and repeat with the
remaining cutlets.

Pour enough olive oil or lamb fat into a frying pan large enough
to comfortably fit all of the cutlets, so it covers the base by about
5 mm (¼ in). Place the pan over medium–high heat and when the
fat is hot, but not at all smoking, add the cutlets – you should hear
a good sizzle when the cutlets are added but the fat shouldn't spit.
Cook for 3 minutes on each side or until golden. Drain on paper
towel and serve with a dollop of the rosemary and raspberry jelly.

KITCHEN NOTE
If your cutlets come with a strip of
fat along the edge, just cut that off
and use it to render for fat.

1 tablespoon duck fat, plus extra
    for frying

1–2 shallots (about 80 g/2¾ oz),
    finely chopped

4–5 good-size sage leaves, coarsely
    chopped

2–3 teaspoons thyme leaves

1 tablespoon 12-month-old Pedro
    Ximénez sherry

120 g (4¼ oz) chicken livers

2 boneless, skinless chicken
    thighs (about 300 g/10½ oz),
    coarsely chopped (see Kitchen
    Note)

freshly ground mix of black, red and
    white pepper, and sea salt to taste

*These patties are so quick to make, and they are superbly moist and
delicious. You can easily use less liver in the recipe if you prefer.
Don't be afraid to use a lot of herbs and pepper – the chicken liver
can take quite a bit of both.*

chicken, sage and liver patties

Place 1 tablespoon duck fat in a small frying pan over medium heat.
Add the shallots, sage and thyme and cook gently, stirring often for
10 minutes or until soft and lightly golden. Stir in the sherry and
cook for a further 1 minute or until reduced. Remove from the heat.

Clean the chicken livers by rinsing them under cold water and
using a sharp knife to remove any veins, bile ducts and sinew.
Pat dry with paper towel and cut into very small pieces.

Place the chopped chicken thighs in a food processor and pulse
until finely chopped but not minced – you are looking for a chunky
texture. Alternatively, cut the chicken into very small pieces by
hand. Place the chicken into a bowl, then stir in the livers and
the shallot mixture. Generously season. To test the mixture, add
enough extra duck fat to a small frying pan to come 2–3 mm
(1/16–1/8 in) up the side of the pan and place over medium–high
heat. When the fat is hot, but not at all smoking, shape a little of
the mixture into a patty and cook for 2–3 minutes, until golden
and cooked. Drain on paper towel, then taste and add more salt,
pepper or herbs to the mixture as required.

Shape the remaining mixture into patties, about 1 tablespoon each
and about 1 cm (½ in) thick. Cook for about 2–3 minutes on each
side, allowing the patty to brown before turning over, or until just
cooked in the centre – the chicken should be opaque and the liver
still a little pink. Drain on paper towel and serve.

KITCHEN NOTE

I prefer buying chicken thighs on the
bone because they're cheaper. The
bones can be used for stock, and to avoid
waste, I put the chicken skin and its fat
in a small frying pan and cook it up to
render some of the fat. Crisp chicken
skin is also delicious to eat, and you
can crumble some of it into the patty
mixture for extra flavour if you like.

213

SLOW DOWN AND SAVOUR THE SEASONS

SWEETNESS

DIETARY INFO VEGETARIAN | WHEAT FREE
SERVES 8-12

4 large peaches (about 650 g/
    1 lb 7 oz)
1–1½ teaspoons golden caster
    (superfine) sugar or maple syrup
750 ml (26 fl oz/3 cups) thickened
    (whipping) cream
1 teaspoon natural vanilla extract

SHORTCAKE BASE
260 g (9¼ oz/2 cups) white
    spelt flour
2 teaspoons baking powder
1½ tablespoons rapadura sugar
    or raw sugar
½ teaspoon bicarbonate of soda
    (baking soda)
1 egg
110 g (3¾ oz) unsalted butter,
    melted and cooled
1 teaspoon apple cider vinegar
125 ml (4 fl oz/½ cup) Cultured
    Buttermilk (page 50)
60 ml (2 fl oz/¼ cup) milk
1 teaspoon natural vanilla extract

KITCHEN NOTE
This recipe can be adapted to make a savoury scone. For a tomato, feta and basil scone, simply reduce the sugar in the base to 2 teaspoons and add ¼ cup chopped herbs and 80 g (2¾ oz) grated cheddar cheese. Before baking, top with 250 g (9 oz) cherry tomatoes, 50 g (1¾ oz/½ cup) grated cheddar cheese and 20 g (¾ oz) crumbled feta.

Shortcakes have just a little more richness than a scone, thanks to an egg and a bit more butter, and they make a wonderful base for fresh fruit. I find the traditional shortcake, with the top and bottom, too much in the way of carbohydrate. I prefer more fruit and cream, with just a little of the shortcake as a base – plus it's super easy to make.

peach shortcake

Preheat the oven to 200°C (400°F) and line a baking tray with baking paper.

To make the shortcake base, place the flour, baking powder and sugar in a medium-size bowl. Sift in the bicarbonate of soda and whisk through to evenly distribute the ingredients.

In another bowl, whisk the egg, butter, vinegar, buttermilk, milk and vanilla together until well combined. Add this to the flour mixture and use a large spoon or spatula to bring it together – do not overmix. Turn onto the lined tray and shape into a rectangle about 25 × 22 cm (10 × 8½ in). Bake for 15–20 minutes or until golden and cooked. Remove from the oven and stand until barely warm.

As soon as the shortcake goes in the oven, peel the peaches and cut them into thick slices, discarding the skin and stones. Place in a bowl with the sugar and stand for 30 minutes.

Place the cream and vanilla in a large mixing bowl and whisk until the cream is firm enough to hold its shape. Take care not to overbeat the cream, but you don't want it to run off the shortcake.

When the shortcake has cooled, spread the cream over the top and arrange the peaches attractively on top, then drizzle over their juices.

1 kg (2 lb 4 oz) ripe plums, halved, stones removed, cut into quarters if very large

40 g (1½ oz/¼ cup) light muscovado sugar, plus 1 teaspoon extra, for sprinkling

1 teaspoon natural vanilla extract

½ teaspoon ground cinnamon

½ teaspoon cornstarch (cornflour), or kudzu (kuzu)

COBBLER TOPPING

130 g (4½ oz/1 cup) white spelt flour

1 teaspoon baking powder

3 teaspoons rapadura sugar or raw sugar

¼ teaspoon bicarbonate of soda (baking soda)

1 egg

55 g (2 oz) unsalted butter, melted and cooled

1 teaspoon natural vanilla extract

90 ml (3 fl oz) Cultured Buttermilk (page 50)

A cobbler is simply fruit with a shortcake topping dolloped on in a cobbler fashion, but when done well it can be one of the most delicious desserts. In essence, it's really another way of having a scone (shortcake) with jam (cooked, sweetened fruit). This can be made with other fruits, especially moist and juicy fruits such as berries.

plum cobbler

Place the plums, sugar, vanilla and cinnamon in a bowl, toss to combine and stand for 30 minutes.

Preheat the oven to 180°C (350°F). Place the plums in an ovenproof dish (I use a 21 cm/8¼ in round × 4.5 cm/1¾ in deep dish), leaving the juices behind in the bowl. Add the cornstarch to the juices and stir until smooth, then add the juice mixture to the plums. Bake for 20–25 minutes, until the plums look just about cooked and have released all their juices.

Meanwhile, to make the cobbler topping, place the flour, baking powder and sugar in a mixing bowl. Sift in the bicarbonate of soda and whisk through to evenly distribute the ingredients. In another bowl, mix the remaining ingredients together well, ensuring the egg is well beaten. Add this wet mix to the dry ingredients and use a large spoon or spatula to bring it together – do not overmix. Dollop spoonfuls (about the size of a walnut) of the mixture onto the plums and into the juices too. Sprinkle with the extra sugar and bake for 15–20 minutes, until the cobbler topping is lightly golden.

KITCHEN NOTE

The success of a cobbler is all in the cooking. Firstly, choose a dish that allows the best transmission of heat (enamel-coated or cast-iron are both good); a wide and shallow dish is best. Secondly, keep an eye on the timing – the juices should have reduced and caramelised around the edges of the dish when it's ready.

DIETARY INFO GLUTEN FREE | DAIRY FREE | VEGAN | EGG FREE
SERVES 4

4–5 freestone peaches (about
750 g/1 lb 10 oz)

CRUMBLE

40 g (1½ oz/¼ cup) macadamia nuts,
roughly chopped
35 g (1¼ oz/½ cup) shredded
coconut
1½ tablespoons quinoa flakes
(rolled quinoa)
1½ tablespoons amaranth flakes
(rolled amaranth)
2 tablespoons coconut oil (if firm,
warm it a little to melt)
1 teaspoon natural vanilla extract
1½–2 tablespoons maple syrup

A wonderful light version of a crumble that is delicious served on a hot summer's day with Mum's Strawberry Ice Cream (opposite) or the Vanilla Buttermilk Ice Cream on page 222.

peach, macadamia and coconut crumble

Preheat the oven to 190°C (375°F).

To make the crumble, place the nuts, coconut, quinoa and amaranth in a mixing bowl. Add the coconut oil, vanilla and maple syrup and stir to combine well. Taste and add more maple syrup if desired, but bear in mind the sweetness of the peaches.

Choose a heavy, shallow ovenproof dish to cook the peaches in – a cast-iron dish is perfect. Peel the peaches over your dish to catch any juices, reserving the skins, then cut into thick slices, removing the stones as you go. Pick up the skins and stones and squeeze any juice into the dish, before discarding. Sprinkle the crumble topping over the peaches and bake for 30–35 minutes, until the crumble is golden and the juices are bubbling around the edges of the dish.

PHOTO ON PAGES 220-221

1½ teaspoons powdered gelatine

60 ml (2 fl oz/¼ cup) hot water

600 g (1 lb 5 oz) strawberries, rinsed and hulled

375 ml (13 fl oz/1½ cups) thin (pouring) cream (or coconut cream for a dairy-free version)

110–165 g (3¾–5¾ oz/½–¾ cup) golden caster (superfine) sugar

Come high summer, Mum would make ice creams – vanilla, peach and strawberry – and it was the highlight of many a family gathering. I love this recipe for its honest flavour. It is, indeed, strawberry – not kind of, or similar to, but actually strawberry – just as it should be. The recipe for this originally comes from Old Fashioned Homemade Ice Cream, *by Ann Creber (Decalon Books, 1979). This is my slightly tweaked version.*

Mum's strawberry ice cream

Dissolve the gelatine in the hot water, stirring well until smooth, then set aside to cool.

Place the strawberries in a blender or food processor and process until smooth. Strain the strawberry puree through a fine sieve into a bowl, pressing well to extract as much liquid as possible. Discard the seeds. You should have about 375 ml (13 fl oz/1½ cups) puree. Add the cooled gelatine, cream and 110 g (3¾ oz/ ½ cup) sugar and combine well. Taste and add more sugar as needed (see Kitchen Notes). Churn the mixture in an ice-cream machine according to the manufacturer's instructions, then freeze overnight or until firm.

PHOTO ON PAGE 220

KITCHEN NOTES

● Taste the mixture once made and adjust the sweetness to your taste. Bear in mind that the ice cream will lose some of its sweetness once frozen.

● For a dairy-free alternative use good-quality coconut cream and, if necessary, remove the thin layer of oil. I'm partial to the Ayam brand of coconut cream.

PEACH, MACADAMIA AND
COCONUT CRUMBLE AND MUM'S
STRAWBERRY ICE CREAM

strawberry amasake ice cream

DIETARY INFO GLUTEN FREE | DAIRY FREE | VEGAN
MAKES 600 ML (21 FL OZ)
YOU WILL NEED TO BEGIN THIS RECIPE THE DAY BEFORE

Taste for sweetness as you add the sugar and the cordial and bear in mind that you may like to make the ice cream slightly sweeter than you would like – once frozen, the ice cream becomes less sweet.

250 g (9 oz/1 cup) amasake
500 g (1 lb 2 oz/3⅓ cups) strawberries, washed and hulled
2–4 tablespoons golden caster (superfine) sugar
   or maple syrup
2 tablespoons raspberry cordial (I like Belvoir cordials)

Place the amasake into a shallow dish and put into the freezer for 3 hours. It won't set solid but will just chill up nicely.

Place the strawberries in a blender or food processor and process until smooth. Strain through a fine sieve into a bowl, pressing on the puree to extract as much liquid as possible. Discard the seeds. Add the chilled amasake, sugar (or maple syrup, if using) and cordial to taste and whisk to combine well. Churn the mixture in an ice-cream machine according to the manufacturer's instructions, then freeze overnight or until firm.

vanilla buttermilk ice cream

DIETARY INFO GLUTEN FREE | VEGETARIAN
EGG FREE
MAKES 1 LITRE (35 FL OZ/4 CUPS)
YOU WILL NEED TO BEGIN THIS RECIPE THE DAY BEFORE

Loosely based on a recipe by David Lebovitz, who is one of my favourite bakers, this buttermilk ice cream is not too rich and is delightfully sharp. The brown rice syrup will colour the buttermilk mixture a little, but you won't even notice it once frozen. It is sublime with the Fig and Bay Syrup (page 98), or indeed any fresh, stewed or frozen fruits and of course, the Peach, Macadamia and Coconut Crumble (page 218).

110 g (3¾ oz/½ cup) golden caster (superfine) sugar
   or 125 ml (4 fl oz/½ cup) maple syrup
60 ml (2 fl oz/¼ cup) brown rice syrup
310 ml (10¾ fl oz/1¼ cups) Cultured Buttermilk (page 50)
375 ml (13 fl oz/1½ cups) thin (pouring) cream
1 vanilla bean

Place the sugar (or maple syrup, if using) and the brown rice syrup in a small saucepan over very low heat until the sugar is dissolved and the rice syrup has loosened. Don't stir it, but rather give the pan a little swirl to combine. Set aside to cool.

Place the buttermilk and cream in a bowl with the cooled syrup. Using the tip of a small sharp knife, cut the vanilla bean in half lengthways, then scrape the seeds out and add them to the milk (see page 104 on how to make vanilla bean sugar). Whisk together well, then refrigerate until chilled. Churn the mixture in an ice-cream machine according to the manufacturer's instructions, then freeze overnight or until firm.

DIETARY INFO GLUTEN FREE | DAIRY FREE | EGG FREE
SERVES 3-4
YOU WILL NEED TO BEGIN THIS RECIPE THE DAY BEFORE

1 kg (2 lb 4 oz) nectarines
1 vanilla bean, halved lengthways
½–1 tablespoon golden caster
   (superfine) sugar, to taste
3 teaspoons powdered gelatine

This recipe is one of those special ones – it will use a lot of nectarines for very little result, but oh my, that result is more than worth it. It's exceptionally luscious and sensual with a gorgeous mouthfeel and perfect for a celebration. This is quite a soft-set jelly so if you'd like it a little firmer, increase the gelatine by a quarter of a teaspoon.

nectarine jelly

Cut the nectarines into quarters and discard the stones. Place in a saucepan with the vanilla bean and 375 ml (13 fl oz/1½ cups) water. Cover and cook over low heat for 30 minutes or until the nectarines are cooked and have released all their juices.

Place a fine sieve over a bowl, making sure that the sieve does not sit too low in the bowl. Pour the cooked nectarines and their liquid into the sieve – do not be tempted to press the nectarines at all – you are looking for lovely clear juices. You should end up with about 500 ml (17 fl oz/2 cups) liquid in the bowl. To release any trapped juices in the nectarines, I very gently put a spoon into the sieve and lift them just a little. You will find that the juice is quite thick – this is because of the pectin in the fruit. Discard the nectarine pulp and vanilla bean (see page 104 on how to make vanilla sugar). Transfer the juice to a small saucepan and sweeten to taste with the sugar. Bring to just below the boil, then remove from the heat and whisk in the gelatine until fully dissolved.

Pour into a container and let cool a little before refrigerating overnight, or until set.

DIETARY INFO VEGETARIAN | WHEAT FREE
SERVES 8-10

130 g (4½ oz/1 cup) white spelt flour
120 g (4¼ oz/1¼ cup) almond meal
1¼ teaspoons baking powder
150 g (5½ oz) unsalted butter, softened
110 g (3¾ oz/½ cup) golden caster (superfine) sugar
3 eggs
2 teaspoons natural vanilla extract
600 g (1 lb 5 oz) apricots (moorpark or royal Blenheim are my favourites, about 15 apricots)
25 g (1 oz/¼ cup) flaked almonds
2 tablespoons honey
rosemary leaves, optional, to serve

Along with the Strawberry Celebration Cake on page 242, this is my quintessential summer cake. Here, baking fruit in a buttery nut batter results in a delicious end result. Apricot is a wonderful match with honey, but any fresh stone fruit will do.

apricot, honey and almond cake

Preheat the oven to 200°C (400°F). Lightly grease a 22 cm (8½ in) spring-form cake tin and line the base with baking paper.

Place the flour, almond meal and baking powder in a bowl and whisk through to evenly distribute the ingredients.

Using a stand mixer fitted with the paddle attachment, beat the butter and sugar until light and creamy. Add the eggs, one at a time, beating well after each addition and stopping from time to time to scrape down the side. Add the vanilla with the last egg. When the mixture is pale, thick and creamy, add the flour mixture and beat very slowly on the lowest speed until the flour is just combined.

Spoon the batter into the prepared tin and gently smooth over. Cut the apricots in half and discard the stones. Press the apricot halves into the batter on their sides, leaving them a little above the batter to caramelise during cooking. Combine the flaked almonds and 1 tablespoon honey in a small bowl and scatter over the cake.

Bake for 40–45 minutes, then reduce the oven temperature to 180°C (350°F) and bake for another 20 minutes or until done and the apricots are lovely and caramelised. If the apricots or almonds start to burn, turn down the heat. To test if it is done, insert a small sharp knife or skewer right into the middle of the cake, under the apricots, and if it comes out with a few crumbs attached, it is ready. Remove from the oven, brush with the remaining honey, sprinkle with rosemary leaves, if using, and serve.

DIETARY INFO VEGETARIAN | DAIRY FREE | WHEAT FREE
MAKES 10

LEMON CURD

90 ml (3 fl oz) strained lemon juice
1½ teaspoons agar powder
2½ teaspoons kudzu (kuzu) or
    cornflour (cornstarch)
250 ml (9 fl oz/1 cup) coconut milk
60 ml (2 fl oz/¼ cup) maple syrup
60 ml (2 fl oz/¼ cup) brown
    rice syrup
½ teaspoon natural vanilla extract
2 teaspoons finely grated lemon zest
tiny pinch of ground turmeric

CUPCAKES

195 g (6¾ oz/1½ cups) white
    spelt flour
1 teaspoon baking powder
¾ teaspoon bicarbonate of soda
    (baking soda)
45 g (1½ oz/½ cup) desiccated
    coconut
2 teaspoons apple cider vinegar
2 teaspoons natural vanilla extract
185 ml (6 fl oz/¾ cup) maple syrup
125 ml (4 fl oz/½ cup) coconut milk
60 ml (2 fl oz/¼ cup) rice milk
80 ml (2½ fl oz/⅓ cup)
    macadamia oil

ITALIAN MERINGUE

150 g (5½ oz/⅔ cup) golden caster
    (superfine) sugar
60 ml (2 fl oz/¼ cup) water
3 large egg whites, at room
    temperature

While at first glance, these might look like a lot of work, they really aren't and they are truly delicious. The lemon curd can be made up to four days ahead of time to help things along. Once put together, they are best eaten that day, but will keep for one or two days in an airtight container in a cool place.

lemon meringue cupcakes

To make the lemon curd, place the strained juice and agar in a small saucepan and whisk until smooth and well combined. Stir over very low heat for about 5 minutes, then increase the heat to medium and bring to a gentle boil. The mixture will be very thick at this stage, but will thin out as the agar dissolves. Immediately reduce the heat a little and continue to cook at a very gentle simmer for 5–8 minutes, stirring often to avoid the agar sinking to the bottom and sticking.

Meanwhile, place the kudzu in a bowl with 60 ml (2 fl oz/¼ cup) coconut milk and mix to a smooth slurry. Stir in the remaining coconut milk, the syrups and vanilla extract. Remove the lemon mixture from the heat, then whisk in the coconut mixture. Return to the heat and stir continuously over very low heat, just until the mixture comes to the boil. Remove from the heat and whisk in the lemon zest and turmeric. Transfer the curd to a small bowl, press a piece of baking paper onto the surface to prevent a skin forming, then refrigerate for 1 hour or until set. Store in an airtight container in the fridge for up to 4 days.

To make the cupcakes, preheat the oven to 170°C (325°F). Line a 12-hole muffin tin with 10 paper cases (leave the middle 2 holes empty).

Sift the flour, baking powder and bicarbonate of soda into a bowl. Add the desiccated coconut and whisk through to combine.

Place the remaining ingredients in another bowl and whisk. Add this to the dry ingredients and mix until just combined. Leave to sit for 1–2 minutes – the mix may appear wet but will firm up as it stands. Divide the batter among the paper cases (using about ¼ cup batter per case). Bake for 25–30 minutes or until a skewer inserted into one of the cupcakes comes out clean. Cool in the tin for 15 minutes before transferring to a wire rack to cool completely.

To make the Italian meringue, place the sugar and water in a small saucepan over medium heat and bring to the boil, brushing down any sugar crystals on the side of the pan with a wet pastry brush. Do not stir or the sugar may crystallise. When the sugar has dissolved, increase the heat to a rapid boil and cook until the syrup reaches 121°C (250°F) on a sugar thermometer.

Meanwhile, place the egg whites in the bowl of a stand mixer fitted with a whisk attachment. As the temperature of the syrup approaches 115°C (239°F), whisk the egg whites on medium speed until soft peaks form, taking care not to overbeat.

When the syrup reaches 121°C (250°F), immediately remove it from the heat, and with the motor running slowly, gradually drizzle the syrup into the egg whites. When all the syrup is added, stop whisking, then use a spatula to scrape the side of the bowl. Increase the speed to medium–high and continue whisking for 5 minutes or until the meringue has cooled down completely and is thick, soft and silky. Use immediately.

To put the cupcakes together, using a small paring knife, cut a 3 cm (1¼ in) round piece of cake from the centre of the cooled cupcakes, ensuring you have 6 mm–1 cm (¼–½ in) border of cake (I freeze these middles to use for a trifle later on). Stir the chilled and set lemon curd until smooth, then place 1 tablespoon curd into the cupcake holes, pressing down a little to fill. Spoon the Italian meringue into a piping (icing) bag fitted with a 2.5 cm (1 in) nozzle and pipe the meringue over the curd. Using a kitchen blowtorch on low flame, gently brown the edges of the meringue while being careful that the flame doesn't set fire to the paper case.

PHOTO ON PAGE 228

KITCHEN NOTES

● Lemons are highly acidic, and this will affect the set of the curd. If using Meyer lemons, reduce the amount of sweetness added. This recipe makes more lemon curd than you will need for the cupcakes. Store the leftover curd in an airtight jar in the fridge for up to 1 week.

● For nut-free cupcakes, replace the macadamia oil with 100 g (3½ oz) melted unsalted butter, and omit the rice milk. You can also replace the macadamia oil with 80 ml (2½ fl oz/ ⅓ cup) coconut oil, melted and cooled a little – this version is best eaten while still fresh.

● The Italian meringue is best used as soon as it is made. Once made, it is extremely stable. This meringue will sit atop your cake and not weep, and will still look just as good the next day.

LEMON MERINGUE CUPCAKES

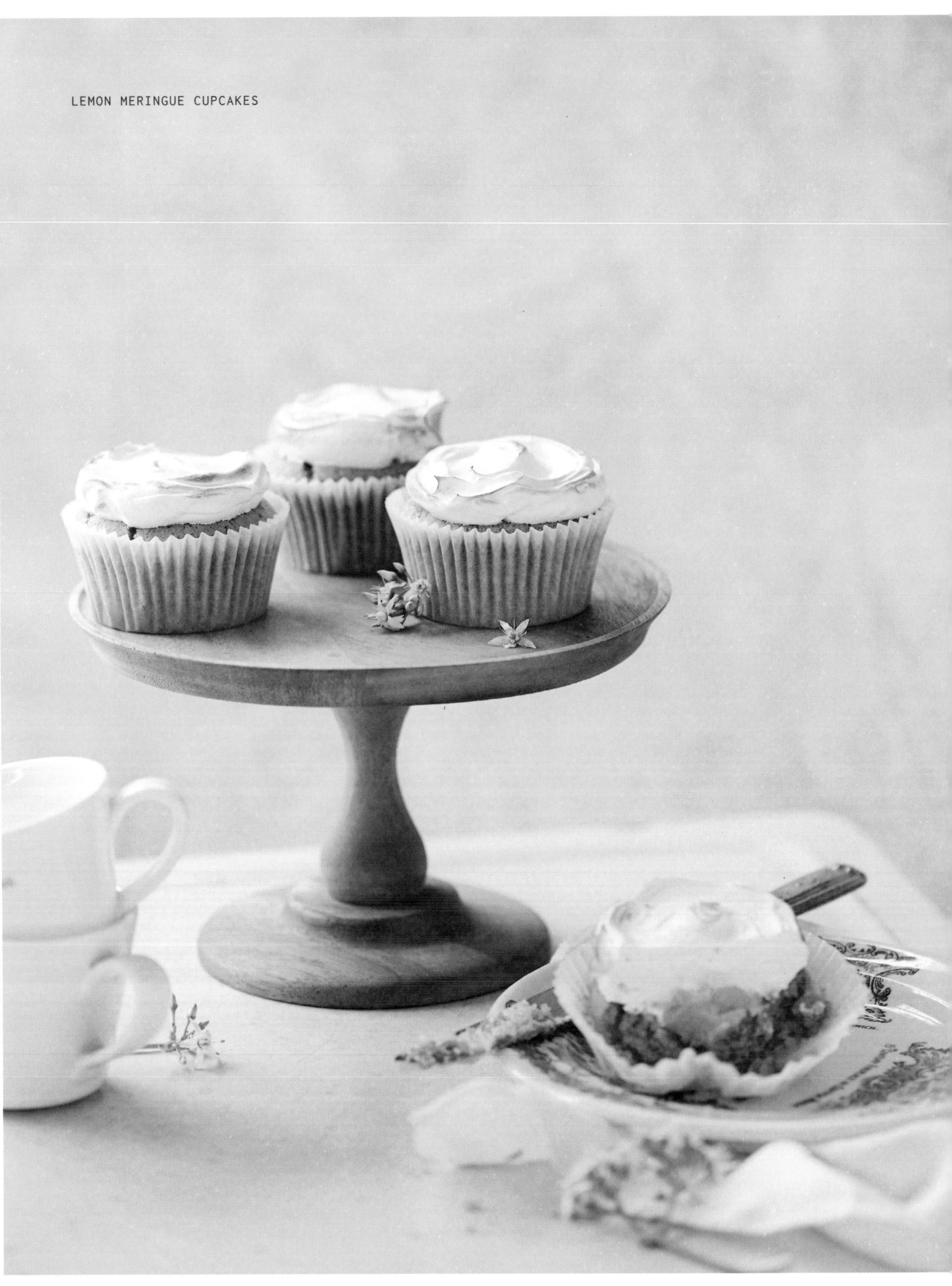

APPLE PICNIC PIE WITH
PASSIONFRUIT ICING

DIETARY INFO WHEAT FREE | VEGETARIAN
SERVES 6–9

1 kg (2 lb 4 oz) apples (see Kitchen
  Notes), peeled, cored and cut into
  quarters, or if very large,
  into eighths
1–2 tablespoons rapadura sugar
  or raw sugar
75 g (2½ oz/½ cup) golden icing
  (confectioners') sugar, sifted
1 teaspoon soft unsalted butter
  (melted is fine)
pulp of 2–3 passionfruit

SHORTCAKE PASTRY
195 g (6¾ oz/1½ cups) white
  spelt flour, plus a little extra
  for dusting
pinch of sea salt
50 g (1¾ oz/½ cup) almond meal
1 teaspoon baking powder
125 g (4½ oz) unsalted butter,
  softened
75 g (2½ oz/½ cup) rapadura sugar
  or raw sugar
1 egg
1 teaspoon natural vanilla extract

230

Mum used to make a version of this pie to take on picnics, and it remains one of my favourites.

apple picnic pie with passionfruit icing

To make the pastry, place the flour, salt, almond meal and the baking powder in a bowl and whisk through to evenly distribute the ingredients.

Using a stand mixer fitted with the paddle attachment, beat the butter and 75 g (2½ oz/½ cup) sugar until light and creamy. Add the egg, then continue beating until soft and creamy. Add the vanilla and, with the motor on low speed, add the flour and beat slowly just until the pastry comes together. Separate the dough into two pieces, one to equal two-thirds of the dough and the other one-third of the dough. Form into rough rectangles, wrap in plastic wrap and refrigerate for 1 hour or until well chilled.

Meanwhile, place the apples in a large frying pan with 1 tablespoon water and 1 tablespoon sugar. Cover and cook over low heat for 10–15 minutes, until the juices have seeped from the fruit and the apples are cooked. At this stage the apple varieties that break down when cooked, will have broken down by now while the others should still be intact. Taste and add extra sugar as desired. Remove from the heat and stand for a few minutes. If you notice any small pools of watery looking liquid, place it back over medium–high heat for a couple of minutes to evaporate the liquid. Set aside to cool.

Preheat the oven to 180°C (350°F). Place a black bottom tray, if available, in the oven to preheat (this will provide a crispier base). Lightly grease your tin (see Kitchen Notes) and line with baking paper, or simply butter the tin well and dust with flour.

As the weather cools it's lovely to pack a simple picnic and head outdoors. This pie will be the star of any picnic blanket.

Roll out the larger piece of pastry between two sheets of baking paper, using just a little bit of flour. You need to do this quite quickly, and if it is cold enough it will be fine. Between rolls you will need to stop, lift the paper off, sprinkle the pastry with a little flour, then replace the paper, turn it over, lift off the paper, sprinkle it with a little flour then replace the paper. This will allow the pastry to roll easily. You are looking to roll this so it comes about half to two-thirds up the sides of the baking tin. Immediately peel off the top sheet of the baking paper and invert the pastry into the tin, allowing a little to come up the sides, then peel off the remaining sheet of baking paper. Don't worry if the pastry breaks, just patch it up. Place the tin in the freezer to chill while you roll the remaining piece of pastry out to the width of the tart (this will be the top of the pie).

Place the cooled apples in the pastry-lined tin. Peel off the top sheet of baking paper and invert the pastry top over and onto the apples, then peel off the remaining paper. Trim the edges with a knife and use a fork to seal the edges together. Place on the preheated tray, if using, and bake for 40–45 minutes, until the top is golden. Bear in mind that if the top appears golden, the base may not be cooked through. If the top looks as if it is browning too much, cover it with foil. Remove from the oven and leave to cool for 20 minutes before transferring onto a wire rack to cool completely.

Place the icing sugar and butter in a bowl, then add enough passionfruit pulp to mix to a spreadable consistency. Spread the icing over the top of the cooled apple pie, then cut into slices and serve.

PHOTO ON PAGE 229

KITCHEN NOTES
- Choose your apples carefully – not just for flavour, but also for texture when cooked. I like to use a mix of apples that will break down during cooking (such as granny smith) and ones that hold their shape (such as golden delicious). Talk to your supplier and ask about flavour and texture when cooked because all apples vary.
- I like to use a 3 cm (1¼ in) deep, 30 × 20 cm (12 × 8 in) rectangular tin to make this as it cuts into nice, easy to handle pieces. You could also use a 24 cm (9½ in) round spring-form tin.

2 tablespoons small pearl tapioca

185 ml (6 fl oz/¾ cup) full-cream (whole), non-homogenised milk or almond milk

60 ml (2 fl oz/¼ cup) sherry, preferably Pedro Ximénez

60 g (2¼ oz) unsalted butter, softened, plus extra for greasing

75 g (2½ oz/½ cup) rapadura or raw sugar, or light or dark muscovado sugar

60 g (2¼ oz/1 cup) breadcrumbs made from day-old bread

1 teaspoon bicarbonate of soda (baking soda), sifted

200 g (7 oz/1 cup) mixed dried fruits (cherries, sultanas/golden raisins, raisins and glace ginger), cut into small pieces

2 teaspoons finely grated lemon zest

½ teaspoon mixed spice

1 teaspoon natural vanilla extract

This recipe is reminiscent of simpler times when delicious food was made with the little that was on hand, and everything was used. Tapioca binds when there are no eggs to do the job, and breadcrumbs are used in place of precious flour. I grew up on this pudding, and it remains a huge favourite. It's especially delicious when made with glorious dried fruits and a stunning sherry such as a Pedro Ximénez.

tapioca plum pudding

The night before, combine the tapioca, milk and sherry in a small bowl, then cover and stand overnight at room temperature. This is a cold weather pudding so it should be able to sit out at room temperature, but if it is warm, place in the fridge.

The next day, grease a 1 litre (35 fl oz/4 cup) pudding basin (mould) with a little butter.

Using a stand mixer fitted with the paddle attachment, beat the butter and sugar until light and creamy. Stir in the tapioca mixture, then add the remaining ingredients and stir to combine well. Transfer to the greased basin and spread the top to even. Cover with a well-fitting lid (or use baking paper secured well with kitchen string). Place a trivet in the base of a large saucepan of water and place the pudding bowl on top, then pour in enough water to come two-thirds up the side of the basin. Cover the pan, bring to the boil, then reduce the heat to very low, cooking it at a very gentle simmer (so it doesn't rattle) for 2½ hours, or until the tapioca is clear and translucent. Turn out onto a plate to serve.

KITCHEN NOTE

Look for tapioca (or sago) that is free from additives, such as sulphur dioxide, which commonly appears. You can make this with whatever bread you have on hand: sourdough, white, wholemeal or seeded will be just fine.

DIETARY INFO GLUTEN FREE
SERVES 10

210 g (7½ oz/1½ cups) teff flour
1 teaspoon ground ginger
2 teaspoons ground cinnamon
½ teaspoon freshly grated nutmeg
2 teaspoons baking powder
125 g (4½ oz) unsalted butter,
   softened, plus extra for greasing
80 ml (2½ fl oz/⅓ cup) honey
60 g (2¼ oz/ ⅓ cup firmly packed)
   dark muscovado sugar
3 eggs
1 teaspoon natural vanilla extract
3 very ripe bananas (about 530 g/
   1 lb 3 oz, unpeeled)
125 ml (4 fl oz/½ cup) Cultured
   Buttermilk (page 50), or plain
   natural yoghurt

MOCK BUTTERCREAM
60 ml (2 fl oz/¼ cup) honey
1 tablespoon full-cream (whole),
   non-homogenised milk
½ teaspoon gelatine
100 g (3½ oz) unsalted butter,
   softened
1 teaspoon vanilla bean paste

One of my favourite cakes when growing up was a honey roll with mock buttercream. This is my version of that cake. Mock buttercream comes from a time when little was on hand, and one had to be ingenious: gelatine is used in place of icing sugar to help give body to the end result. This is a perfect autumn banana cake, rich with spice and honey. It keeps exceptionally well, but because it is so moist, when the weather is warmer it is best kept in the fridge. When it's cooler, it's best under a glass dome as this will keep the crumb and buttercream lovely and moist.

honey and banana cake with mock buttercream

Preheat the oven to 180°C (350°F). Lightly grease a 1 litre (35 fl oz/ 4 cup) capacity loaf (bar) tin and line the base with baking paper.

Place the flour, spices and baking powder in a mixing bowl and whisk through to evenly distribute the ingredients.

Using a stand mixer fitted with the paddle attachment, beat the butter, honey and sugar until pale and creamy, scraping the side and base of the bowl a couple of times as you go. Add the eggs, one at a time, beating well after each addition. Add the vanilla, then peel the bananas and break into chunks into the bowl. With the mixer on low speed, beat slowly to break up the bananas for 5–6 seconds. Add the flour mixture and the buttermilk and mix through slowly, scraping down the side until well combined. Transfer to the lined tin and bake for 45 minutes or until a skewer inserted into the middle comes out clean. Remove from the oven and leave in the tin to cool completely.

To make the mock buttercream, place the honey, milk and 1 tablespoon water in a small saucepan and stir over low heat,

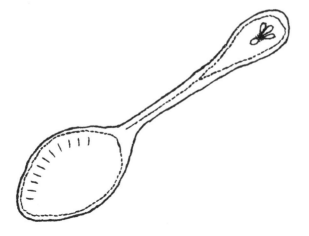

Mock buttercream comes from a time when little was on hand, and one had to be ingenious.

just until the honey has dissolved. (Make sure you use just enough heat to dissolve the honey.) Remove from the heat and set aside to cool briefly.

Place the gelatine and 1 tablespoon boiling water in a very small bowl and stir until dissolved. Stir this into the honey mixture.

Using a stand mixer fitted with the paddle attachment, beat the butter until light and fluffy, scraping down the side from time to time. Add the vanilla bean paste, then very slowly drizzle in the honey and gelatine mixture. Take care to drizzle it in very gradually in the beginning, then slowly increasing the amount as you go. If the mixture looks a bit wet, stop adding the honey mix and continue to beat until creamy. You can also pick up the bowl and place it in a sink filled with a little hot water to soften the butter slightly from time to time. Continue until all the honey mixture is incorporated and beat until creamy and fluffy.

When the cake is cool, turn it out onto a wire rack and cut it in half horizontally. Spread the buttercream on the bottom half and replace the top layer of the cake.

KITCHEN NOTES

● Here, I've broken my rule of not heating honey, but I just love the flavour and texture that honey gives to a cake. I like to use a well-flavoured, dark honey in this cake.

● The icing is best used soon after it is made, but can be made ahead of time and refrigerated until needed. If making it ahead, take it out of the fridge well before using to allow it to come to room temperature. If it is still too firm to spread, simply use an electric hand-held beater to whisk until creamy.

● This cake can easily be up-scaled into a three-tiered layer cake. Simply divide the batter into three separate 15 cm (6 in) round cake tins and bake them for 35–45 minutes. Double the amount of icing, then spread between the layers and around the outside of the cakes once completely cooled.

DIETARY INFO LOW GLUTEN OPTION | DAIRY FREE | VEGETARIAN
MAKES 8 POCKET PIES

1 quantity Sweet Barley and Spelt Pastry (page 84) or Dairy-free Sweet Vanilla and Coconut Pastry (page 87)
1 egg, lightly beaten
2 tablespoons golden caster (superfine) sugar, or demerara, raw or rapadura sugar

FILLING

400 g (14 oz) apricots
200 g (7 oz) raspberries
2 teaspoons cornflour (cornstarch) or kudzu (kuzu)
1–2 teaspoons golden caster (superfine) sugar or maple syrup, or to taste
½ teaspoon vanilla bean paste or scraped seeds from ½ vanilla bean

KITCHEN NOTES

● Use fresh fruit rather than frozen. If it must be frozen, thaw the fruit first.
● The smaller you cut the fruit, the more you'll be able to fit in the pies. And the amount of fruit you add will depend on the kind of pastry used. Because dairy-free pastry is not as flexible, I tend to fill it with less fruit to prevent breakage.
● Too much moisture can ruin the pie so the drier the filling, the better.
● Adjust the cornflour (cornstarch) as required, for example, berries have more juice than apples and would need more cornflour.
● Adjust the sweetness as desired depending on the fruit.

Like the savoury pocket pies on pages 158–162, this recipe is endlessly versatile. Use this recipe as a template – the fillings can be made with any seasonal stone fruit and/or berries you like.

apricot and raspberry pocket pies

For the filling, cut the apricots in half, remove the stones and cut the flesh into 5 mm (¼ in) slices. If your apricots are very large, cut them into smaller lengths. Add to a bowl with the raspberries and the remaining filling ingredients and gently toss through.

Divide the pastry into two and place one half in the fridge. Roll out the remaining half of the pastry into a 23–24 cm (9–9½ in) square, 2–3 mm (¹⁄₁₆ in) thick. Cut into four and leave it exactly where it is (that is, don't separate it once you have cut it). Divide half the quantity of fruit mix between the bottom half of each piece of pastry, laying the straight edge of the apricot slices facing the fold line, overlapping the apricot as you go, trying to fit as much in as you can and leaving no more than a 1 cm (½ in) border. Use a large palette knife to carefully fold the pastry over the filling, gradually moving the pie away from the other pastry squares as you do so. Next, use a fork to press the edges of the pastry to seal, and then transfer to a baking tray lined with baking paper. Repeat with the remaining pastry and filling.

Brush the beaten egg generously over the pies. If using the barley and spelt pastry, use a sharp knife to make a small cross on top of each pie. Sprinkle over the sugar, then bake for 30–35 minutes, until golden and the juices are sizzling at the sides of the pie. Remove from the oven, allow to cool enough to handle, then eat.

DIETARY INFO VEGETARIAN | WHEAT FREE
SERVES 8-10

1 egg, lightly beaten
1 tablespoon golden caster
   (superfine) sugar, for sprinkling

PASTRY
300 g (10½ oz/2½ cups) unbleached
   spelt flour, plus a little extra
   for dusting
200 g (7 oz) cold unsalted butter,
   cut into small chunks
2 tablespoons golden caster
   (superfine) sugar, optional
1 egg
1 teaspoon vanilla bean paste
1–4 tablespoons ice-cold water

FILLING
2 x 680 g (1 lb 8 oz) jars pitted
   preserved morello (or similar)
   cherries
3 tablespoons cornflour (cornstarch)
   or kudzu (kuzu)
2–3 tablespoons golden caster
   (superfine) sugar
1 vanilla bean, halved lengthways and
   seeds scraped
1–2 drops almond essence (I like the
   Nielsen-Massey brand), optional

I would rank a fruit pie of any description one of my favourite desserts – especially when there is a lot of fruit, and just a little pastry. This pastry is incredibly easy to make and is enriched with an egg to give it a slightly sexier biscuity crumb. This pie is at its glorious best when made from morello cherries that have been picked and cooked or preserved yourself, rather than purchased in generic imported jars.

truly madly deeply cherry pie

To make the pastry, place the flour, butter and sugar, if using, in a food processor and pulse 1–2 times, just until the mixture resembles very coarse breadcrumbs. Turn the mixture out into a bowl. Alternatively, to combine by hand, place the dry ingredients in a bowl and, using your fingertips and thumbs, rub the butter into the flour mixture to achieve flat chips of butter. I tend to lift the butter and flour that I am working on and let it fall back into the bowl to help aerate the mixture. Try to work quickly and lightly. When ready, the butter pieces should range in size from small breadcrumbs to small lentils.

Place the egg, vanilla and 1 tablespoon ice-cold water in a small bowl and beat with a fork until well combined. Add to the flour mixture and use a butter knife to cut the liquid into the dry ingredients. Add extra cold water as needed, a little at a time, being very careful not to add too much; the mixture should appear moist but not at all wet. Bring the dough together into a ball, do not knead or work it as this will cause the pastry to become tough. Take one-third of the pastry, shape into a rough ball and flatten, then do the same with the remaining pastry. Wrap both lots of pastry in plastic wrap and refrigerate for at least 1 hour.

Meanwhile, lightly grease a 24 cm (9½ in) round, 3 cm (1¼ in) deep tart (flan) tin with butter and place in the freezer to chill.

To make the filling, drain the cherries in a sieve placed over a bowl. Measure out 625 ml (21½ fl oz/2½ cups) cherry juice (keep the rest for another recipe). Place the cornflour in a medium-size saucepan and add enough of the cherry juice to make a smooth slurry.

Add 1 tablespoon sugar and the remaining juice, followed by the cherries, vanilla seeds and bean, and a drop of almond essence. Cook over medium heat, stirring continuously until it comes to the boil. Taste and add extra sweetness or almond essence if desired. Remove from the heat, take out the vanilla bean (see page 104 on how to make vanilla bean sugar with this) and set aside to cool briefly.

To roll and blind bake the pastry, use as little flour as possible, but enough to make sure your work surface is lightly dusted. Roll out the larger ball of pastry until about 3 mm (⅛ in) thick and large enough to fit the base and sides of the prepared tin. Gently ease the pastry into the tin and trim the edges with scissors, leaving about 2 mm (1/12 in) of pastry sitting above the edge. Place in the freezer to chill for 5–10 minutes.

Preheat the oven to 200°C (400°F). Place a black bottom tray, if you have one, in the oven to preheat (this will give you a crispier base). Line the pastry shell with baking paper, then fill with pastry weights, dried beans or uncooked rice, ensuring the weights come up the sides. Place on the hot tray and bake for 10–15 minutes or until the edges are very lightly golden. Remove from the oven, remove the weights and paper and return the pastry to the oven. Reduce the temperature to 180°C (350°F) and bake for 15–20 minutes, until the pastry is light golden and almost cooked. If you find the pastry is puffing on the base, reduce the temperature. Remove from the oven and set aside to cool briefly (you can put the tray back into the oven).

To assemble the pie, ensure your oven is preheated to 200°C (400°F) and the tray is inside.

On a surface lightly dusted with flour, roll out the remaining pastry into a rectangle 30 x 23 cm (12 × 9 in) and about 3 mm (⅛ in) thick. Place on a baking tray lined with baking paper, then run a knife along the pastry, cutting it into 2 cm (¾ in) wide strips. Separate the strips ever so slightly and place the tray in the freezer. Very cold pastry will allow you to get through the latticing without it melting and losing shape.

Place the cherry filling in the blind-baked tart shell. Remove the cold pastry strips from the freezer and lattice the top, then brush with the beaten egg and sprinkle with the sugar. Immediately place the pie on the preheated tray in the hot oven and bake for 10–15 minutes, until the lattice is light golden. Reduce the oven temperature to 180°C (350°F) and bake for another 30–45 minutes, until golden, and the juices are running. Remove from the oven and allow the pie to cool slightly before eating.

PHOTO ON PAGE 240

KITCHEN NOTE
This recipe calls for cooked and preserved cherries in their sweetened juices.

FROM LEFT: TRULY MADLY DEEPLY
CHERRY PIE AND STRAWBERRY
CELEBRATION CAKE

DIETARY INFO VEGETARIAN | WHEAT FREE
SERVES 8-10

500 g (1 lb 2 oz/3⅓ cups)
  strawberries, hulled
  and halved or quartered,
  depending on their size, plus
  250 g (9 oz/1⅔ cups) extra for
  decorating (optional)
150 g (5½ oz/1 cup) rapadura sugar
  or raw sugar
1 teaspoon natural vanilla extract
195 g (6¾ oz/1½ cups) white
  spelt flour
1 teaspoon baking powder
½ teaspoon bicarbonate of soda
  (baking soda)
60 g (½ cup) almond meal
125 g (4½ oz) unsalted butter,
  softened
½ teaspoon vanilla bean paste or
  1 teaspoon natural vanilla extract
3 eggs, separated
125 ml (4 fl oz/½ cup) Cultured
  Buttermilk (page 50)

STRAWBERRY CHEESECAKE ICING

125 g (4½ oz/1⅓ cups) strawberries,
  hulled
125 g (4½ oz) cream cheese,
  softened
60 g (2¼ oz) unsalted butter,
  softened
½ teaspoon vanilla extract
75 g (½ cup) golden icing
  (confectioners') sugar, sifted

This cake is my new go-to quintessential spring-into-summer cake, and my take on the classic Southern strawberry cake. The strawberry cheesecake icing is insanely good, and if there is more than you can use, it will keep for a week in the fridge and is perfect in a bowl with fresh strawberries as a treat.

strawberry celebration cake

Make the icing at least 5 hours before using it. Place the strawberries in a blender and puree until smooth. Place in a fine sieve over a bowl and use the back of a large serving spoon to press through – discard the seeds that remain. You should have about 80–125 ml (2¾–4½ fl oz/⅓–½ cup) puree. Using ½ a cup of puree will give you runnier icing, which is good for a slab cake.

Beat the softened cream cheese, butter and vanilla in the bowl of stand mixer fitted with the paddle attachment on medium speed, until creamy and smooth. Add the icing sugar and strawberry puree and continue to beat on slow speed until well combined. Increase the speed to medium–high and beat until deliciously creamy. You may need to stop and scrape down the side, to the bottom of the bowl, from time to time. Transfer to a small bowl, cover with plastic wrap and refrigerate for at least 5 hours to firm up before using.

Meanwhile, preheat the oven to 190°C (375°F). Place the strawberries in a baking dish that is big enough so they are not too crowded. Sprinkle with 2 tablespoons of the sugar, add the vanilla extract and toss through. Bake for 20 minutes or until the strawberries are slightly singed at the edges and the juices are thick. Remove from the oven and set aside to cool. Reduce the oven temperature to 170°C (325°F). Grease the base and sides of a 30 × 22 cm (12 × 8¾ in) slab tin (see also Kitchen Notes), and line the base with baking paper.

Sift the flour, baking powder and bicarbonate of soda into a large bowl, then whisk in the almond meal and set aside.

242

Place the butter, remaining sugar and vanilla paste in the bowl of a stand mixer fitted with the paddle attachment. Beat on medium speed until creamy and smooth, scraping down the side, to the bottom of the bowl, from time to time. Add the egg yolks and beat until light and creamy.

In a separate bowl, whisk the egg whites until very soft peaks form and set aside.

Add the flour mixture and buttermilk to the butter mixture and beat on the lowest setting until just mixed through – do not overbeat. Remove the bowl from the mixer and very gently fold in the egg whites, until just incorporated. Gently stir in the cooled roasted strawberries until just combined. At all stages, avoid overmixing. Spoon the batter into your prepared tin and carefully smooth out. Bake for 30–35 minutes, or until golden and a skewer inserted into the middle comes out clean. Remove from the oven and leave to cool in the tin for 10 minutes before you invert the cake onto a wire rack to cool completely.

To put the cake together: Pour the desired amount of icing over the cake, or cut the cake in half horizontally and layer with icing in between.

If making a two-tiered cake (or three-tiered cake, see Notes)
Place one of the cakes on a cardboard round, then place this on a rotating cake stand. Using a small offset spatula, spread about ½ cup of the icing on the top of the cake. Place the next cake on top of this and spread this with ½ cup of icing. Top with the final cake. You are going to apply the icing two separate times – the first layer will seal in the crumbs and make a smooth surface to work on. I like to use my 15 cm (6 in) straight spatula to spread an even coating of icing around the edges and top of the cake. Then take your stainless steel dough scraper, and with the squared side on the base of the cake stand and against the side of the cake, gently rotate the cake stand in an even manner with your other hand. Make sure you only apply light pressure on the icing, giving you a smooth spread of icing. Use your spatula to even off the top, and again. Place in the fridge for 30 minutes. Remove and apply another layer of icing and repeat the process with the spatula and dough scraper until the cake is how you would like it. Place the cake in the fridge to firm up a little before topping with fresh strawberries, if desired.

PHOTO ON PAGE 241

KITCHEN NOTES

● This cake can be made as a three-tiered 15–20 cm (6–8 in) or a two-tiered 22 cm (8¾ in) cake. For these sizes, the baking time will be around 45–55 minutes. If making a tiered cake, double the amount of icing and use 170 ml (5½ fl oz/⅔ cup) strawberry puree.

● In very hot weather, you may need to refrigerate the cake and bring it out about 30 minutes before serving for the cake and icing to relax. Leftovers keep very well covered with a glass dome for a couple of days, or in an airtight container in the fridge.

● While not absolutely essential, a rotating cake stand, an offset spatula and a dough scraper makes light work of icing and decorating this cake.

DIETARY INFO VEGETARIAN | WHEAT FREE | EGG FREE
MAKES 10-12 GOOD-SIZE SCONES

APPLES

30 g (1 oz) unsalted butter

3 tablespoons rapadura sugar or
   raw sugar

½ teaspoon ground cinnamon

1 teaspoon natural vanilla extract

4 apples (about 550 g/1 lb 4 oz),
   peeled, quartered, cored and cut
   into 5 mm (¼ in) slices
   (see Kitchen Notes)

finely grated zest of 1 lemon

SCONES

130 g (4½ oz/1 cup) white spelt
   flour, plus extra for dusting

75 g (2½ oz/½ cup) wholemeal
   (whole-wheat) spelt flour

60 g (2¼ oz/½ cup) oatmeal

2 teaspoons baking powder

3 teaspoons rapadura sugar or
   raw sugar

¼ teaspoon bicarbonate of soda
   (baking soda)

1 teaspoon apple cider vinegar

125 ml (4 fl oz/½ cup) milk

125 ml (4 fl oz/½ cup) Cultured
   Buttermilk (page 50) or plain
   natural yoghurt

100 g (3½ oz) very cold unsalted
   butter, cut into rough 1 cm
   (½ in) pieces

CINNAMON GLAZE

150 g (5½ oz) golden icing
   (confectioners') sugar, sifted

20 g (¾ oz) unsalted butter,
   softened

1 teaspoon finely grated lemon zest

½ teaspoon natural vanilla extract

1 teaspoon ground cinnamon

This is a scone for an autumn or winter morning when you are looking for a sweet something rather than a big breakfast, or for a wonderful morning tea.

apple pie scones

To make the apple mix, melt the butter, sugar, cinnamon and vanilla extract in a large frying pan over low–medium heat. Add the apples and cook for 15–20 minutes or until just tender and a knife inserted into them meets little resistance. The moisture content of apples varies enormously, if your apples have very little, you will need to cover with a lid, to help the juices sweat out. If you have juicier apples, you will need to reduce most (but not all) of the juice off towards the end of cooking time – you should have no more than 1 tablespoon of juice. Ideally, some apples will have broken down a little and others will still be intact. Stir through the lemon zest and set aside to cool.

To make the scones, preheat the oven to 200°C (400°F) and line a baking tray with baking paper. Place another piece of baking paper on the work surface, sprinkle it with a little extra spelt flour, and give yourself another 30 g (1 oz/¼ cup) spelt flour for your hands and knife.

Place the flours, oatmeal, baking powder and sugar in a mixing bowl and sift in the bicarbonate of soda. Mix through with a whisk to combine, breaking up any lumps of flour.

Place the vinegar in a cup measure, add 90 ml (3 fl oz) milk and the same amount of buttermilk and set aside.

Using your fingertips or a pastry cutter, cut the butter into the flour until the mixture resembles coarse breadcrumbs – some bits should be the size of a pea. Add the milk and vinegar mixture and mix with a large spoon until just combined – do not overmix. Gradually add the remaining milks, as needed, to form a moist, but not at all sloppy dough. Try to use as little extra milk and buttermilk as possible.

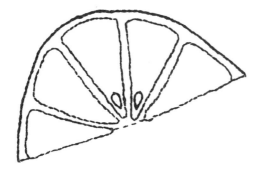

Slightly trickier than your average scone, but so worthwhile! Please try these, I know you will love them.

Dollop bits of the dough onto the baking paper, then gently pat the dough together to make a rectangle about 23–26 cm (9–10½ in) long and 20 cm (8 in) wide. Use the reserved extra flour to help you pat the dough out to size. Lay the apple along the left side of the scone mix, ensuring it is right to the edge along the length, and the top and bottom. Use the baking paper to pick up the right side of the dough and fold it over to cover the apple. Using floured fingertips, slowly peel off the paper from the top, then using a large sharp, floured knife, cut the scone dough into 10–12 slices, moving each slice to the baking tray as you go. Don't worry if the slices fall apart a little, they will still bake up beautifully. Bake the scones for 15–20 minutes or until golden and cooked through.

Meanwhile, to make the glaze, place all the ingredients in a small bowl. Add 2 tablespoons boiling water and mix together well until the butter is melted and the mixture is smooth. Drizzle the glaze over the scones as soon as they come out of the oven and serve warm. Any leftovers will keep for 1 day in an airtight container in the fridge, or can be frozen.

KITCHEN NOTE

Choose a mix of apples from those that break down a little, to those that stay intact for this recipe. I have limited varieties of apples where I live, but have found Fuji, mutsu or golden delicious are firmer apples that hold their shape well. I would encourage you to explore the many varieties out there and ask your grocer or farmer about the apples you are buying.

DIETARY INFO VEGETARIAN | WHEAT FREE | LOW GLUTEN
SERVES 8–10

130 g (4½ oz/1 cup) white spelt flour
110 g (3¾ oz/1 cup) barley flour
1½ teaspoons baking powder
1 tablespoon finely chopped
   fresh rosemary
finely grated zest of 1 medium–
   large lemon
115 g (4 oz/¾ cup) rapadura sugar
   or raw sugar
sea salt and freshly ground
   black pepper
3 eggs
1 teaspoon natural vanilla extract
185 ml (6 fl oz/¾ cup) extra virgin
   olive oil
185 ml (6 fl oz/¾ cup) Cultured
   Buttermilk (page 50)

LEMON SYRUP
185 ml (6 fl oz/¾ cup) strained
   lemon juice
75 g (2½ oz/½ cup) rapadura sugar
   or 70 g (2½ oz/⅓ cup) raw sugar,
   plus extra as needed
4–5 rosemary sprigs, about 2–3 cm
   (¾–1¼ in) long

KITCHEN NOTE
Although the amount of sugar in the syrup may seem excessive, lemons vary enormously in their acidity, and rapadura sugar is only about 75 per cent sucrose. Add what works for you, to your taste. You may prefer to add a bit of rapadura and bring it to a syrup consistency, then add some honey to the mix.

Most likely my favourite teacake in the book, this is delicious and rustic. It is best enjoyed in cooler weather and thanks to the syrup, keeps exceptionally moist.

rosemary, olive oil and lemon teacake

Preheat the oven to 180°C (350°F). Lightly grease and line a 1 litre (35 fl oz/4 cup) capacity loaf (bar) tin with baking paper. Don't cut the corners of the baking paper to fit – fold them instead. This will allow you to pour the lemon syrup onto the cake when it is cooked without it seeping onto the tin.

Place the flours, baking powder, rosemary, lemon zest, sugar, a few grinds of pepper and a pinch of salt in a mixing bowl and whisk together to evenly distribute the ingredients.

Place the eggs, vanilla, olive oil and buttermilk in another bowl and whisk together. Add the wet mix to the dry mix and stir gently to combine. Transfer to the lined tin and bake for 60–70 minutes or until a skewer inserted into the middle of the cake comes out clean.

About 10 minutes before the cake is ready, start making the lemon syrup. Place the lemon juice, rapadura sugar and the rosemary sprigs in a small saucepan. Bring to the boil and simmer for 5 minutes, then taste and add extra sweetness as desired (see Kitchen Note). Continue to simmer until it has reduced by one-third and has a syrupy consistency.

Remove the cake from the oven and, while still hot, use a cake skewer to pierce the cake right to the bottom in 12 places. Pour the hot syrup over the top, making sure it flows into any cracks. Leave to cool briefly before serving. Store for up to 4 days in an airtight container, in a cool dark place.

DIETARY INFO VEGETARIAN | WHEAT FREE | DAIRY FREE
SERVES 8–10

90 g (9 oz/½ cup) dried apricots, chopped into small pieces
75 g (2½ oz/¾ cup) stabilised rolled (porridge) oats
30 g (1 oz/¼ cup) pumpkin seeds (pepitas)
40 g (1½ oz/¼ cup) sunflower seeds
60 g (2¼ oz/½ cup) pecans or walnuts, coarsely chopped
75 g (2½ oz/½ cup) wholemeal (whole-wheat) spelt flour
½ teaspoon baking powder
1 teaspoon finely grated lemon zest
85 g (3 oz/½ cup) dried cherries or raisins, coarsely chopped (remove any seeds)
1 egg
80 ml (2½ fl oz/⅓ cup) macadamia oil
1 teaspoon natural vanilla extract
2 tablespoons brown rice syrup
2 tablespoons maple syrup

KITCHEN NOTE
If preferred, replace the macadamia oil with 125 ml (4 fl oz/½ cup) melted butter.

This is my take on a wholesome morning tea slice. It offers extended fuel from nutrient-dense nuts and seeds, and dried fruits. I prefer something a little more cake-like rather than muesli-bar-like as I find the latter a little too dry for my tastes. Apricots could be replaced easily with other stone fruit such as nectarines or peaches.

apricot and cherry morning tea slice

Preheat the oven to 180°C (350°F) and line a 27 × 18 cm (10¾ × 7 in) shallow baking tin with baking paper.

Place the dried apricots in a small saucepan with 60 ml (2 fl oz/ ¼ cup) water. Cover and bring to a very gentle simmer over low heat, then cook for 5–10 minutes, until the apricots have absorbed all the liquid and are plump. Set aside to cool.

Meanwhile, place the oats, seeds and nuts on a baking tray and put them in the oven for 10 minutes or until lightly toasted. Set aside to cool a little before adding to a bowl along with the flour, baking powder, lemon zest and dried cherries. Whisk through to ensure that all the ingredients are evenly distributed.

In a separate bowl, whisk together the egg, macadamia oil, vanilla, brown rice and maple syrups. Add to the dry ingredients, along with the apricots and combine well. Turn into the prepared tin, smooth over the top and bake for 30–35 minutes, until golden on top and slightly crisp around the edges. Leave to cool completely before cutting into bars. Store in an airtight container in a cool place for up to 1 week.

DIETARY INFO GLUTEN FREE | VEGETARIAN
MAKES 6 SMALL POTS

100 g (3½ oz) dark chocolate
 (70% cocoa solids)
2 eggs, separated
1½–3 tablespoons maple syrup
250 g (9 oz/1 cup) Cultured Cream
 (see page 50)
2 teaspoons natural vanilla extract

A classic chocolate mousse, but when made with cultured cream it provides a slight sour edge, and a serving of good bacteria to help your gut. Perfect.

chocolate mousse with cultured cream

Place the chocolate in a food processor and process until finely chopped – the smaller the pieces, the better.

Place the egg yolks and 1½ tablespoons maple syrup in a heatproof bowl and whisk until well combined. Place over a saucepan of hot water over low heat, making sure the base of the bowl does not touch the water. Whisk for about 8 minutes, or until the mixture is thick and creamy and quite warm, taking care that the water does not boil. If the mixture looks too hot, remove the bowl from the pan and whisk, off the heat, to cool it down a little. When ready, take off the heat and set aside for 1 minute, leaving the hot water in the pan, but the flame turned off.

Whisk the cultured cream until soft peaks form. Whisk the egg whites in another, spotlessly clean bowl until soft peaks form and they are not at all solid or dry.

Place the egg yolk mixture back on the saucepan of hot water and whisk for a couple of seconds until lovely and creamy again. Remove from the heat, then add the chocolate and whisk for 1–2 minutes, or until melted, smooth and silky. It will become quite thick but keep whisking (or stirring with a wooden spoon). Using a spatula, gently fold in the cream. Taste at this point and add extra maple syrup, if desired. Add the vanilla, then gently fold in the egg whites until incorporated. Spoon into six small pots, then cover and refrigerate for 1 hour, or until set.

KITCHEN NOTES

● It's best to use a Cultured Cream (page 50) that is softly thick but pourable. At this particular stage, it will whip well and will not be too strongly flavoured.

● The mousse contains culture that is still alive and as it is allowed to sit, it will become more sour and slightly fluffier in texture. I make the mousse in small glass pots with a lid, and try to eat them within 1–2 days.

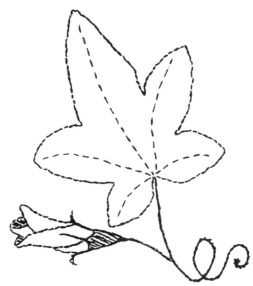

index

PAGE NUMBERS IN *ITALICS* REFER TO PHOTOGRAPHS.

251

253

ACKNOWLEDGEMENTS

A book is never the work of just one person; it takes a village, and I am blessed to 'live within' a wonderful village of family, friends and publishers. My beautiful daughter, Nessie, continues to encourage and support all I do. She still rolls her eyes when she thinks I have gone too far, and gives honest feedback on everything I cook. Mum, Lisa, Kim, Peter, Kate, Pip, Anne and Mark, Michael and Louise, Stephen and Martina, Fran, Josh, Zac and Charlie are my close and loving family, and I couldn't imagine my life without them.

I've learnt a lot about true friendship over the past year and I can't tell you how much I value the real thing: Nene, Holly Davis, Katrina Lane, Denise and Julie especially are such supportive, wise and talented women. A special thank you to Holly and to one of my Whole and Natural Foods Chef Training graduates, Trudie Fenwick; they both worked so hard at the book shoot to help me produce the beautiful food you see within these pages.

Thanks to the Murdoch Books team: to Sue Hines, my publisher Corinne Roberts, to Katie Bosher and Madeleine Kane. Thanks to Christine Osmond, Kate Wanwimolruk, Lauren Camilleri and Melody Lord. Photographer Cath Muscat and stylist Michelle Noriento brought this book to life with such skill and beauty, thank you. But a part of that village is you, dear reader — as you invite me into your home, we are still building a brave new world and we're doing together.

I say with deep gratitude and love to you all, thank you.

Published in 2016 by Murdoch Books, an imprint of Allen & Unwin

Murdoch Books Australia
83 Alexander Street
Crows Nest NSW 2065
Phone: +61 (0) 2 8425 0100
Fax: +61 (0) 2 9906 2218
murdochbooks.com.au
info@murdochbooks.com.au

Murdoch Books UK
Ormond House
26-27 Boswell Street
London, WC1N 3JZ
Phone: +44 (0) 20 8785 5995
murdochbooks.co.uk
info@murdochbooks.co.uk

For Corporate Orders & Custom Publishing, contact our Business Development Team at salesenquiries@murdochbooks.com.au.

Publisher: Corinne Roberts
Editorial Manager: Katie Bosher
Design Manager: Madeleine Kane
Designer: Lauren Camilleri
Editor: Kate Wanwimolruk
Photographer: Cath Muscat
Needlework: Melody Lord

Stylist: Michelle Noriento
Food Editor: Christine Osmond
Home Economist: Holly Davis
Assistant at shoot: Trudie Fenwick
Production Manager: Alexandra Gonzalez

Text © Jude Blereau 2016
The moral rights of the author have been asserted.
Design © Murdoch Books 2016
Photography © Cath Muscat 2016

A cataloguing-in-publication entry is available from the catalogue of the National Library of Australia at nla.gov.au.

ISBN 978 1 74336 5373 Australia
ISBN 978 1 74336 5380 UK

A catalogue record for this book is available from the British Library.

Colour reproduction by Splitting Image Colour Studio Pty Ltd, Clayton, Victoria
Printed by 1010 Printing International Limited, China

IMPORTANT: Those who might be at risk from the effects of salmonella poisoning (the elderly, pregnant women, young children and those suffering from immune deficiency diseases) should consult their doctor with any concerns about eating raw eggs.

OVEN GUIDE: You may find cooking times vary depending on the oven you are using. For fan-forced ovens, as a general rule, set the oven temperature to 20°C (35°F) lower than indicated in the recipe.

MEASURES GUIDE: We have used 20 ml (4 teaspoon) tablespoon measures. If you are using a 15 ml (3 teaspoon) tablespoon add an extra teaspoon of the ingredient for each tablespoon specified.